THE IRISH TIMES

BOOK

of the

YEAR

2013

EDITED BY

PETER MURTAGH

Gill & Macmillan

Gill & Macmillan
Hume Avenue
Park West
Dublin 12
with associated companies throughout the world
www.gillmacmillanbooks.ie

© *The Irish Times* 2013
978 07171 5785 3

Design by Identikit Design Consultants, Dublin
Print origination by Carole Lynch
Index compiled by Cliff Murphy
Printed and bound in Italy by Castelli Bolis

*The paper used in this book is made from the wood pulp
of managed forests. For every tree felled, at least one tree
is planted, thereby renewing natural resources.*

A CIP catalogue record is available for this book
from the British Library.

5 4 3 2 1

Contents

Introduction

The single most significant piece of reporting in *The Irish Times* for the 12 months from October 2012 to September 2013 was Kitty Holland's report of 14 November 2012 (which she wrote with Paul Cullen) disclosing the tragic circumstances in which Savita Halappanavar died at Galway University Hospital. Just as the case of Anne Lovett – the 15-year-old schoolgirl who died beside a grotto in Granard, Co. Longford, while giving birth alone and unaided in 1984 – forced the country to take a good, hard look at itself, so too does the case of Savita Halappanavar.

It was clear from the outset of the controversy that erupted when news of Mrs Halappanavar's tragedy emerged that Ireland could no longer pretend that abortion was an issue to be ignored. Since 1992, the procedure had been legal, on foot of a Supreme Court judgment concerning the pregnancy following rape of a 14-year-old girl. It was legal when, in the words of the judgment, there was 'a real and substantial risk' to the life of the mother. And yet every government since had avoided the imperative to legislate to this effect, including urgings from the European Court of Human Rights. It took the death of Mrs Halappanavar, and the uncertain position in which her condition put the medical team trying to treat her, to jolt a government into action.

It is its own comment on the quality of both debate and political leadership in Irish public life today that none of the central issues raised during the heated debate that followed Mrs Halappanavar's death was different in substance to those raised during previous abortion debates. This time, however, the political establishment was shamed into action, albeit the bare minimum required.

Thirty years later, Holland's dispassionate reporting of one of the consequences of all that – the paralysing uncertainty for medics as to the parameters of what they could and could not do to save their patient's life – was a model of putting the facts first and letting the arguments fall where they will.

Peter Murtagh
September 2013

Contributors

Paddy Agnew is Rome Correspondent.

Bono is a musician and lead singer with the rock band U2.

Brian Boyd writes about music and comedy.

Tara Brady is a film critic and feature writer.

Simon Carswell is Washington Correspondent.

Donald Clarke is Film Critic and an *Irish Times* columnist.

Malachy Clerkin is a sports journalist.

Stephen Collins is Political Editor.

Peter Crawley is Chief Theatre Critic at the *Irish Times*.

Kevin Cullen is a reporter and columnist with the *Boston Globe*.

Paul Cullen is Health Correspondent.

Gavin Cummiskey is a sports journalist.

Marie-Claire Digby is a food writer.

Keith Duggan is a sports and feature writer currently based in the United States.

Aidan Dunne is Art Critic.

Ken Early is a sports journalist.

Hilary Fannin is an *Irish Times* columnist.

Patrick Freyne is a feature writer.

Michael Harding is a writer and *Irish Times* columnist.

Bernice Harrison is TV Reviewer.

Shane Hegarty was Arts Editor until taking a sabbatical to write children's books. However, he continues to write a column in Saturday's *Weekend Review*.

Mark Hennessy is London Editor.

Kitty Holland is an *Irish Times* reporter.

Ann Marie Hourihane is a freelance writer.

Joanne Hunt is an *Irish Times* news and features writer.

Róisín Ingle is an *Irish Times* journalist and writes a weekly column, 'Up Front', in the Saturday magazine.

Michael Jansen is a Middle East expert and analyst, reporting regularly from Lebanon, Syria and Egypt.

Colm Keena is Public Affairs Correspondent.

Anna Kenny is an *Irish Times* journalist.

Conor Lally is Crime Correspondent.

Miriam Lord is a colour writer, member of the *Irish Times* political staff and parliamentary sketch writer.

Ruadhán Mac Cormaic is Legal Affairs Correspondent.

Manchán Magan is a freelance writer, specialising in travel writing.

Lara Marlowe was Washington Correspondent until early 2013 when she returned to France as Paris Correspondent.

Frank McDonald is Environment Editor.

John McManus is Business Editor.

Frank McNally writes 'An Irishman's Diary'.

Eoin McVey is a managing editor.

Seán Moran is GAA correspondent.

Ines Novacic is a freelance writer based in New York.

Carl O'Brien is Chief Reporter.

Dan O'Brien is Economics Editor.

Ross O'Carroll-Kelly is the alter ego of Paul Howard.

Jennifer O'Connell is an *Irish Times* columnist.

Brian O'Connor is Racing Correspondent.

Enda O'Doherty is Opinion Editor.

Olivia O'Leary is a broadcaster and former *Irish Times* political journalist.

Ian O'Riordan is Athletics Correspondent.

Fintan O'Toole is Literary Editor and an *Irish Times* columnist.

Richard Pine writes from Greece where he lives in Corfu.

Conor Pope is Consumer Affairs Correspondent.

Derek Scally is Berlin Correspondent.

Kathy Sheridan is a features writer.

Lorna Siggins is Western Correspondent.

Laura Slattery is a business reporter who also writes a Media & Marketing weekly column.

Gerry Thornley is Rugby Correspondent.

Michael Viney is a nature writer and weekly columnist writing 'Another Life' from his and his wife, Ethna's, cottage in west Mayo, for the Saturday edition of *Weekend Review*.

Arminta Wallace is a feature writer.

Noel Whelan is an *Irish Times* columnist.

Photographers and illustrators whose work features in this year's edition include *Irish Times* staff members: Alan Betson, Brenda Fitzsimons, Bryan O'Brien, Cyril Byrne, Dara Mac Dónaill, Eric Luke and Frank Miller. Martyn Turner is *Irish Times* cartoonist. Michael Viney paints illustrations for his weekly column, 'Another Life'.

Other photographers in this volume are either freelance photographers or work for the organisations identified following their name. They include: Alan Crowhurst/Getty Images, Alan Lewis, Alessandro Bianchi/Reuters, Alex Livesey/Getty, Andrew Cowie/Getty, Andrew Downes, Andrew Redington/Getty, Andrew Winning/Reuters, Antonio Calanni/Associated Press, Billy Stickland/Inpho, Christine Cornell, Ciara Wilkinson, Collins/Collins Courts, Dan Sheridan/Inpho, Dave Thompson/Press Association, Domnick Walsh/Eye Focus, Doug Mills/Reuters, Eddie Mallin, Eoin Coveney, Eric Bouvet, Feng Li/Getty, Gianluigi Guercia/Agence France Presse, James Crombie/Inpho, Joe O'Shaughnessy, Joe Raedle/Getty, John Tlumacki/The Boston Globe/Getty, Joseph Eid/AFP/Getty, Josh Haner/*The New York Times*, Julien Behal/PA, Justin Sullivan/ Getty, Keith Heneghan/Phocus, *L'Osservatore Romano*, Larry Busacca/Getty, Laura Hutton/Photocall Ireland, Lucas Jackson/Reuters, Luis Davilla/Getty, Michael Appleton/*The New York Times*, Michael Kelly, Michael Prior, *New York Daily News*/Getty, Niall Carson/PA, Pascal Le Segretain/Getty, Peter Macdiarmid/Getty, Sean Curtin/Sean Curtin Photo, Shelley Corcoran, Simon Duggan/Provision, Spencer Platt/Getty, Will Oliver/the estate of John Ryan, Youen Jacob/Provision, and Yves Herman/Reuters

Jacket cover photographs were taken by AP Photo/*L'Osservatore Romano*, Inpho/Dan Sheridan, Joe O'Shaughnessy, Reuters/Andrew Winning, Camera Press/Neil Drabble, Loic Venance/AFP/Getty Images, Alex Livesey/Getty Images, Eric Luke/*The Irish Times*, Reuters/Doug Mills/Pool, Domnick Walsh/Eye Focus, Alan Betson/*The Irish Times*, Alan Lewis, Brenda Fitzsimons/*The Irish Times*, AP, Inpho/Billy Stickland, PA Wire/Press Association Images

TUESDAY, 2 OCTOBER 2012

'The sound of a dying pig didn't put children off their dinner'

Michael Harding

Joe Brady was having an open day on his organic farm near Lough Owel last week, and when I got to the farm gate his mother said: 'They're in the shed.'

It was a huge galvanised shed, busy with things men do well: timber logs were stacked 10ft high, and a mountain of turf was heaped in the corner.

Two musicians played fiddle and guitar underneath an oil drum and a chef was stir-frying beef on a gigantic pan.

An elderly man was serving organic potatoes. The remnants of a roasted pig lay on a stainless-steel tray and Joe was making pork sandwiches.

The place was humming with an elegant masculinity and the pleasures of farming life.

The women seemed happy, too; posh ladies in mohair jumpers and leather boots trying to suck

Enda Kenny with Germany's Chancellor Angela Merkel during a European Union leaders summit at the European Council headquarters in Brussels. Photograph: Yves Herman/Reuters.

the juice out of their burgers without wetting their fingers.

But it was the pig that I was interested in; the pig that sleeps in the human psyche. Even Churchill recognised that a cat looks down at you, a dog looks up at you, but only the pig looks you in the eye.

I asked one woman who breeds pigs if her children were bothered when a pig died.

'It's difficult coming up to the day,' she admitted. 'But once it's over you get on with life. When we're bringing the carcass home from the abattoir, I'm usually in the back seat of the car keeping the blood stirred in the bucket.'

'So you make your own black pudding,' I remarked.

Another woman with long black hair and sunglasses on her head was balancing a sliver of pork on her plastic fork. 'There's a beautiful pig out the back,' she said.

So out I went and saw a fat sow in a sty, lying on her flank while her little piglets suckled and slept. It was a comforting sight.

But I wasn't fooled. There's nothing comforting about the life of a pig. All that mollycoddling on an organic farm is nothing more than preparation for the abattoir.

I grew up beside a pig factory. I heard them squeal every evening when I was coming from school as the conveyer belt dragged each animal by the hooves to the boiling vats, and gullies below collected the blood, and men walked about the factory yard with long knives, their white rubber aprons smeared with glistening guts.

In Kinnegad last year, I spoke to an old man for whom pig killing was an annual ritual.

'We hung him from an oak beam in the old days,' he told me, 'and we finished him off with sledgehammers. We tied a rope around his legs. And we pulled him up, suspended him in midair, and mother would come with a pan and a pot stick to catch the blood when it flowed. We'd hit the pig with the hammer to stun him, and maybe sometimes take his eye out by accident.

'But me father was ready, when the pig was stunned, and he had a type of a rod – it was a long knife – and he'd stick it right between the ribs and then me mother would put the pan underneath and, as me father let the knife down through the pig, the blood followed the blade all the way to the basin and we'd be there stirring it to make sure it didn't thicken.

'Then we'd make a fire in an old barrel, and we'd get boiling water going, and scald the pig and scrape his skin with knives. And some people made pickles out of the jowl. And if a man came to do the killing, then he took the bones away with him as well as his five shillings.

'And the next morning we'd wash out the kidneys and fry them on a pan. And we'd be fighting for the kidneys.'

In those days, the sound of a dying pig didn't put children off their dinner. I suppose the ritual of slaughter allowed them to acknowledge the warrior-hunter within themselves. Whereas nowadays some young people grow up thinking that rashers grow on trees and foxes knit jumpers to pass the winter.

Much more alarming is the fact that a mythic black pig is still ploughing furrows through the interior landscape of some Irish males. A wild boar runs amok in their unconscious minds as they vomit in taxis and urinate on homeless people in the streets, in a pathetic attempt to release the 'warrior' from their deeply constipated psyches.

THURSDAY, 4 OCTOBER 2012

Multiplier Effect Leaves Reilly on Dicey Ground

Miriam Lord

Dáil sketch: the Minister for Health struggles to come to grips with selection criteria for care centres.

James Reilly furnished the Dáil with the verbal equivalent of a doctor's prescription yesterday – unintelligible, as opposed to illegible.

For a man so anxious to explain he wasn't responsible for the Great Bump-Up of Balbriggan, the Minister for Health baffled and bamboozled instead of clarifying and enlightening.

Here's the stand-out highlight from Dicey Reilly's brain-frying exercise in obfuscation: 'I have laid it out three or four times to you: the criteria. They're quite extensive criteria and, because all of them act in different ways, it's a bit like a multiplier.

'One and one makes two and two and two make four but four by four makes 16 and not four and four makes eight and so it is with this. It's a logistical, logarithmic progression, so there is nothing, there is nothing simple about it.'

You can't beat a university education.

Labour's Ruairí Quinn, who took Leaders' Questions because the Taoiseach, Tánaiste and most of the Cabinet were on an awayday to Brussels, went in to bat for his fellow Minister at the start of Dáil business. Reilly – not in Brussels but not inclined to show his face in the chamber either – was dish of the day.

Sliced, diced and served up by the Opposition after fresh information emerged about his spot of off-list skiing with the primary care centres of North Dublin. But Ruairí wasn't concerned in the least, giving the impression he didn't know what the fuss was all about.

'I'm quite satisfied with the information I'm getting from Dr Reilly,' said the Minister for Education, with a totally straight face.

Melanie Verwoerd, former partner of the late Gerry Ryan, speaking after a High Court settlement over her memoir of life with the broadcaster. Photograph: Collins Courts.

The Reverend Dr Heather Morris, president designate of The Methodist Church in Ireland, with Mrs Justice Susan Denham, photographed after the Michaelmas Law Term service at St Michan's Church, Dublin. Photograph: Brenda Fitzsimons.

If Fianna Fáil's health spokesman Billy Kelleher wasn't happy with the explanations already given by Dr Reilly about how two towns in his constituency were bumped up a carefully compiled list of locations for these care centres, well, perhaps he hadn't asked the right questions. 'I've put down the questions, but I haven't got the answers,' protested Billy.

Back in 1995, when Quinn was in a different government, his taoiseach John Bruton was accused of withholding information and he famously replied that the opposition hadn't 'asked the right question'. Some of the old-timers in the chamber felt a bit of a shiver when Quinn rehashed that little episode of Rainbow Coalition infamy.

Was it not supposed to be different this time? So many questions about how Balbriggan and Swords slithered up the list, although Róisín Shortall resigned as Reilly's junior minister because she thinks she knows the answer. She insists it's a case of 'stroke politics' – Dicey diverting a little gravy to his home patch.

Judging by the private reaction of many Government and Fianna Fáil deputies – not to mention a few media folk – in Leinster House over the past week, it's just your average, run-of-the-mill 'stroke'. And sure doesn't everyone do it? Back to Quinn, who couldn't answer most of the questions yesterday morning.

But there was one. 'Am I satisfied that Minister Reilly will deal comprehensively with these issues? The answer is "yes".'

After the Minister for Health's matinée performance, you'd have to have serious questions about Quinn's judgement. Dicey Reilly muddied and fudged comprehensively, protested ignorance and innocence vehemently, and left his audience utterly confused in the process.

In fairness to Quinn, he teed things up nicely for his Fine Gael colleague by declaring that the contentious Balbriggan site had nothing to do with Dr Reilly. It was 'selected' by Mary Harney when she was minister for health.

The Government backbenchers cheered and taunted. Game, set and match. Or so they thought. On to the afternoon session, with Reilly in the chamber to answer opposition concerns over the primary care centres issue. He sounded and looked strained, talking quietly as he read from a script. They say if you're explaining, you're losing.

Therefore, when Dicey finished his opening statement, he must have been winning because there wasn't really a proper explanation in it. All he had to do was supply an answer and accompanying documentation to show how the final list of locations was compiled. And why some, like Swords and Balbriggan, leapfrogged areas that had been considered more urgent in the original list.

But there were loads of lists, blustered Reilly, and all sorts of additional criteria, which he spoke about in incomprehensible detail, but there was no breakdown of how these criteria were applied, what marks were awarded to what locations and what weightings were used.

For all the time he has had to supply this vital information, with all his advisers and important people with access to information in the HSE, James Reilly could not explain – apparently because the whole story has nothing to do with him.

In the morning, his defence – put forward by Quinn in the Dáil and himself on radio – seemed to be that Harney had 'selected' and chosen the Balbriggan site. By the afternoon, the explanation had changed. It wasn't Harney who earmarked the site. In fact, it might have been him, but he can't be sure.

It doesn't matter anyway, because Dicey Reilly was certain of one thing: 'I had no hand, act or part in this.' Oh dear God, we're getting terrible visions of Bertie at the tribunal now.

The Opposition stressed that it wasn't against Swords or Balbriggan getting a centre, but what about those towns they displaced on the list of 20? Joe Higgins said the Labour Party, by standing by Reilly, had developed an 'acute strain of Stockholm syndrome'. It was unfortunate, he sighed, to see 'political stroke pulling and cronyism' returning to North Dublin.

Maybe the Government is operating on a three-strokes-and-you're-out policy. Dicey Reilly must be on a last warning, so.

'This is a situation that's in flux,' he said.

The silence from the Government benches that greeted his statement indicated that many others are wondering if they're going to be fluxed too by the end of all this.

FRIDAY, 5 OCTOBER 2012

A People with Bizarre Attitudes to Tax and Spending

Dan O'Brien

We Irish are unusual in our attitude to tax and Government spending in at least three respects: we meekly accept increases in 'invisible' taxes but revolt when asked to write even small cheques to the Government; once we have paid our taxes, we care little about how politicians spend our money; and despite being a politically right-of-centre nation, civil society voices are much more likely to advocate more taxes and a bigger state than vice versa.

Start with the respective public reactions to two changes to the tax code made earlier in the year – the introduction of a €100 annual household charge and the hiking of the main value added tax rate (from 21 per cent to 23).

The VAT increase will already have cost the overwhelming majority of people multiples of the

Parents for Children against Children's Referendum chairwoman Maria MhicMheanmain, and editor of **Alive** *newspaper, Fr Brian McKevitt, at a press conference in Dublin. Photo: Laura Hutton/Photocall Ireland.*

household charge, yet there has hardly been mention of this additional burden over the course of the year.

By contrast, the household charge has triggered a tax revolt that is enormous in scale. Hundreds of thousands have refused to pay and Phil Hogan, the minister levying the tax, faces protests wherever he goes. For a nation that has often appeared to have under reacted to austerity, the response to the €2-a-week charge looks like an overreaction.

Nor is this an aberration. The response to the €50 sceptic tank charge was similar.

Yet more evidence of Irish taxpayers' allergy to writing cheques to Government came in last week's Comptroller and Auditor General's report, which suggested that non-payment of motor tax is

seven times higher in Ireland than in Britain.

The lesson for politicians (and the troika) appears to be that the most effective way to raise revenue is to tax people as stealthily as possible.

A second unusual characteristic of Irish taxpayers is how little we seem to care about what the Government does with our money once the State has relieved us of it.

In most EU countries, taxpayer organisations exist to highlight Government waste and counter-balance lobbying from interest groups, which seek more from the exchequer's coffers or fight to hang on to the share they have already secured. Taxpayer alliances are even more common in the Anglophone world. Yet no such entity exists in Ireland. This is all the more curious given the enormous expansion in public spending in recent times. In 1997, when the Fianna Fáil–Progressive Democrat administration came to power, general government expenditure stood at €26 billion. A decade later, the coalition, labelled 'neoliberal' by its fiscally innumerate critics, was spending €70 billion. This 163 per cent increase was by far the biggest among peer countries and four times the increase in the euro zone as a whole.

As a resident abroad until 2010, I watched from afar with some amazement. It was clear that little of the extra cash was being allocated on the basis of rigorous analysis, evaluation or consideration of value for money. Much of the spending was targeted at pleasing vested interests or buying them off.

When interviewing politicians on trips to Dublin, my pet concluding question was to ask whether voters on doorsteps or at constituency clinics raised issues of waste/excess in public spending. Before the crash, not a single politician could recall the issue ever coming up.

A third curious aspect of the tax/spending debate is ideological. According to international attitudes surveys, Irish people are unusually right of centre. This is reflected in the unique state of affairs in the democratic world whereby the two largest parties have always been conservative-leaning.

Given this orientation, one might have expected a US-style Tea Party movement to rise across the land, with protests against tax increases of all kinds spreading like wildfire. But that has not happened. Nor has a single civil society organisation or lobby group advocated going beyond the current administration's two-thirds cuts/one-third taxes budget adjustment strategy.

By contrast, plenty of groupings have advocated going the other way. Social Justice Ireland just this week urged that two-thirds of the adjustment comes from higher taxes, while last week the Nevin Institute think tank proposed 85 per cent comes from more taxes with spending cuts of just 15 per cent. Irish redistributionists may be in the minority, but they are more motivated and better organised than the inarticulate libertarian majority.

Gap Closing between Loving and Mourning Greece

Richard Pine

I am frequently criticised by Greeks, both at home and in the diaspora (especially the diaspora), for writing harshly about the Greek political and economic systems. And I am also applauded by non-Greeks, especially those who have difficulty operating a business in Greece, for saying the same things. Both criticism and applause are misplaced.

The Irish historian Roy Foster wrote to me: 'Greece is a country I both love and mourn.' What is there to love about Greece? Quite apart from its spectacular scenery, its climate, its extant antiquities, and the fact that it was – perhaps still is – the cradle of civilisation, there is something much more fundamental – the intimate relationship between landscape and character – which makes Greece and its people so attractive and so challenging.

This relationship has created a grittiness that inheres in all Greeks, whether townies or villagers. It enabled the Greek army to repel the Italians on the Albanian border in 1941 – the first victory by the Allied countries in the Second World War. During that war, it enabled the Greeks to form an effective resistance movement against occupying German forces, despite appalling famine in Athens and other cities. It fuelled the debate about the future identity of the country during the ensuing civil war, and it provided the animus that preserved it from the military junta of 1967–1974, especially the students (many of whom were killed) who eventually defeated that regime.

What is there to mourn about Greece? First, the perennial irredentism that makes Greeks long for restitution of its antique glory, including the idea of recapturing Constantinople (Istanbul), which led to the Anatolian catastrophe of 1922 and which, it can be argued, was a major factor in the political and economic upheavals from the 1920s onwards.

Next, the era following the exit of the colonels in 1974, when successive governments, first under New Democracy and then Pasok, created a 'welfare state' based on clientelism and cronyism, encouraging a dependence on a fixer mentality which, along with other factors, has contributed to the present crisis.

Other aspects of Greek society that must be bewailed include the education system, inferior at all levels, which sees billions of euro spent privately by parents to try to ensure a better life for their children.

The lack of industrial development, which Ireland has overcome by attracting multinational manufacturing and financial services, has been a major absence in the Greek economy: there was an ambition, a part of the irredentism in the heart of every Greek, that Athens could become the financial hub of the burgeoning Balkan economic world, but that was never realised.

The lack of planning in the development of tourism, which is not only Greece's major export industry but also coterminous with its attraction as a social and cultural magnet, leaves Greece competing badly with neighbouring countries in the provision of, for example, marinas and golf courses (there are only 12 courses in the entire country).

Perhaps most serious of all is the transition from a rural to an urban society, which leaves many villages depopulated but without creating any technological or wealth-creating nodes on which to build.

And, since accession to the EU, Greece, like Ireland, used the begging bowl to attract adhesion funds which have now led to today's loss of sovereignty.

Loving or mourning. Which? The love and the pluses outweigh the bewailing and the minuses. But the gap is closing.

One could never despair of a country and a people that exhibit, in the face of adversity, such *joie de vivre* which pushes their bewilderment and misery into a corner. In the village where I live on the island of Corfu, local expressions of opinion on the current situation are heated to the point of violence but subside at the *kafeneion*, as evening continues, into equally heated games of cards and backgammon (perhaps the national pastime).

I for one could never forsake the country where I have made my home, but the gap is closing. Even if a 'Grexit' from the euro results in not only the collapse of the Greek economy, but also possibly the euro itself, and, as many are now arguing across Europe, of the EU as a credible entity, I would not blame the Greeks. I never loved the EU and I would not mourn it.

Even if we had a military regime – and that is not impossible – I would join the Greeks in resisting it, as they did in 1967–1974, and living in its shadow.

Greece may not be a modern, forward-looking society, keeping pace with the northern march towards unification and 'progress'. Not least because of that idea of *terroir*, as the French call it – the rootedness of people in their locale, that intimate relationship between land and people which makes them more concerned about their vines and their olives (the grape harvest comes in the third week of September, followed by the long cropping of the olives) than about a factory in a nearby town. Only the sea – *thalassa* – has been a challenge to the land, and even then, despite Greece's continuing domination of the shipping industries, benefiting only a few millionaires.

Greece's potential is untapped in so many areas, even though the areas highlighted by economists and technocrats may not be those I am thinking of. The areas to be exploited are those that create the reasons for loving Greece, and the areas in which Greece is mourned are possibly those where mourning is inappropriate. But the gap is closing.

Up Front

Róisín Ingle

Out of the blue I am invited to a ball. I immediately think of the last ball I attended and squirm. That was back when I had money. I didn't actually have money, of course, but the excesses of those days were catching and occasionally I behaved like somebody who did.

Because, and this is what I would have argued back then, it's impossible to find clothes for a ball when you are what retailers kindly label plus-size. (Plus what? VAT?) So, obviously, I rang a fashion designer I had met once in my life and asked her to make something up for me. When I think about it now I say to my old-self: 'What were you thinking, asking a fashion designer to make you an outfit, you madser?' My old-self replies: 'Look, I couldn't find anything. Anyway, I'm loaded. I do my weekly shop in the fanciest grocery store in town. What? You know how I adore their chocolate-covered dried mangos.' That woman is dead to me now, dead, thank Merkel.

Deep down I thought the designer might whip me something up for €20. She whipped something up alright, but it cost quite a bit more. I happily produced the credit card; delighted to shell out completely unnecessary cash back then, I was. These days you'll find me in the vegetable aisle of Lidl wondering if I should splash out on vine-ripened tomatoes or just stick with the ordinary ones.

Times change, you know. People change.

It was black of course, the custom-made designer outfit, black being the plus-sized ball-goer's friend. I thought it was the business. I went to the ball and was not a bit surprised when almost immediately a photographer approached wishing to take my picture in my custom-made designer gear.

I was put in a photograph with another woman. I smiled a sort of enigmatic grin, conscious that eventually people might be gazing at the photograph in magazines wondering where I got my gear. The grin said: 'Sorry babe, it's a one-of-a-kind designer number.' The other woman in the picture was wearing dressy black trousers and a generously proportioned silk black top. When the photographer finished, she turned to me and said: 'Don't worry, that photo won't get used anywhere. They just put us together because we are fat and in black.' It put me right off balls to be honest.

But here I am down the back of the coach on my way to another ball, trying to start a sing-song. I am wearing a sparkly, taffeta coat-dress belonging to my mother. Cost: €14 for the dry cleaning. There is a woman down the back of the coach called Melky Jean, a sister of Wyclef Jean, who has travelled from California to entertain the revellers. 'Give us a tune,' I say. '99 bottles of beer on the wall,' she begins, which is the American version of 'Ten Green Bottles'. And that's when I know tonight's going to be a good night.

At the ball some fun things happen. Melky's husband is a cool dude called Supreme and I call him Soup all night, which I, if nobody else, find hilarious. A brilliant a cappella harmony group called Keynotes do a duet with Brian Kennedy. Melky sings a Tina Turner song and my rule about never dancing in public is momentarily forgotten. I'm rollin' (rollin') rollin' (rollin') rollin' on a river. I win something in the raffle. Suddenly, I love these events again.

But never mind all the high-octane messing, the thing I remember best about the night is a woman called Shirley making a speech about her son, Luke. It was the Make-A-Wish Ireland Ball. They grant wishes to seriously ill children and already this year they've granted wishes to 140 children, who want to be train drivers for the day, or go to the Paralympics, or ride a Lipizzaner horse in Vienna. Shirley spoke about nine-year-old Luke who was born with Prune belly syndrome, a condition that affects one in 40,000 babies, most of whom don't survive beyond a few weeks. He was born with no tummy muscles, abnormalities in the urinary tract, end-stage kidney failure, chronic lung problems – the list went on and on.

Luke's wish was to be Sonic the Hedgehog. Not just dress up as him but also be him, actually turn into sonic and flip and run at supersonic speed.

Impossible? That's a dirty word in Make-A-Wish Ireland. They drafted in some IADT students and after months of meticulous planning Luke was able to star in his own adaptation of a Sonic the Hedgehog game. Luke was thrilled that his exact idea came to life on the screen and Shirley said it gave her and her husband 'a day off from worrying'.

'It was a day where our whole focus was on Luke but only about what made him truly happy,' she said. 'I can honestly say I didn't think about medications, infections, future surgeries, battles with the hospital and HSE or blood results the whole day. I just kept looking at his face, and every time he said "wow this is awesome" it was like winning the Lotto for his dad and me.'

Simara Martinez and Libya Wilson, who were travelling with the 'Bain bus', highlighting the business practices of US Republican presidential candidate Mitt Romney. Photograph: Carl O'Brien.

The recession has driven a wrecking ball through the charity ball sector, but I'm glad I got the chance to hear about Luke, to put on my mother's best frock and to dance like nobody was watching in support of a magical cause that's well worth celebrating.

MONDAY, 8 OCTOBER 2012

'Bain Bus' Protest a Vehicle for Bigger Debate about Workers

Carl O'Brien in Arlington, Virginia

It hardly looks like a towering threat to Mitt Romney's election hopes, but try telling that to the occupants of this flimsy, 24-seat Ford minivan.

The 'Bain bus', which includes current and former employees of companies bought by Bain Capital, is rolling through swing states such as Ohio, Virginia and Florida to protest at the business practices and economic plans of the company's long-time chief executive, Republican presidential candidate Mitt Romney.

Today, midway through its 7,500-mile journey, it is stopped at Quincy Park and a small group of about 150 people has gathered to lend support. They're about to demonstrate outside the local Republican headquarters. The bus is yellow and emblazoned with red and black signs that scream: 'Stop the Romney economy'.

There are employees like Libya Wilson (19), a mother of two from Pittsburg, who works for Dunkin' Donuts. She tells of how conditions in her $8-an-hour job have deteriorated since it was taken over by the private equity firm, with unreliable hours, unpaid breaks and expanding responsibilities without pay increases.

'We were told we'd get a small raise every six months, and more if we worked beyond what was

expected. That's all changed,' she says. 'How do I pay for diapers, clothes or shoes for my kids?'

There are also employees from Sensata Technologies, a profitable motor sensors firm that was bought up by Bain and is about to be relocated to China.

Tom Gaulrapp, from Freeport in Illinois, will lose his job after 23 years. He says he was earning a decent wage of up to $18 an hour, or $40,000 a year. Now, he fears scrabbling to find low-paid work.

'If all of this continues, then we won't have any middle class left,' he says. 'All that we're left with are minimum-wage jobs with no benefits.'

Bain Capital isn't to blame for the slew of problems facing low-paid workers in the United States, but it has become a lightning rod for much of the fear and anxiety among voters over job security, outsourcing and the good of the wider community.

In short, it has become a vehicle for a larger conversation about the state of the American worker. While a majority of jobs lost during the economic downturn in the US have been in the middle range of wages, most of those added during the recovery have been low-paying, according to a National Employment Law Project report. The disappearance of mid-wage, mid-skill jobs is part of a longer-term trend that some refer to as a hollowing out of the workforce.

'The overarching message here is we don't just have a jobs deficit; we have a "good jobs" deficit,' Annette Bernhardt, the report's author and a policy co-director at the National Employment Law Project, said at the report's launch.

Low-paid jobs or minimum-wage jobs accounted for just over 20 per cent of job losses during the recession. Many of these jobs were out-sourced. Since employment started growing in recent times, low-paid jobs accounted for almost 60 per cent of all job growth.

Bain Capital's story is just a small symptom of a much bigger overall shift in the economy, and of globalisation in general.

In his campaign for presidency, Romney – a champion of free markets and small government – has sought to use his business experience to his advantage. He has argued that his private-sector knowledge of building companies makes him the best candidate to turn around the ailing US economy.

While some firms he invested in were over-leveraged with debt and collapsed, leaving many workers high and dry, others flourished and went on to create even more jobs.

'Bain Capital invested in many businesses,' a Romney spokesman said in a written statement. 'While not every business was successful, the firm had an excellent overall track record and created jobs with well-known companies like Staples, Domino's Pizza and Sports Authority.'

The Obama campaign, in the mean time, has been portraying Romney as a heartless capitalist and 'outsourcing pioneer', more interested in making money than in creating jobs. But the president has yet to move beyond blunt criticism of outsourcing to outline a detailed strategy of how to take advantage of the inevitable march of globalisation.

On the Bain Bus there's little doubt over which candidate will offer them a more secure future – but there's also recognition that miracles won't happen overnight.

'Barack Obama needs our support,' says Libya Wilson. 'The bad things he was left with won't change overnight; I was always told patience is key to life – and that's what we need to remember.'

Simara Martinez (21) from Boston worked for Dunkin' Donuts until recently. She helps her mother out, who also works two low-paid jobs. 'I just don't want a cold-hearted businessman who's on the side of the rich,' she says. 'I want someone who cares for people. We might as well vote for

Former Anglo Irish Bank chairman Seán FitzPatrick leaving the Criminal Courts of Justice in Dublin after being sent for trial on charges of giving illegal financial assistance to 16 others in July 2008. Photograph: Dara Mac Dónaill.

someone who will try to change things for us, rather than someone who doesn't give a damn.'

TUESDAY, 9 OCTOBER 2012

Book of Evidence a Blockbuster as Trio of Anglo Bankers Sent for Trial

Kathy Sheridan

It lasted just 10 minutes, with few public witnesses and no visual record. But it was a portentous moment in Irish commercial and social history. Lined up in the dock of the Criminal Courts of Justice were three former senior bankers of Anglo Irish Bank, a defunct institution that has already cost the State €29 billion.

Shortly before 10.30am in court No. 1, Seán FitzPatrick, Willie McAteer and Pat Whelan were occupying separate benches, FitzPatrick supported by his daughter, sister and brother-in-law, McAteer and Whelan by their wives. All three defendants wore the bankers' uniform of blue shirts and navy suits, although Whelan – at 50, the youngest by more than 10 years – had opted to go tie-less.

Meanwhile, lawyers were heaving 12 boxes of evidence through the door. The nine hefty volumes for the defendants (plus a set for the judge) represented the fruits of an investigation that has already taken three and a half years, and which could take another year to come to trial.

As the court clock struck 10.30, a hooter sounded with the warning that the building might have to be evacuated due to an 'incident'. No one moved. Outside, a 30-year-old who announced he was homeless and up on charges of being drunk and disorderly mistook a besuited detective for a banker and loudly berated him for ripping off the country. His girlfriend – who said he was an

attention-seeker – started to read out a letter he wanted delivered to FitzPatrick. The brief protest ended with his arrest for a 'public order incident', according to gardaí.

Back inside, the low, chaotic mutterings of defendants before the criminal branch of the District Court were oddly absent, replaced by serried, slickly groomed lawyers, bankers and smartly dressed investigators. Also yesterday, another case involving the embattled Seán FitzPatrick was being heard farther up the quays in the bankruptcy court, where an application to fix a date for examination of his financial situation was adjourned after arguments that the criminal case against him might be prejudiced.

In court No. 1, the three bankers were sitting awkwardly together in the dock, where an attempt to present the book of evidence to them foundered on the sheer size of the 'book'. As lawyers started heaving the nine boxes across the court and into the clearly inadequately sized dock, the judge looked askance: 'There's no need to physically, personally deliver the files . . .' Whereupon the boxes were heaved out of the dock again. It took only a few minutes to send the three forward for trial at the Circuit Criminal Court.

It was all over by 11.18. 'Lock him up for life!' shouted a youth half-heartedly, loitering on the steps, before urgently demanding a light for his cigarette.

WEDNESDAY, 24 OCTOBER 2012

Obama Bags it as Foreign Policies Hit Home

Lara Marlowe in Delray Beach, Florida

The queue stretched farther than I could see; some 11,000 Americans waited good-naturedly to see President Barack Obama in a tennis stadium yesterday morning. Under blue sky, with palm trees

Republican presidential candidate Mitt Romney with his wife, Ann Romney, at the conclusion of his public debate with President Barack Obama in Boca Raton, Florida. Photograph: Justin Sullivan/Getty Images.

US President Barack Obama waves on stage with first lady Michelle Obama after his public debate in Boca Raton, Florida, with Republican challenger Mitt Romney. Photograph: Joe Raedle/Getty Images.

quivering above the stars and stripes, they chanted, 'Four more years. Four more years'.

Down the road in Boca Raton, Obama's victory in the foreign policy debate had given them a boost. For half an hour in Delray Beach, hope lived again.

Somehow, Mitt Romney's rallies never attain the warm and fuzzy brotherhood thing Obama does so well. With post-debate polls giving Obama a victory ranging from eight to 16 percentage points, the president was in top form. True, it was nothing like the 45 per cent lead Romney scored on his 3 October debate performance. If Obama loses 12 days from now, history will trace his defeat back to Denver.

Obama's at his best when he wields humour. Google reported a rush on the word 'bayonets' on Monday night, after the president mocked Romney's desire to spend 'an extra $2 trillion on defence that the military haven't even asked for'. The US navy is smaller than it's been since 1917; the air force at its most ill-equipped since 1947, Romney moaned.

'I think Governor Romney maybe hasn't spent enough time looking at how our military works,' Obama said.

'You mentioned the navy, for example, that we have fewer ships than we did in 1916. Well, governor, we also have fewer horses and bayonets.' Laughter erupted in the press room.

At yesterday's rally, Obama revisited the debate, using a new term he's coined to describe Romney's shifting policies.

Romney's foreign policy 'has been wrong and reckless', Obama said. 'Last night, he was all over the map . . . During the debate he said he didn't want more troops in Iraq, but he was caught on video saying it was unthinkable not to leave 20,000 troops in Iraq . . . Last night, he claimed to support my plan to end the war in Afghanistan. I'm glad he supports it. But he's opposed a timeline that would actually bring our troops home.' At the debate, Romney said he always supported killing Osama

bin Laden. 'But in 2007, he said it wasn't worth moving heaven and earth to catch one man,' Obama reminded the crowd. 'Now we've come up with a name for this condition: it's called Romnesia.'

By now, anyone following the campaign has heard of 'Romnesia'. The crowd nonetheless roared with laughter. 'Romnesia! Romnesia! Romnesia!' they chanted. 'We had a severe outbreak last night,' Obama continued. 'It was at least stage three Romnesia.'

Over the past three weeks, Romney has bolted for the centre: in domestic policies on 3 October and in foreign policy on Monday night. Seeking to reassure voters who fear he would drag the US into another war, Romney talked mostly of peace. His most memorable line: 'We can't kill our way out of this mess' in the Middle East.

Yesterday, Obama pivoted to domestic issues, mocking Romney's 'Romnesia' on the auto bailout, the hiring of teachers and the saving of Medicare. Romnesia means 'you can't seem to remember the policies on your website, or the promises that you've been making over the six years that you've been running for president,' he said.

'Don't worry, Obamacare covers pre-existing conditions. We can fix you up. We can cure this disease!' Many of the supporters in the Delray stadium were true believers. African American Natalie King (33), a customer services representative for a local newspaper in Boca Raton, said proudly: 'I volunteered for the Obama campaign. I'm a phone bank captain.' She brought her 93-year-old mother to the rally, and refuses to believe polls that give Romney a slight edge in Florida. I mentioned seeing plenty of Romney signs but no Obama signs. 'Everything the Romney campaign does is dirty and nasty,' King says. 'They're stealing Obama signs. We don't steal theirs.'

Catherine Belle (68) wore an Obama T-shirt, an Obama watch, three Obama bracelets and dangly Obama earrings. Belle, who is also African

American, boasted that her nephew in Tallahassee is often mistaken for Obama. A retired school bus attendant for special needs children, Belle travelled to Washington for the inauguration in 2009.

'He stands for women and healthcare and all of us,' she says. 'I don't like the things that Romney stands for; from what I understand, he stands for the rich.' Because she is Jewish, Sheri Jacobs (46) is concerned that Obama has not visited Israel. But she'll vote for him anyway, because 'I think he needs more of a chance. Nobody could solve these problems in four years'.

The 'Romnesia' angle appears to have swayed Jacobs and her husband Jack (60) with whom she shares a catering business. Sheri Jacobs is a registered Independent and considered voting Romney 'but he never stayed the same. He's a moderate when he's with moderates, and something else when he's not. If the Republicans had a truly moderate candidate, I'd have voted for him'.

If Obama can convince people like Jack Jacobs, he should win 12 days from now. Jacobs is afraid Romney would take the US back to the Bush years, which 'did not benefit the middle class and upper middle class – people like us – only the rich.' After the first debate, Jacobs leaned towards Romney. Now he's leaning back towards Obama.

'It seemed like Romney's tail was tucked between his legs' in the foreign policy debate, Jacobs says. 'Romney changes his mind every other week. I don't like that, and I don't like his stand on women's rights either.'

Unlike the Romney event I attended last week, no one left the Obama rally before it ended. Instead, supporters stood in the bleachers, cheering their candidate as he plunged into the crowd. Bruce Springsteen's 'We Take Care of Our Own' blared from the loudspeakers, and many in the audience sang along. I thought of Obama's tardy appropriation of the term 'Obamacare', which the Republicans meant to be derogatory. 'I do care,' Obama says now. If Mitt Romney loses the election, it will be because he couldn't convince Americans that he cared too.

FRIDAY, 2 NOVEMBER 2012

'A fireman who helped clean up 9/11 – and he's crying'

Ines Novacic in New York

Streets where water is so high only four-wheel drives can wade through them and skeletons of houses stripped of windows, doors and walls – that's what residents in the storm-ravaged Irish-American neighbourhoods of Breezy Point and the Rockaways in Queens are trying to cope with.

'Three-foot water on the main road, the puddles are ponds,' said A.J. Smith, a community leader and lifelong resident of Breezy Point, whose family emigrated to New York during the Great Famine.

'I met a friend yesterday, a fireman who helped clean up 9/11 – and he's crying, talking to me. His house just isn't there anymore. People are just stunned.'

Apart from flood damage, 111 houses in Breezy Point were destroyed by a fire that broke out during the hurricane late on Monday night.

'Our firemen fought in waist-deep water and extremely high sustained winds,' a spokesman from the New York Fire Department told *The Irish Times*.

Smith described the morning after the storm as one of the 'most emotional' for anyone from the community, comparing it to a war evacuation scene: 'People being rescued on the back of pick-up trucks, people being ferried to look at what's left of their homes, trying to pick things from piles of debris.'

*People embrace amidst the remains of homes that were destroyed by a fire during Superstorm Sandy, in the Breezy Point neighbourhood in New York. Photograph: Michael Appleton/*The New York Times.

A sense of disbelief lingers throughout the neighbourhood. Another resident, Christina Fischer, whose family comes from Sligo, said that she hopes the Government realises how much help is required of them.

'We're a strong little town, with a faith in God and belief in the community. But we really are in need of immense assistance. I've got five kids and I don't know where to put my little ones in school – there was irreparable damage to the local one.'

When he visited the area two days ago, New York's mayor Michael Bloomberg said, 'To describe it as looking like the pictures we've seen of the end of World War II is not overstating it. It was completely levelled.'

Fischer said that, in hindsight, the city should have issued martial rather than mandatory evacuation notices, forcing people to leave their homes before the storm.

'Some of the elderly residents, like those from the former summer bungalows, wedged between the bigger renovated houses, insisted they've waited out 70 years of storms and wouldn't leave,' said Fischer.

'One neighbour diagonally behind us, Danny Sullivan, is a fireman and his folks refused to leave. So in the middle of the night when ember from the fire across the street started hitting their home, he carried out his parents. Neighbours started helping the people that stayed.'

The local fire department said up to 25 trucks were lost trying to get through floodwaters to the fire. Public transport to Breezy Point and the Rockaways remains closed, and there's still no power or electricity, with very limited running water.

'You can get close, but they're trying to keep just residents coming in, and since there's no power, the bridges close when it starts getting dark,' said Jarad Astin, a Rockaways local.

Astin and his wife Christel Rice, an Irish flute and tin whistle musician and teacher, said they were trying to drive to their home yesterday afternoon but could not find a station stocked with petrol anywhere in Brooklyn or Queens.

'I feel so helpless,' said Rice, fighting back tears. 'All those people, who have nothing now . . . We're very fortunate, we just had flooding.'

The couple added that the situation was turning particularly dire for people from the poorer downtown Rockaways neighbourhood, saying they wouldn't be surprised if looting started very soon.

Dan Dennehy, a chairman at the Ancient Order of Hibernians in America, said that the most important thing for every community is to reach out and check in on its members.

'Like right now, we in the Irish community are waiting for the smoke to blow away so we can start getting the people what they need,' said Dennehy. 'Those guys that have no homes, we'll help them to rebuild.'

SATURDAY, 3 NOVEMBER 2012

New Reality Dawns for Quinn as Garda Van Arrives

Kathy Sheridan

To the end, Seán Quinn retained his ability to surprise. A stately, almost funereal procession from a Four Courts holding cell along Byzantine corridors ended abruptly at an exit, where the 66-year-old took a startlingly athletic running jump into the narrow, black cage of a garda van.

The vehicle had been reversed almost to the steps, frustrating attempts to photograph the historic moment when the first big beast of the Irish business jungle was taken away to join the 20 to 30 new prisoners committed to Mountjoy every Friday afternoon.

It was only three years since the new inmate had controlled a €5 billion empire and – in the words of his lawyer – 'stood tall as a leading light of the Celtic Tiger'.

Three weeks ago, he told the *Financial Times* that he deserved public gratitude. 'Overall I don't think that I owe the Irish taxpayer any apology.'

Yesterday he was emotional but unbowed. 'They have tried to drag us through the muck. They took all my money. They took my companies. They took my reputation and they put me in jail, but yet they have proven nothing,' he told the media.

Then a garda finally lost patience, tapped him firmly on the shoulder and, with a wag of an index finger, gestured towards the cells downstairs.

Still, he was taken at a time of his choosing and without handcuffs. He could have requested a stay on the nine-week sentence – the IBRC had made no objection – but from early morning, his drained, hollow-eyed face suggested his mind was made up.

As Ms Justice Elizabeth Dunne read her 11-page judgment, terms such as 'evasive and unco-operative', 'not credible', 'serious misconduct' and 'outrageous' were dropped into the crammed and silent court.

Tears welled in his eyes when she mentioned his background, his education, the start of his business and 'its development into what became one of the largest business enterprises in this country'.

She spoke of his links with the GAA and numerous charities and of his medical problems. She also referred to his affidavit, in which he spoke of how 'these proceedings had "negatively consumed" his life and that of his wider family'.

But, she concluded briskly, 'he has only himself to blame'.

His supporters, seated around him, looked increasingly downcast as he dabbed at his eyes and mouth with a big white handkerchief, pulled at his ear, worked his jaw in a nervous tic and repeatedly

Seán Quinn arriving at the High Court in Dublin where he was jailed for nine weeks over his role in a multimillion-euro, asset-stripping plot designed to frustrate the former Anglo Irish Bank recover assets for the tax-payer. Julien Behal/Press Association.

brought his head down, then straightened up and folded his arms.

It hardly helped that his nemesis, Mike Aynsley, the group chief executive of the IBRC, was seated directly in front of him.

When sentence was pronounced, Quinn blinked and fitfully massaged his throat. The court adjourned to give him time to consider a stay, but there was obviously little left to be decided. He and his son Seán jnr used the time to sup pints in a downstairs bar.

There was no surprise when his lawyer told the court that his client wanted to begin his sentence immediately.

Quinn told the media: 'I suppose I was always proactive in life and never waited around for somebody else to make decisions . . . It's as well getting it dealt with.'

The only problem with the timing was that he wanted to be out for a grandchild's christening on 22 December. That wasn't for the court to decide, said the judge. By then the new reality had been signalled by the appearance of a uniformed garda.

As the courtroom emptied, supporters surrounded him and shook his hand. Tears trickled down his face while a woman hugged him, then he was led away.

Out in the corridor, Seán jnr made phone calls, watching alone through a window as the garda van backed into the yard.

Outside, a successful 55-year-old Dublin-based businessman in a pinstriped suit leaned against a wall and wept openly for the man who had been his first employer.

'Twenty-five years later, when I was fundraising for youth development for Fermanagh

Savita Halappanavar and her husband, Praveen, photographed at their home in Galway.

GAA, he gave me €100,000 and said "spend it well". That's only seven years ago. I felt I owed it to him to take two days here to support him.'

Woman 'Denied a Termination' Dies in Hospital

Kitty Holland and Paul Cullen

Two investigations are under way into the death of a woman, who was 17 weeks pregnant, at University Hospital Galway last month.

Savita Halappanavar (31), a dentist, presented with back pain at the hospital on 21 October, was found to be miscarrying and died of septicaemia a week later.

Her husband, Praveen Halappanavar (34), an engineer at Boston Scientific in Galway, says she asked several times over a three-day period that the pregnancy be terminated. He says that having been told she was miscarrying, and after one day in severe pain, Ms Halappanavar asked for a medical termination.

This was refused, he says, because the foetal heartbeat was still present and they were told, 'this is a Catholic country'.

She spent a further two and a half days 'in agony' until the foetal heartbeat stopped.

Intensive care

The dead foetus was removed and Savita was taken to the high dependency unit and then the intensive care unit, where she died of septicaemia on the 28th.

A family photograph of Savita Halappanavar.

An autopsy carried out by Dr Grace Callagy two days later found she died of septicaemia 'documented ante-mortem' and E.coli ESBL.

A hospital spokesman confirmed the Health Service Executive had begun an investigation, while the hospital had also instigated an internal investigation. He said the hospital extended its sympathy to the family and friends of Ms Halappanavar but could not discuss the details of any individual case.

Speaking from Belgaum in the Karnataka region of southwest India, Mr Halappanavar said an internal examination was performed when she first presented.

'The doctor told us the cervix was fully dilated, amniotic fluid was leaking and unfortunately the baby wouldn't survive.' The doctor, he says, said it should be over in a few hours. There followed three days, he says, of the foetal heartbeat being checked several times a day.

'Savita was really in agony. She was very upset, but she accepted she was losing the baby. When the consultant came on the ward rounds on Monday morning, Savita asked if they could not save the baby, could they induce to end the pregnancy. The consultant said, 'As long as there is a foetal heartbeat, we can't do anything.'

'Again on Tuesday morning, the ward rounds and the same discussion. The consultant said it was the law, that this is a Catholic country. Savita [a Hindu] said: "I am neither Irish nor Catholic" but they said there was nothing they could do.

'That evening she developed shakes and shivering and she was vomiting. She went to use the toilet and she collapsed. There were big alarms and a doctor took bloods and started her on antibiotics.

'The next morning I said she was so sick and asked again that they just end it, but they said they couldn't.'

At lunchtime the foetal heart had stopped and Ms Halappanavar was brought to theatre to have the womb contents removed. 'When she came out

she was talking okay but she was very sick. That's the last time I spoke to her.'

At 11pm he got a call from the hospital. 'They said they were shifting her to intensive care. Her heart and pulse were low; her temperature was high. She was sedated and critical but stable. She stayed stable on Friday but by 7pm on Saturday they said her heart, kidneys and liver weren't functioning. She was critically ill. That night, we lost her.'

Mr Halappanavar took his wife's body home on Thursday, 1 November, where she was cremated and laid to rest on 3 November.

The hospital spokesman said that, in general, sudden hospital deaths were reported to the coroner. In the case of maternal deaths, a risk review of the case was carried out.

External experts were involved in this review and the family consulted on the terms of reference. They were also interviewed by the review team and given a copy of the report.

THURSDAY, 15 NOVEMBER 2012

People ask, 'How can this happen in the 21st century?'

Kitty Holland

Praveen Halappanavar, husband of Savita, has spoken of how Ireland's reputation as a 'good place to have a baby' was among the factors in their decision to start a family here.

Speaking to *The Irish Times* yesterday from Belgaum in southwest India, where his wife was from, he said most of their friends in Galway had had babies there. The couple moved to Galway in 2008.

'All our friends, you know, had great stories to tell about the babies they had in Ireland. So we

People outside the Dáil demanding legislation to protect women's lives following the death of Savita Halappanavar. Photograph: Brenda Fitzsimons.

decided we'd go there. We had heard Ireland was a good place to have a baby. Most of our friends there had babies there and they're all fine, and so we decided: have a baby in Ireland.'

He said he and Savita held a gathering at home in the Roscam area of Galway, on Saturday, 20 October – the night before she presented at Galway University Hospital with severe back pain – to announce they were expecting a baby.

'Savita was very excited, very happy . . . All our close friends came to congratulate us. We had a dinner at home, and it was early morning on Sunday she had the severe back pains.'

That Sunday morning she presented at Galway University Hospital and was told she was losing the pregnancy.

Despite her making a number of requests for the pregnancy to be terminated – given the distress she was in and the fact the baby could not be saved – this was repeatedly refused because the foetal heartbeat was still present, her husband said.

The heartbeat stopped on Wednesday, 24 October, the womb contents were removed and Savita was taken to the high-dependency unit before being moved to ICU, where she died on Sunday, 28 October. She had contracted E.coli and septicaemia, a pathologist found. She was cremated in India on 3 November.

Explaining to family in India what had happened had been very difficult, her husband said.

'[Savita] has a lot of doctors in her family, a lot of medical people – her uncle, her aunt, many people who are in medicine – and they are all asking, "How can this happen in the 21st century, when the medical field is so advanced?" and "Why didn't they abort her?"'

'So I had to explain the whole thing, about the law there and how the foetus is live . . . and they were all just . . . some people even laughed at me, "That's crazy," they said. And I just had to tell them, that's the way it is, that unfortunately that's the country we were in at the time.'

'People keep asking me, "How could they leave the womb open for two days? There is a high risk of infection there."'

'A common thing I'm asked: "The mother's life is a bigger life. They knew that they couldn't save the baby. Why didn't they look at the bigger life?"'

Asked whether if there had been a termination he thought things could have been different, he said: 'Yes, of course. She was perfectly all right the day she went in, until Wednesday. I think, and it's just my take, I think on the Tuesday night things got worse, when she picked up that fever, when she started shivering, I think the infection was already taking hold and taking over her entire body. It was too late then.'

Her parents were still in shock, he continued. 'Her dad is in very bad shape. They are giving him medication to make sure that he gets some sleep. No one, including me, we can't believe she's not with us. She was such a lovely person, full of life. It's been just so very hard for them, their only daughter.'

They had been in Galway with the couple for two months before returning to India just before these events unfolded.

'At the airport, when I went to drop them, you know, they said, "We are so lucky to have her, such a wonderful daughter."'

Stoat's Dainty Steps a Vital Part of the Great Dance of Life

Michael Viney

The tracks at the tideline were those of tiny feet: a sinuous line of marks in the sand, now being licked away by foamy wavelets pushing up the strand.

I am used to seeing tracks of fox scavenging at first light well ahead of me, but this was finer stitching altogether: two little paws together at the front, the others spaced aslant in the length of one wellington-boot print – about 30cm.

The skipping gait of a stoat suddenly sprang to mind, an idea that would have taken longer to arrive some years ago. Among the earliest observations to Eye on Nature was that of a Co. Clare naturalist who had watched a stoat circling a little pocket of rock-pool in the limestone shore of the Burren. The tide had left a small fish – perhaps a blenny – locked up in the pool, and the stoat, by this account, had mesmerised it by its circling before pouncing to hook it out.

I was, perhaps, a tad sceptical at the time, but others offered similar stories of stoats haunting the shore for prey or fresh carrion. The beachcombing fox, too, helped my education. And the tracks of the stoat now reminded me of Paddy Sleeman's island badgers.

Dr Sleeman, a zoologist with UCC, has spent years studying badgers as part of research towards a vaccine to protect them from bovine TB. Among them are animals that have colonised offshore islands – two off Donegal, others off Sligo, Cork and Waterford. The badgers seem simply to have walked to them, on short causeways at low spring tides, and decided to stay, sometimes making their setts in sand dunes. And their food, analysed from droppings, is rich in sandhoppers, crab and other

Stoat on shore by Michael Viney.

marine life – the reason, perhaps, they wandered out on the shore in the first place.

This is interesting in itself. Badgers are supposed to eat earthworms, beetles and frogs. This is certainly their staple menu on pastures of intensive farming, where cattle and ryegrass dominate the local ecosystem. But Ireland's mustelid mammal family – of which the badger is the largest, the stoat the smallest, the otter somewhere in the middle – also includes the pine marten, notoriously omnivorous in its food, eating everything from squirrels and birds to berries and bees.

The island badgers are fine and healthy – not one of them with TB. That you might expect from their glorious isolation, remote from dairy cattle. But Sleeman is one of the legion of scientists alert to every nuance of the link between biodiversity and the general health of the world, not least of its human population.

A recent manifesto is the weighty (but attractive and engaging) book *Sustaining Life: How Human Health Depends on Biodiversity* (Oxford,

2008), in which Harvard Medical School enlisted 100 scientists to spell out the consequences of the current cascade of extinction.

The value of 'ecosystem services' to human life, such as clean water, breathable air and nourishing crops, may now be broadly appreciated, but nature's complexity and fragility are not.

The interplay of biodiversity and the spread of infectious diseases has captured Sleeman's special interest. Many such diseases are spread by biting insects, such as malaria by mosquitoes, and where biodiversity is rich these have a wider choice of animals to bite. Gabon, in west Africa, still has plenty of trees and monkeys, and the level of malaria is low; Ivory Coast is denuded of forests, and the only biteable primates are people, so malaria is widespread. Haiti and the Dominican Republic offer similar contrasts, even as they share one island.

Ireland's biodiversity is not half bad, if you count in our migrant birds, our species-rich shore and sea, the newly plumbed genetic inheritance of our native wildlife. Even our diversity of snails, creatures so derided by a certain strain of politicians, can have important agricultural value. In a public lecture now offered on YouTube by UCC, Sleeman explains how the liver fluke, damaging parasite of sheep and cattle, needs one particular snail to host part of its life cycle. With so many snail species available, it meets a lot of failure and so its harmful impact is diluted.

A classic ecological lesson is the story of Lyme disease, a tick-borne illness potentially debilitating in people and now making some headway in Ireland. It is named for a town in Connecticut in the US, where suburbs expanded rapidly into woodland. The woods originally had 15 kinds of mammal the tick could latch on to, but few of which would give them the disease in their blood.

After the woods were invaded by houses and people, the mammals were reduced to one, a mouse that could pass on Lyme disease. Now free of predators, the mice were concentrated in the remaining undergrowth, so were more and more infected ticks. This pattern and its consequences helped to spread the pathogen to people across the north-east of the US – and now, it seems, beyond.

MONDAY, 19 NOVEMBER 2012

Better to Light a Scented Candle than Curse the Darkness of Leinster House

Miriam Lord

They lit candles in the abortion capital of Ireland and stood in silent protest. But it was a small gathering in London.

Dublin was different.

Saturday's 'March for Savita' was a solemn occasion – tinged with sorrow at the death of a young woman and suffused with anger at the failure of successive Irish governments to legislate on abortion.

It's been 20 years since the Supreme Court handed down judgment in the X case, but politicians have dodged their responsibility to act on it. And it's 30 years since a poisonous referendum campaign (on both sides) ended with a constitutional ban on abortion.

What has changed over those years? Nothing much.

The arguments grind on, the marchers march, the legislators ignore and the furtive trips by Irish women to English clinics continue.

But the candles are classier.

On Saturday, when winter darkness fell and the temperature dropped, an unmistakable scent of summer hung in the air around the Dáil.

Pleasing pockets of fragrance punctuated the long lines of people moving slowly towards Leinster House, hints of lavender and vanilla and rose wafting up from flickering candles cupped in cold hands.

A man crosses a lock as bright blue skies and sunshine are reflected in the waters of the Grand Canal near Baggot Street in Dublin. Photograph: Bryan O'Brien.

That's women for ya, as a certain former taoiseach might say.

But this wasn't only a women's march, even if the floral nature of many flames added a feminine note to the candlelight vigil.

The crowd mustered in late afternoon. The turnout looked poor, made up of what seasoned protest observers might call 'the usual suspects'. Some took the opportunity to hand out flyers for this weekend's austerity protest.

But after the appointed hour, people suddenly converged on Cavendish Row in great numbers, with homemade placards and candles, children and buggies and dogs in tow.

For older people preparing to march, there was a weary familiarity about this event – been there, done that, admired the slogans decades ago . . .

'Am I going to have to do this again when I'm

50?' was the question on one young woman's placard; '20 years later and we're still protesting' proclaimed another, held by a girl wearing a hat with furry ears on it and surrounded by her furry-hatted friends. They were barely out of their teens.

The march moved off in driving rain, the crowd swelling all the time.

Vickey Curtis from Dublin 7 was with 15 friends, all wearing headbands displaying a large letter X. 'I thought of Savita and what happened to her, and I thought about the X case. If it was any of us, we'd just be deemed another X too. We want to show unity and want to call for change.'

A man in a bobble hat walked along, holding up a piece of cardboard. It read: 'My mother is a woman.' There was a quietness about onlookers along the route. Perhaps it was the sight of the large coloured banners. Made by NCAD students,

Thousands gather at Merrion Square, Dublin, to demand legislation on abortion after the death of Savita Halappanavar. Photograph: Dara Mac Dónaill.

they featured a stylised image of Savita Halappanavar's face.

Chris Murray waved a painted paper lantern on a stick. 'My children, Jack and Ruby, made this on St Martin's Day last weekend – it's a German festival. I'm meeting them on Kildare Street and you'll see us all holding up our lanterns.'

'Never again! Never again!' chanted the marchers.

Trinity College students Alison Connolly (Dublin), Tara Roche (Galway) and Clare Kealey (Dublin) were part of a 30-strong group.

'Woman Up and Legislate!' demanded Alison's placard. Tara carried a scented candle in a glass. 'And I've brought my mom,' said Clare.

The mom, Bernie, held a candle (pomegranate fragrance) in a little ceramic bowl. 'My daughter Anna is in America and would love to be here. She

sent me this candle and asked me to carry it for her today,' she said. Kathleen Lynch, from UCD and 'a proud Clare woman', marched with her daughter Nora (24), along with Kathleen's golden Labradors, Poppy and Bonnie.

The light faded significantly by the time we got to Grafton Street and the candles came into their own.

When the head of the protest reached the gates of Leinster House, people were still rounding College Green. There were speeches from the back of a truck and the crowd cheered when a turnout of up to 20,000 was announced.

Gráinne Griffin (24) from the Choice Network ran out of candles. 'I had about 500 in the bag and I thought I'd be ages giving them away, but they went in no time,' she said. 'I'm here because I'm furious. I'm just so angry.' It was dark and circles of white lights now framed the images of Savita on the banners.

Gráinne pointed towards them. 'People haven't been listened to for 20 years and this is what it's led to.' In her impassioned address, ULA deputy Clare Daly castigated Taoiseach Enda Kenny for saying he would not be rushed into a decision. 'He sat in the Dáil for over 30 years while 150,000 Irish women were exported out of here . . . to maintain the hypocrisy that there are no Irish abortions.'

When speakers made political points, it was abundantly clear that the crowd wasn't interested. Attempts to start a 'Shame on Labour' chant went nowhere.

A minute's silence was observed in memory of Savita. The only sound was the rasping of flints as candles were lit.

The crowd dispersed and the flames were extinguished. A bright light glowed above the main entrance to Leinster House.

But the building was in darkness and the doors were closed. And it remains to be seen whether all those touchingly optimistic girls in their furry-eared hats will still be marching when they are 50 – assisting the cynical 80-year-olds to light their candles so they don't set fire to themselves in frustration.

WEDNESDAY, 21 NOVEMBER 2012

An Irishman's Diary

Frank McNally

The good news is that this is World Hello Day, a small but worthy initiative designed to advance the cause of peace. You may not have heard of it before, but in fact this is its 40th anniversary. And you can mark the milestone, as people have marked the previous 39 instalments, by saying hello today to 10 different people.

The bad news is that the initiative was begun in 1973 – by two Irish-American brothers – as a response to the Yom Kippur war. So four decades on, World Hello Day doesn't seem to have made much of an impression yet on the Middle East. The integrity of the Arab-Israeli conflict remains unblemished. If its participants don't organise a World Goodbye Day eventually, we'll be lucky.

Maybe the event's ambitions need to be downgraded slightly. In which vein, I think it would be worthwhile even if it persuaded a few grumpy Dublin shop assistants, who currently consider it beneath them, to greet customers. Or, among those who do greet, it could be a useful restraint on the global march of 'Have a Nice Day', which is still spreading faster than Starbucks.

Mind you, viewed in certain lights, 'Hello' can be an equally controversial choice as peace envoy. In one of its more recent mutations, it isn't a greeting at all, but a one-word, sarcasm-laced question. Which, depending on the extent of its rising intonation, can mean anything from 'Is anybody listening?' to 'Are you out of your tiny little mind?'

Even before that development, the word sometimes had unwelcome connotations. The stereotypical English policeman was famous for using it – in triplicate, like an official document – as an opening gambit in any investigation. And its duplicate form has been satirised too. Among non-Anglophone peoples, the word's reputation as something that otherwise gibberish-speaking foreigners say was immortalised in the title of a BBC sit-com, *'Allo 'Allo*.

It is also one of the least precise words in English having been spelt 'Hallo', 'Hullo' and even 'Hollo' at different periods before settling – most of the time – on the vowel E. It may have been the telephone that sealed its popularity in this form. Certainly the phone remains its biggest ally. Even in Ireland, where 'Howya' and 'Is it yerself?' might rival it as face-to-face greetings, 'Hello' remains, almost always, the first word you say into the receiver.

But in any case, as befits a global initiative, the event inaugurated by Michael and Brian McCormack in 1973 did not confine itself to the

John Byrne, who has been homeless and on the streets of Dublin for 25 years, with his pet rabbit Barney and dog Roxy. Another man, Gary Kearney, pleaded guilty to animal cruelty after throwing Barney into the Liffey. Byrne rescued the pet. Photograph: Julien Behal/Press Association.

Anglophone 'Hello'. After all, getting people to say 'Shalom' and 'As-salamu alaykum' to each other was arguably more important.

And when they wrote to the world's political and cultural leaders seeking endorsement, the brothers did indeed speak other people's languages. Although I note from the website that, in his reply, Seamus Heaney had to correct them on the spelling of 'Dia duit'.

The website proudly proclaims this year's event to be the 40th World Hello Day. But the archive of good wishes has a somewhat dated look these days, suggesting the letter-writing campaign, at least, peaked during the 1990s. Queen Elizabeth II is one of the few current heads of state listed, and her reply is from 1987.

Still, it continues to seem like a good cause. So as a contribution to World Hello Day 2012, and even though we don't normally do this sort of thing, I'm going to mention a touching email we received yesterday, seeking this newspaper's help in a matter of the heart.

It came from India and a man named Abhishek, who earlier this month, on 15 November, met two female Irish tourists at a place called Anjuna in Goa. He spent several hours chatting to them, 'mostly on topics to do with Ireland and India'. As a result of which, he became severely smitten by one of the pair.

In case of embarrassment, I shall withhold the first name of the woman who did the smiting – innocent as it clearly was – except to say that it sounds like an Irish county and was once the subject of a hit record for Gilbert O'Sullivan.

Anyway, either because he was 'extremely stupid' or 'too shy' (his words), Abhishek didn't ask for her contact details. He doesn't even know what part of Ireland she's from. All he knows is that she works as a broadcasting technician, maybe in sport. So if that sounds like you, and you want to mark World Hello Day by reintroducing yourself, we have his address.

THURSDAY, 22 NOVEMBER 2012

Bomb on a Lunchtime Bus Was 'Like a Punch in the Stomach'

Ruadhán Mac Cormaic in Tel Aviv

Noémie Douek was on her break, sitting on a step outside the cafe where she works on Sha'ul HaMelech Boulevard, when she heard the explosion. What she saw, about 20m away, was black smoke billowing from a stationary bus and the cars all around coming to a sudden stop.

'We knew very quickly it was a bomb. With a rocket there's always a siren before the bang,' the 22-year-old said. 'I wanted to go and help them but there was a chance that there would be another explosion, so we felt it was too dangerous to get close.'

Within minutes there was pandemonium. Ambulances and police cars zoomed in and out. A helicopter circled overhead. Armed detectives fanned out into surrounding streets. From the nearby military complex that houses Israel's defence ministry, loudspeakers ordered soldiers on to high alert.

Word of the first major bombing in Tel Aviv since 2006 spread quickly around the city, and at first the police struggled to hold back the crowds that descended on the scene.

The bomb exploded on the 142 bus just after

midday as it approached the vast military headquarters – what one onlooker described as 'Israel's Pentagon'.

Police said it was not a suicide attack and suggested that someone might have left the device on the bus.

The explosion left 15 people injured, three of them seriously, and reduced the bus to a shell of twisted metal and shattered windows.

The last time a bomb blast hit Israel's commercial capital was in April 2006, when a Palestinian suicide bomber killed 11 people at a sandwich stand near the old central bus station.

Hamas militants have fired at least four rockets at the city over the past week, the first such attacks since Saddam Hussein launched Scud missiles at the city in 1991, but they caused no casualties.

'It's like a punch in the stomach,' said Odeya Koren, a middle-aged woman who stopped at the scene. 'What should I do as a mother? Should I tell my kids not to take a bus? What if they walk and the bus blows up beside them? Should we stay at home? How can you live?'

Although the rocket attacks of the past week had broken Tel Aviv's sense of isolation from the Gaza crisis, ordinary life had largely continued unaffected. Yesterday, a question politicians, analysts and citizens were grappling with was whether the bombing could – or should – scupper attempts to agree a ceasefire between Israel and Hamas.

For Ms Douek, the answer was straightforward. 'It frightens me, and that's why we have to respond. There comes a point when you have to defend yourself.'

Others hoped the talks would remain on track and that the bombing would not embolden cheerleaders for a ground invasion.

Nathan Datner, a Tel Aviv-based actor, said he was furious that Palestinian militants were targeting civilians with bombs and rockets – that 'they are trying hard to kill us' – but he hoped, nonetheless, that hostilities would soon end.

'There has got to be a ceasefire,' he said. 'People have got to sit down and talk.'

Participants in the Westport Sea2Summit adventure race on the top of Croagh Patrick in Co. Mayo.
Photograph: Andrew Downes.

WEDNESDAY, 28 NOVEMBER 2012

Begrudgery Hasn't Worked. It's Time to Break our Addiction to 'Failure Porn'

Jennifer O'Connell

Look away now, those of you revelling in our collective misery – it's not all bad news for Ireland Inc. In the past year, 300 new start-ups have opened their doors in Ireland, and average weekly earnings are up by 1.1 per cent.

Consumer-sentiment indices published in September showed a slight upward kink. Despite a wobble this year, the Irish gaming industry has doubled the number of people it employs in three years, to 2,800. McDonald's, the Danish brand Only and the DocMorris pharmacy group all recently announced expansions.

Of course, we don't want to read any of that. We are a nation of begrudgers, and as such, we fetishise failure and are enjoying the prolonged period of schadenfreude the recession has brought. That's the script, right?

Just ask Bono, who famously said: 'In the US, you look at the guy that lives in the mansion on the hill, and you think, "You know, one day, if I work really hard, I could live in that mansion". In Ireland, people look up at the guy in the mansion on the hill

Garda Eabhach Dineen (left) and Garda David Campbell, from Pearse Street station in Dublin, patrolling on their Segways in Grafton Street. Photograph: Eric Luke.

and go, "One day, I'm going to get that bastard".'

Alternatively, consult the current edition of the *Lonely Planet*, which describes begrudgery as our 'national sport' and accuses us of being 'fatalistic and pessimistic to the core'.

Dylan Collins, the chairman of video games company Fight My Monster and start-up ambassador for Enterprise Ireland, wrote about a similar phenomenon this week in a short blog post, in which he criticised Irish people's appetite for 'failure porn'.

'A lot of property developers lost a lot of money. Yes, by all means analyse how it happened. But stop turning it into some kind of fetish,' he wrote. 'Stop perving on the failure porn.'

As Collins rightly points out, we don't want to hear about the number of new start-ups when we could be reading in newspapers, like this one, about all the Icaruses who flew too close to the sun and got burned.

For all our rich literary heritage, it's surprising that we left it to the Germans to come up with a word for deriving pleasure from someone else's misfortune. But we've taken their schadenfreude and raised them a word of our own.

'Begrudgery' is the very Irish art of not being able to take pleasure in the success of perfectly nice, talented people such as Cecelia Ahern, Ryan Tubridy, Bill Cullen, Harry Crosbie or Rosanna Davison. It's that urge you get to stick pins in your own fingernails when you see a photo of Rory McIlroy and Caroline Wozniacki gazing at each other lovingly.

In the light of everything we've been through in the past few years, it's not surprising that 'failure porn' has emerged as something of a cultural meme. *Anglo the Musical* – that's about failure. The *Four Angry Men* tour? More failure.

It is worth bearing in mind that begrudgery is not a uniquely Irish characteristic: the Scandinavians have a similar phenomenon they call the Law of Jante, and the Australians have tall poppy syndrome. But we've got the best word for it and I'm willing to bet we do it better than anyone else.

But let's not be too hard on ourselves. For a small and relatively insular population, begrudgery might actually serve a purpose.

The sociologist Max Weber argued that in certain, closed societies with fixed hierarchies, the perception exists that there may only be a limited amount of attention, authority and material resources to go around. In this type of society, for someone to rise in status, another must fall.

In the closed society we call home, with its hierarchy of builders, developers, bankers and senior politicians, Weber's theory seems particularly relevant. As things 'got boomier', in the words of one former taoiseach, it was the golden circle that benefited most.

And later, when things 'went bustier', their yachts floated up on the rising tide of misery – and then sailed off to stiller, sunnier climes.

The begrudgers, of course, expected all this. They looked at the guy in the mansion on the hill and they knew that he would never have got there without over-generous lending on the part of banks, an absence of proper planning, lax financial regulation, and a property bubble fuelled by Government-funded tax breaks.

But here's the rub. Resentment towards the kind of people who bought the hot tubs, took out the expensive golf club memberships and drove the 2006 SUVs didn't do anything to curtail the madness, any more than being proved right will bring the naysayers much solace now.

If begrudgery's purpose is to put a brake on the hubris, then it's safe to say it hasn't worked.

So yes, our inability to appreciate the success of others might be part of who we are, a natural response to finding yourself part of a small, closed society – a society where, historically, a privileged few called the shots and opportunities for advancement were largely determined by who you knew – but it probably isn't doing us any good.

And that's why Collins is right. Maybe it is time we stop fetishising failure and focus on the good news.

FRIDAY, 30 NOVEMBER 2012

All Aboard the Hope and Hen Popemobile

Hilary Fannin

My father was a cartoonist. He drew a daily box cartoon for the *Evening Herald* and a weekly box cartoon for *Business & Finance* magazine, and in between he drank miniature bottles of Merlot and ate beef-and-onion sandwiches in O'Donoghue's on Baggot Street.

Bob went to work every day with a drawing pad and a pencil case; in the pencil case he had pencils, a scalpel to pare those pencils, and a selection of fine-nibbed felt pens – the instruments of his trade.

Cartooning may look like child's play, but it is not an easy job. All right, it's hardly going down the pit; it's not exactly negotiating fiscal stability in an igloo, or whatever it is busy people do these days, but, you know, as gigs go, there is pressure. Always pressure.

My abiding memory of Bob is of early mornings in the strange panto-set kitchen of one of the last houses my parents lived in, and of him gently heating a small measure of Paddy in the bottom of a bumpy saucepan to pour on his

Ruby Walsh, riding There's No Panic, takes a huge leap at a fence during the Fuller's Pride Novices' Steeple Chase at Newbury racecourse, England. Photograph: Alan Crowhurst/Getty Images.

porridge, while simultaneously berating the radio.

'Say something funny,' he would shout at the newscaster, 'for Christ's sake, say something funny.' He liked drawing cows, liked their eyelashes and their coy ankles. The beef tribunal made him happy. Mad cow disease was a godsend – all those crazy cattle jumping over a crescent moon.

But, day in day out, the news can be a poker-faced old bag in the corner who just won't give a man a break.

Anyway, I bring this up because recently I've begun to empathise with his plight. It's been a relentlessly grim time on our po-faced little island, and there just hasn't been a whole heap to smile about. I sit down to write and I find the keyboard dressed in black.

And then I picked up the newspaper and there was a front-page story about the Popemobile, which has had a makeover courtesy of its entre-preneurial owner, and has now become available to hire for stag and hen nights and corporate events. God, Bob would have loved it: all those eyelash extensions and diamanté tooth jewels, all that fake tan, all those blood-red acrylic fingernails and luminous thongs – and that's just the groom's party.

I was there in 1979 when pope John Paul II appeared in the Popemobile to the rapturous ecstasy of the youthful crowds. Well, I wasn't there actually: me and a handful of the damned were working in a hamburger bar on Talbot Street, which, despite our special offer of sanctifying grace on the French fries, remained empty (all right, I'm making up the sanctifying grace bit, but it seemed that nobody in Dublin could stomach a milkshake that night).

It's extraordinarily symbolic of how the times have changed: a hen party in the Popemobile. You could capitalise on this one and have a fleet of mobile-ettes in its wake offering a Brazilian and cocktail-shaking course, a shoulder wax and sushi bar.

I don't mean to offend anyone for whom the symbolic value of the vehicle has been demeaned by its new commercial status. As someone who grew up in a time when the wallpaper of repression was slowly being stripped away, it kind of feels healthy to recycle our past, to re-imagine some of its more peculiar relics. Hell, it's probably just a matter of time before some entrepreneurial type buys up the country's cobwebbed confessionals and turns them into tanning booths.

There are other less hedonistic plans for the Popemobile. The vehicle's owner has also spoken of his desire to get a sponsor on board to take the van around the country as a 'hopemobile', gathering stories about local heroes.

A fine and worthy enterprise indeed. And once the plastic ball-and-chains, the giant condoms, the glittering little cats' ears that hens wear on their heads to enhance their impersonations of scalded felines as they screech up and down the cobble-stones, once all this has been cleared out, along with the last banished strains of Boss and Polo, of eau-de-désirée and eau-de-credit-card-nuptials, people will flock to it.

It will be fantastic if the pope's chariot becomes a receptacle for stories of how neighbours bailed out floodwaters and skint relatives, of how skills were bartered and resources shared, of how communities coped in the flickering light of this stormy recession. We may be rolling in debt, we may be courting despair like hungry lovers, but, hey, at least the country's cartoonists have something to get their rubber fangs into. What is that old adage about an ill wind again?

SATURDAY, 1 DECEMBER 2012

Waiter, Waiter, There's a Lie in My Soup

Shane Hegarty

Does Bono watch Graham Norton on a Friday night, perhaps flicking over from the *Late Late* when the disease-of-the-week slot starts?

If he watched it last week he will have heard, from an Irish member of the audience, a story he's already familiar with. It went something like this: a guy and his girlfriend go to a fancy Dublin restaurant. They spy Bono and a friend at a table opposite. When Bono nips to the toilet, they ask his friend if he'll take a picture of them with Bono when he returns. Friend takes picture. They later ask for the bill. The waiter tells them it has already been covered. 'Did Bono pay for our meal?' they ask. 'No, his friend Bruce Springsteen paid for it.'

Cue laughter from star guests and audience. Cue many viewers enjoying this fun encounter. Cue other viewers shouting at the telly that it did not happen.

The Bono-and-Bruce restaurant story has become one of the most repeated urban myths of recent years. The details can alter – it might happen in Copenhagen, London, a variety of Dublin restaurants (most commonly Chapter One); some-times it's an autograph rather than a photograph – but the punchline is always the same: they didn't recognise Bruce Springsteen!

I'm going to go out on a limb and say that the man who appeared on Graham Norton is not the ground zero of this amazing anecdote that has spread far and wide.

The origin is uncertain: online there are references to it as far back as 2009 at least, and it appeared in Hugh O'Donoghue's 2010 book *Urban Legends Heard in Ireland*. The most recent edition of *The Encyclopedia of Urban Legends* uses it

A humpback whale breaches at the mouth of Baltimore Harbour in Cork. Photograph: Simon Duggan/Provision.

as an example of positive celebrity lore.

Bono is the central character in more negative urban myths, such as one that tells of him standing on stage, clapping his hands slowly while pronouncing: 'Every time I clap my hands a child dies in Africa.' During a pause a wag in the crowd calls out, 'Well, stop clapping your bloody hands.'

This is a mutation of a Bono-free Jimmy Carr joke, based on a real Make Poverty History campaign. It gained legs when the *Daily Telegraph* printed the Bono version as fact in 2006, and it still pops up occasionally in pieces that give the U2 singer a dig for tax double standards.

Why did it grow? Because people are keen to suspend belief for a story that feeds off the perception that Bono is a self-righteous prat who could do with having a notch or two taken off his

heel lifts. The Bono-Bruce story also flourishes because it can sound just on the right side of plausible, if told in sincere friend-of-a-friend fashion.

Both, though, are in essence jokes: a set-up and a punchline at odds with how most such Irish celebrity stories usually go. They tend not to be funny. And the joke is seldom on the teller.

In Ireland the most prevalent tend to be those that take on a particular nastiness; rumours that have run around and around until they've taken on a dark certainty that blackens the subject's name.

You'll all know one. You'll probably know a few. They are effectively slices of malicious gossip, but they often come framed in the 'I know the garda/nurse' context of urban myth. In several cases the subjects have had to publicly dispel fictional stories that have got out of hand.

Among the most pervasive urban myth of the late 1990s and early 2000s, for instance, was the Ronan Keating/Brian Kennedy/lovers/row/car crash, the kernel of which Kennedy and Keating have each been forced to dismiss more than once. Yes, I know you know the garda . . .

Those myths have stickiness because in a country in which everyone is connected, it's easier to accept it when someone says, 'It really did happen to a friend of mine. Or a friend of that friend, anyway.'

In the villages of twitching curtains, where secrets genuinely were hidden from view, and rumour filled the void, the greater focus put on a celebrity or sportsperson leads to greater rumours. And in the gap between the people and the establishment, you'll always hear the words, 'Sure, everybody knows it's true; they just won't print it.'

Anyway, the next time Bono is interviewed, maybe someone will ask him for his version of the restaurant story. Everyone has a Bono story. He'll surely have a few himself.

SATURDAY, 1 DECEMBER 2012

Artane Days Stayed with Ship Crooner

Mark Hennessy in London

In life, singer Matt Munro was a favourite of Dubliner John Ryan. In death, the strains of the crooner's 'Softly As I Leave You' greeted mourners as they gathered for his funeral this week.

The congregation at Golders Green crematorium in north London was small but select – friends Ryan had made over years attending the London Irish Centre's elderly lunch club.

Few of them, however, knew of his past: of life in Dolphin's Barn and then of years – too painful to speak about afterwards to all but a handful, and

John Ryan disembarking from the Canberra on a date unknown. Photograph: Will Oliver/the estate of John Ryan.

then only briefly – in the Artane industrial school in Dublin.

Born in 1928, Ryan's mother and father, Annie and James, died of TB before he was 12: the nine children went into homes, the four boys to

Artane. He never knew where his sisters had been taken.

For being an orphan, Ryan was sentenced to four and a half years for 'destitution', though he refused to go before the Residential Institutions Redress Board for compensation.

'He didn't want to go there, too many memories, none of them good. He said he saw his brothers frequently at the beginning but over time they were placed in separate sections,' said Cllr Sally Mulready.

'By the time he left he did not know whether his brothers had left before him or were still there when he left. In any case, he never saw them again,' she told *The Irish Times*.

Mulready had frequent contact in the London Irish Centre with Ryan, who spent years singing on cruise ships, in the weeks before he died in early November.

'He said to me, "I am really worried that they will put me down a hole when I die. I don't want to be buried down a hole. I am just a nobody and nobody will care",' she went on.

In late October, the two travelled to Levitons funeral directors in Camden to make arrangements: 'The taxi driver – he was an Asian man – asked us if we were going to a funeral.

'John said "I am going to see my own funeral. I want to see what it's like." He had a dry sense of humour. The driver swung around in his seat, totally taken by the story,' she continued.

The undertaker asked his religion. 'That was a long time ago. I want no priest or prayers at my funeral. I just want to go,' replied the single 84-year-old.

Ryan and Mulready left Levitons and went to his bank, where he drew down a cheque for £3,093 to pay for his last rites. 'He was a happy man coming back,' she commented.

Less than a fortnight later, he contracted septicaemia and was rushed from his sheltered accommodation in Camden to University College Hospital in Euston.

Before drifting into unconsciousness, he named Mulready as his next-of-kin, leaving her to organise a simple ceremony in Golders Green in accordance with his wishes.

Most of them in their seventies and eighties, and all Irish, the dozen-and-a-half mourners were discomfited by the lack of a religious service, but they complied, despite quiet murmurs of unhappiness.

Mary Allen read Yeats's 'Lake Isle of Innisfree', while Ann Sherwin sang 'Smiling Through', a song made famous by Richard Tauber. 'He had a philosophy of smiling through,' said Mulready.

Failing to hold back the tears, Maria Connolly, one of those who run the popular lunch club in Camden, was, nevertheless, joyful that so many had come to mark his passing.

'I will always remember him. The world goes on, but you wonder why it doesn't stop because such a lovely man has gone,' she said, speaking just feet from his funeral bier.

The people in the pews were asked for memories or tributes.

Neighbour, Eddie Carey, originally from Mitchelstown, Co. Cork, said: 'I never knew that he was in that hell-hole of a place.'

Later, back in the London Irish Centre, where he went three times a week, it was clear that Ryan had told few, if any, of the dark Artane days.

Penny Clune, from Ballina, Co. Tipperary, sat beside him for two years before he mentioned it, and then only briefly: 'He just said he couldn't talk about it, just said that they were bad. He didn't bring it up afterwards.'

If Artane was a past not to be reopened, Ryan happily shared memories of his days on the cruise ships 'singing Frankie Sinatra' all over the world: 'In the photographs, he was absolutely stunning,' she said with a smile.

The photographs of days on board the PO flagship SS Canberra were carefully kept in his flat in Ashton Court on the Camden Road, often still in much-thumbed company display cards.

Back in Golders Green, his coffin retreated behind the heavy metal doors, flanked by green curtains, to the sound of Seán O'Riada's 'Mise Éire'.

For now, his ashes will stay there as Mulready tries to track his relations. 'We'll scatter his ashes there in a year or so, if we can't find them. Or maybe we'll take them to Dublin and cast them into the Liffey. He was proud of being Irish, despite everything. Yes, maybe we'll do that,' she told *The Irish Times*.

His death certificate lists the details of his life and passing simply: 'John Joseph Ryan, born December 16th, 1928, died November 2nd, 2012. Labourer, Singer and Showman (Retired).'

'I've come to court . . . to ask you to assist me in having a peaceful, dignified death'

Kathy Sheridan

The imagery represented justice at its most humane. Three judges of the High Court deserting their lofty dais for a bench usually occupied by the

Wheelchair-confined Marie Fleming, an MS sufferer, leaving the High Court with her partner Tom Curran and family members after her hearing on whether she has a constitutional right to be assisted in taking her own life. Photograph: Cyril Byrne.

media, in order to sit at eye-level with a plaintiff.

They had little choice. The architects of the venerable, old courtroom off the Four Courts' Round Hall clearly never envisaged a plaintiff like 58-year-old Marie Fleming, formerly the assistant director of a university department, now terminally ill with multiple sclerosis and begging the court to be spared a 'horrible' death.

Shortly before 2pm, she came into court in her wheelchair with her partner of 18 years, Tom Curran, and her two children and stepson, her russet hair and jewel-red brocade jacket bringing a flash of colour to a sombre courtroom, packed with lawyers.

Only as her partner performed the slow, infinitely gentle tasks of a carer did the full extent of her disability become evident: carefully removing the blankets on her lap showing glimpses of the three-stone weight loss; peeling off the black gloves revealing the special, splinted gloves beneath, then gently rearranging her stiff, useless fingers; offering her sips of water through a straw; and tenderly moistening her lips with ointment.

Later she would give evidence of the collapsed shoulder which impinges on her lung and breathing function, of the 22 pills she needs to ensure her limbs are pliable and supple for the seven carers who come in to shower, toilet, dress her and put her back in the wheelchair.

'That takes two and a half hours. I often pass the afternoon sleeping, trying to overcome the tiredness of getting showered.'

On good days, she tries to get on with a book she is writing, with the help of a friend who types up her dictation. Then another carer 'comes back at 6 o'clock to put me to bed. Then the day starts all over again the next morning . . .'

She described the pain – 'so severe I'm afraid my head will burst open' – and the spasms 'which wreck my body, which pierce my very heart . . . My voice and swallow have progressively got worse. I would choke at least four times a day, when my back has to be thumped to get me starting to breathe again'.

Her death would most likely be caused by choking but first her speech – her only means of communication – will get worse. 'I've come to court today, whilst I still can use my speech, my voice, to ask you to assist me in having a peaceful, dignified death . . . in the arms of Tom and my children.'

None of her family winced or wept as Ronan Murphy SC led her through this evidence. This was nothing new to them. 'I have talked to all of my children and they know how I feel,' she said in slow, laboured but clearly enunciated words.

'There were a lot of tears shed and questions asked. But they see me and how my life has deteriorated . . . And they are very, very supportive.'

As the judges listened intently, lined along the hard bench with their hands in their laps, she told them she knew a woman with MS who had starved to death, who had died of hunger and thirst. 'That's not what I want. I want to go peacefully in my own home, with the people I love around me.'

Palliative care is 'not acceptable' to her. 'I don't want to be kept in a state whereby you're being given ingestions of massive doses of painkillers that may alleviate the symptoms of pain but leave you in a comatose state. To be kept in a state of not being able to smell the flowers, or to see my beautiful garden or just see the changing of the seasons. That's not acceptable to me to miss all that. I would be doing myself an injustice.'

She has no fear of death. 'I am at peace with the world . . . I have arranged my funeral – a wicker coffin, jazz music to play and my life to be celebrated.' She had even asked that her coffin be transported to the crematorium in the back of a car to spare expense.

She and her family discussed her method of assisted suicide 'non-stop', she said.

She had squarely confronted the methods of suicide available to her now in her paralysed state. 'The only way that is left for me to die is with the use of gas. By this I mean the usage of gas through a face mask. I could assist myself, either by moving my head to initiate the flow of gas or by blowing into a tube that would release the gas . . . I know I would be able to do it. I have practised it in my mind over and over again . . .'

Or a doctor could put a cannula into her arm to pass poison into her veins, she said. 'My physician has stated she wouldn't kill me but that she would help if it were lawful . . .'

She would welcome the presence of an independent observer, she said. 'We have nothing to hide . . .' After some 30 minutes, the questions ceased. None of the opposing counsel chose to cross-examine nor did the judges have any questions. As the courtroom emptied, the slow, agonising tasks were performed in reverse and the dignified little group moved slowly back to the van in the yard.

SATURDAY, 8 DECEMBER 2012

A Real Good Thing

Marie-Claire Digby

His food activism campaigns have changed the way millions of us shop, cook and eat, but it seems there's only one thing people want to know about Hugh Fearnley-Whittingstall, and it's got nothing to do with fish quotas or stressed chickens. No, it's his hairstyle that has people talking.

Stephen Fry once described it as 'the silliest hair in Europe', which the food writer and TV presenter says is 'a bit harsh – I had quite long, curly locks, like lots of people'.

Not any more, though. Sipping a pint of Guinness in a Dublin hotel, HFW sports a sleek short back and sides, and the transformation is quite remarkable.

'I actually just felt like a haircut for quite a while, and I couldn't do it for about a year because of continuity; I can't get a haircut in the middle of a series. When we began filming the first *Fish*

Hugh Fearnley-Whittingstall.
Photograph: Brenda Fitzsimons.

Fight series two years ago, there was a window of opportunity.'

His French wife, Marie, who was a reporter for the BBC World Service in Africa when they met, approved of the change, but 'the children were quite disconcerted for a while, though, because I looked so different'. The couple have four children, ranging in age from two to 16.

They don't live in the quaint farmhouse often seen in *River Cottage* TV footage – their home is another property nearby – so they weren't at risk when in February of this year, a renovated barn and kitchen at Park Farm, the *River Cottage* HQ, burned down. It was 36 hours before Fearnley-Whittingstall, who was away filming *Fish Fight*, learned of the setback. 'It was quite a surreal feeling. I was 500 metres from an iceberg, watching the penguins and seals while digesting the news of the fire.'

Putting that inauspicious start to the year firmly behind him, Fearnley-Whittingstall is in Dublin to promote his latest book, *Three Good Things . . . on a Plate*.

'It started as an idea that just popped into my head about how many great plates of food seem to comprise three good things that go together well – such as the great Irish classic, bacon, cabbage and potatoes, which has always been one of my favourite plates of food.

'I think the book is packed with original combinations, because once you've set the idea rolling it does encourage experimentation, and that's most of all what I hope the book is going to do for readers and for cooks at home.'

At his own home, Fearnley-Whittingstall will be bending the rule of three to embrace a Christmas of plenty. 'Because my wife is French and her parents and brother will be with us, it is quite full-on from a culinary point of view as the French will expect the big festive meal on Christmas Eve and then of course the English want it again the next day. We tend to have a fishy Christmas Eve and a meaty Christmas Day.'

So will it be turkey and all the trimmings, or will the cook formerly known as Hugh Fearlessly-Eatsitall, who has previously advocated the consumption of road kill, human placenta and puppies, have something more challenging on the menu? 'This year we've had a very good year of raising our own meat at home, so I'm not going to go out and get a goose or a turkey. It's going to be beef – sirloin – cooked very rare.'

But wait a minute, wasn't it just last year that

he eschewed his carnivorous ways in favour of a meat-free diet, appearing on the cover of *River Cottage, Veg Every Day* with shorn locks, sculpted cheekbones and a sissyish plate of salad?

Yet here he is, enthusiastically working his way through beef carpaccio, Carlingford oysters and venison – pausing only to enquire if it is Irish – for dinner in Fallon & Byrne. It's clear that if he did become a vegetarian, it was a short-lived experiment.

'There is an interesting, and possibly pedantic, semantic point there, because I would say I didn't become vegetarian, because it was never my intention not to go back to meat and fish. But I did four months that summer with no meat or fish, with almost no exceptions.

'I've never had any truck with the vegetarian-bashing that some conspicuously carnivorous chefs and food writers have gone in for in the past. I don't get it, as if there's something inadequate about not being a meat-eater. I completely respect it.'

Respect is something that is central to Fearnley-Whittingstall's belief structure. He puts his food activism down to a combination of things. 'On one level it's probably a family thing – my parents have always been a little bit politically engaged. They're both thoughtful people; they brought me and my sister up to question why we do certain things.

'Also, at university I studied philosophy and one of the things that interested me most was the ethical side of philosophy. When I first started rearing my own animals, I felt a huge sense of responsibility for that act of raising meat for my own plate. We all have a responsibility there and once you've gone down that route, there's no going back.'

He wasn't always such a driven, focused individual though. His mother, the gardening writer Jane Fearnley-Whittingstall, has said: 'There were times we despaired of Hugh ever finding a proper career.'

But he was unaware of his parents' concerns – 'they were always very supportive' – even as his early career segued from animal conservation in

Africa to cooking at the River Café in London – a position from which he was let go, he says, due to his lack of discipline in the kitchen; others have said he was a famously messy and disorganised cook.

He also worked in the media, as a sub-editor and as a restaurant critic. There was a spell on the obituary desk at the *Telegraph*, where he prepared Michael Jackson's obit, among others.

'I've never had a career plan and to some extent I still don't. Of course I have to plan ahead a little more than I used to and I have a big responsibility to the many people I work with, but a lot of what we all do together is talk about what shall we do next, what would be an interesting line to pursue.'

Next up, he is taking the River Cottage model to Australia, having signed a deal with Foxtel and the Lifestyle Channel, which has launched a hunt for 'the Aussie Hugh'. There are two more River Cottage Canteens and delis on the agenda too. So can we expect a River Cottage Canteen in Ireland?

'Wouldn't that be lovely. I've got a real soft spot for Ireland, which I haven't explored very much. But probably not just yet,' he says.

If the warm reaction Fearnley-Whittingstall got on this visit to Dublin is anything to go by, a River Cottage Canteen would give Jamie's Italian a run for its money. Midway through our chat, a young admirer – more biker than baker – bangs on the window to give him an enthusiastic thumbs-up. In Fallon & Byrne, where he insists on checking out the butcher counter before dinner, he's followed around the shop by fans.

He seems relaxed about the attention, but being in the public eye hasn't all been positive. 'I have had a little bit of flack for being a posh boy, for having a double-barrelled name, for hectoring the nation on eating organic food, or whatever. But I can take that. I can't change who I am or where I came from,' he says with the conviction of a man who's comfortable in his own skin – and his regulation corduroys and cardigan.

Public Outcry Unlikely to Change Gun Culture

Kevin Cullen in Boston

From the outside looking in, it would appear that the slaughter in Newtown, Connecticut, which took the lives of 28 people, including 20 children between the ages of six and seven, is the atrocity that would finally force Americans to drastically limit access to high-powered weapons and ammunition.

But it is not that simple. American gun culture has proved immune to public outcry and political pressure spawned by previous atrocities. Recent polls taken before the massacre showed that support among Americans for gun control measures was at the lowest point since the aftermath of the school shooting in Columbine, Colorado, in 1999 that left 12 high school students and a teacher dead.

Consider that on Thursday, the day before Adam Lanza used a legally purchased and registered military rifle to carry out the second-worst school shooting in American history, state legislators in Michigan passed a Bill that allows licensed gun owners to carry concealed weapons into schools.

On the same day, in the neighbouring state of Ohio, legislators voted to allow guns to be stored in cars parked in the garage of the Statehouse where they cast their votes.

In Florida, meanwhile, the state is preparing for a milestone: hitting the one-million mark for issuing firearm and concealed weapon permits. In Florida, the idea of a million people walking around with hidden weapons is something to be celebrated.

Like just about everything else, Americans are deeply divided about the need for, and the potential efficacy of, gun control.

Even as a nation weeps over what happened in Newtown, the reality is that nearly half of

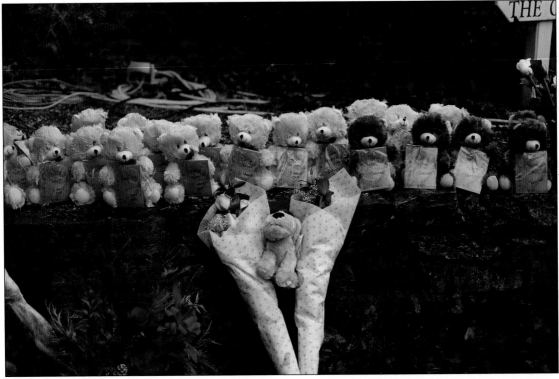

Teddy bears and flowers in memory of the 26 children and adults murdered by a gunman at Sandy Hook School in Newtown, Connecticut. Photograph: Spencer Platt/Getty Images.

Americans legally own guns, and they don't believe they are the problem. They believe that the criminals who will get guns, even if they are banned, are the problem.

They believe mentally unstable people, like those who shoot up schools or shopping malls, are the problem.

For every American who thinks it is absolutely ludicrous that guns – including those that can kill many people in a short period of time – and military-grade ammunition are so easily available, there are those who believe the number of fatalities in Newtown would have been lower if only the teachers who had rushed at Adam Lanza were carrying guns themselves.

'It's madness,' says Dr Judy Palfrey, a paediatrician at Boston's Children's Hospital and past president of the American Academy of Paediatrics.

Palfrey's group has been trying for years to have American gun policy reshaped as health policy, and to create a wider debate on how to create laws and strategies to reduce the incidence of gun violence.

But after the academy produced guidelines that required paediatricians to ask parents and caregivers whether there were guns in the home, and what steps had been taken to secure them, legislators in Florida created a law that exposed those doctors who asked that question to sanctions by the state's board of medicine.

The paediatrician's academy took the matter to court and, late last year, prevailed when a federal judge sided with them.

But the mere fact that a measure that was, on the face of it, aimed at safeguarding children could be construed by a state legislature as a meddling

A hearse carrying the casket of six-year-old Jack Pinto, one of the Sandy Hook murdered children, is driven to the Newtown Village Cemetery during his funeral service. Photograph: Lucas Jackson/Reuters.

intrusion into the rights of gun owners shows how difficult it is to reach a consensus on gun control in America.

Palfrey said the tragedy in Connecticut may be the catalyst to launch the first serious, sustained conversation in America about limiting access to weapons. 'If not this, then what?' she asked.

In the wake of the Newtown massacre, President Obama has offered vague assurances that he is willing to confront the issue, whatever the political fallout. But up to this point, Obama has shown little appetite to do battle with Republicans who are supported by the robustly funded and influential National Rifle Association and other gun enthusiasts.

During the recently concluded presidential campaign, the issue of gun control surfaced only once during the three debates between Obama and

Mitt Romney, and even then it was quickly shifted off the stage.

Obama said he was in favour of reinstituting an assault rifle ban that was passed in 1994 under Bill Clinton, but which expired in 2004 under George W. Bush.

Romney said he opposed reinstituting the ban, which if it had been in place would have made illegal the military-style rifle Adam Lanza used to kill his mother, 20 children, six teachers and himself.

But Obama's enthusiasm for the issue is in doubt. On Sunday, the *New York Times* reported that after the 2011 mass shooting in Tucson, Arizona, which killed six people and wounded 13 others, including Congresswoman Gabrielle Giffords, the US justice department drew up proposals to expand background checks designed to keep guns out of the hands of criminals and the mentally ill.

Those proposals were dropped, however, in the midst of a campaign during which Obama's aides were wary of antagonising the NRA, and as Republicans made political hay out of a gun-trafficking case in which federal drug agents surreptitiously passed guns to Mexican criminals, one of which was used to kill a US border guard.

Violent crime in general is declining in America, but mass shootings are one of the few instances of crime that is on the increase.

Gun control advocates like Palfrey say they believe a rational approach could start with reinst-ituting the assault rifle ban and by requiring background checks for those who buy weapons at gun shows or in private sales.

She is not naive about the influence of the NRA, the opposition to such measures at local level in many states, and how much work it would take to change a culture where individual rights often trump communal ones, even in the area of personal safety.

'We need leadership, and hopefully President Obama is up for this. We have to have this conversation, openly and honestly,' Palfrey said. 'What are we afraid of?'

TUESDAY, 18 DECEMBER 2012

The Year of Slut-Shaming, Creepshots, Malala and More

Laura Slattery

Adele was cut short. Donna Summer left us. We learned about the Red Room of Pain and Naomi Wolf's orgasms . . . a look back on 12 months of women in the news.

A is for Adele. In February the singer gave the finger to Brit Awards' organisers who disrespectfully cut her acceptance speech short. 'It was like the music industry's attitude to women played out as a metaphor,' tweeted Lily Allen.

B is for 'Binders full of women'. What Mitt Romney said he was given as governor when he asked for lists of qualified women for his cabinet. Tumblr-loving ladies were soon photo-graphing themselves bound between giant sheets of cardboard almost as wooden as Romney himself.

B is also for Bikini. Writer-filmmaker Nora Ephron, who died in June aged 71, was unequivocal: 'Oh how I regret not having worn a bikini for the entire year I was 26. If anyone young is reading this, go, right this minute, put on a bikini, and don't take it off until you're 34.' Not long to go now.

C is for Creepshots. Also known as 'revenge porn', creepshots are stalker-style photographs taken and/or distributed without consent by upskirt-loving predators. All the rage in 2012, a particularly nasty creepshots forum on the site Reddit was banned in October.

D is for Dowager Countess. In February, Downton Abbey's Cousin Violet (Maggie Smith) was praised in a BBC-commissioned ageism report for ranking among a select group of 'strong characters who did not seem to deteriorate as they aged'. What would the countess say? Probably something like this: 'At my age, one must ration one's excitement.'

E is for @EverydaySexism. The Twitter account of the year retweets stories from women about casual, 'everyday' sexism, from old-school street harassment to even older-school 'white with two sugars' workplace culture. They all add up to something far from casual.

F is for Feminist Ryan Gosling. 'Hey girl . . . I mean woman.' The internet meme by Danielle Henderson made feminists swoon by imagining the actor as a card-carrying gender deconstructionist. Now available in book form.

G is for Gillard, Julia. The Australian prime minister's blistering speech on the sexism of

The coffin of former Gaelic footballer Páidí Ó Sé is brought to the local cemetery at Ventry, Co. Kerry. Photograph: Niall Carson/PA.

opposition leader Tony Abbott comprised the perfect mix of anger and composure and was delivered with style, force and dignity. A good thing no one saw her stumble a week later when her high heels got stuck in soft grass. It was during a wreath-laying ceremony? Ah.

G also for #GoKatieTaylor. The feelgood Twitter hashtag of the summer. Right hook. Left hook. Gold medal.

H is for Hillary 2016. President Barack Obama had barely secured re-election with the aid of the female vote when the backs were peeled off the bumper stickers promoting a Clinton bid in four years' time.

I is for Intersectionality. Sparked by feminist/critic Caitlin Moran's tweet that she 'literally couldn't give a shit' that everyone in Lena Dunham's HBO comedy *Girls* was white, people who did care staged a heated debate around the not-so-controversial idea that prejudices on the basis of gender, race, class and sexuality are linked.

J is for 'Just the women'. When suspended *Newsnight* editor Peter Rippon noted in an email that his team had 'just the women' lined up for their report on Jimmy Savile, he was citing the journalistic need for multiple story sources. But the much-tweeted phrase also seemed to sum up the way in which victims had been dismissed and disbelieved for decades.

K is for Killing, The. All good things must come to an end, and so Sarah Lund (Sofie Gråbøl), one of the best heroines in television history, has completed her last case. As we now know they say in Denmark, tak! (Thanks!)

L is for Legitimate rape. If it's a 'legitimate rape', opined Republican Senate nominee Todd Akin, there's no need to worry about getting pregnant, as 'the female body has ways to try to shut that whole thing down'. Voters proceeded to shut Akin down.

M is for Mantel, Hilary. The *Bring Up the Bodies* author became the first woman to have won the Man Booker Prize twice. The second book in her Thomas Cromwell trilogy centred on the end-days of much-maligned queen Anne Boleyn, aka Cate Blanchett's mother.

N is for Never Again. The campaigning slogan was adopted by the pro-choice movement as it held marches and vigils in the wake of the tragic, anger-inducing death of Savita Halappanavar.

Abbey Fortune (left) and Grace O'Donnell, both aged four and pupils at St Josephs Nursery, Morning Star Road in Dublin, dressed as angels at the Mansion House opening of the IFA Live Animal Crib by lord mayor Naoise Ó Muirí. Photograph: Bryan O'Brien.

O is for Olson, Peggy. In *Mad Men*'s fifth season, working woman role model Peggy (Elisabeth Moss) finally escaped Don Draper's shadow.

P is for Pink lipstick. As featured in *Science: It's a Girl Thing*, a video released to launch the European Commission's campaign to get more teenage girls to study science. Its 'girl science' seemed to revolve around a love of cosmetics.

Q is for the Queen of Disco. Donna Summer, singer of 'I Feel Love', 'Bad Girls' and 1980s feminist anthem 'She Works Hard for the Money', died in May.

R is for Rabbit-food questions. At a Marvel's *Avengers Assemble* press conference, a male journalist asked Robert Downey Jnr about the conflict between Iron Man's egotism and maturity, and followed up by inquiring about Scarlett Johansson's Black Widow diet. 'How come you get the really interesting existential question, and I get the, like, "rabbit food" question?' an unimpressed Johansson rhetorically wondered to her co-star.

R is also for Red Room of Pain. 2012 will forever be remembered as the year *Fifty Shades of*

Helen Ngoma with her daughter Jacqueline during a HIV avoidance workshop by
Precious Kawinga. Photograph: Frank Miller.

Grey's sadist-in-residence threw down an architectural gauntlet to *Grand Designs*.

S is for 'Slut-shaming'. The new name for this age-old practice surfaced during the backlash to *Twilight* star Kristen Stewart, who had the temerity to sleep with someone who was not her boyfriend.

T is for Troublemaker. The translation of *La Frondeuse*, the title of a new biography of French president Francois Hollande's controversy-sparking partner Valerie Trierweiler. Hint: if they call you a 'troublemaker', you're probably doing something right.

U is for Unapologetic. The new album by Rihanna on which she duets with Chris Brown, the ex who once kept her in a headlock and punched her repeatedly until her cut face swelled and she screamed for help. Romance really has taken an odd turn.

V is for Vagina: A New Biography by Naomi Wolf, in which she extrapolated her latest goddess-infused pseudo-philosophies from the quality of her orgasms. Coming soon: *The G-Spot: A Memoir.*

W is for Women Bishops. A woman can be governor of the Church of England (Queen Liz) or a priest in it, but after the General Synod laity had their say in November, they remain barred from middle management.

X is for XX Factor. If you're outside the paid workforce for domestic reasons, you very likely have two X chromosomes. A Central Statistics Office study found paltry evidence of a 'househusband' trend, noting that 98 per cent of people looking after home or family are women.

Y is for Yousafzai, Malala. The 14-year-old Pakistani schoolgirl was shot in the head by the Taliban for defending girls' right to education. In November, the UN held 'Malala Day' in her honour.

Y is also for Yahoo, which in July became the first Fortune 500 company to appoint a pregnant chief executive, Marissa Mayer (37). She took two weeks' maternity leave and later shrugged off suggestions that having a baby is, like, hard. 'The baby's been way easier than everyone made it out to be,' she laughed in everybody's face.

Z is for Zoe Smith. The Olympic weight-lifter wrote a blog post on haters who trolled that it was unfeminine to do the clean and jerk (a weightlifting move). 'This may be shocking to you, but we actually would rather be attractive to people who aren't closed-minded and ignorant. Crazy, eh?!' Mad.

FRIDAY, 28 DECEMBER 2012

Some Like it Hoff

Donald Clarke

We all think we know Dustin Hoffman. It's not just that the great actor has been on our cinema screens for more than four decades. In 1982, he made the mistake (possibly) of appearing in a film that seemed to offer us a portrait of the artist as he then behaved. Michael Dorsey, protagonist of Sidney Pollack's imperishable *Tootsie*, is charming, irritating, fidgety and – most significantly – fanatical about his work. He won't sit down when playing a tomato in a commercial because it's not realistic.

By this stage in his career, Hoffman had established just that reputation. He was rumoured to argue incessantly with directors. No take was ever good enough. Tootsie seemed to confirm the impression.

'Tootsie was all my idea,' he chortles. 'And my friend Murray Schisgal. We wrote the first draft. It was meant to be a satire on myself. Actors who saw the movie saw it on a different level. We studied with acting teachers like Stella Adler or Lee Strasberg and we saw acting as a craft like writing. You had to know what kind of tomato you were. A writer would know that.'

Did he really cause as much trouble for his associates as Dorsey did for his own colleagues? A key scene finds Michael's agent, played by Pollack, solidly intoning the words 'nobody will hire you'.

'Hey, I had to convince Sidney to play the part,' he says. 'I said, "We are having these arguments every day. Let's put them on film".'

Hoffman looks impressively unchanged. The hair is grey. The face is creased. But he still comes across as an only slightly less hyper-charged version of the young man who energised American cinema in such movies as *The Graduate*, *Midnight Cowboy* and *All the President's Men*.

More encouraging still, not a scent of the rumoured stroppiness comes through. Now 75, Hoffman could hardly be warmer or more helpful. Talking at Gatling-gun pace, he powers his way through the entire career without pausing for breath. He laughs at his own mistakes. He drags up embarrassing moments. He's either an extremely nice fellow, a very good actor or . . . well, he's obviously both of those things.

We've been brought together to consider his delayed debut as feature director. The amiable *Quartet* stars Maggie Smith, Billy Connolly, Tom Courtenay and Pauline Collins as squabbling residents of a retirement home for classical musicians. I had heard that he had held off directing for so long out of a strange loyalty to his late father. The old man had always wanted to be a film director, but never quite managed it.

'Yes. I would say that's right. But it was never conscious on my part. I didn't want to invade his territory. After years of therapy, that did finally come to me. It might have hurt his feelings if I'd done it when he was still alive.'

Dustin Hoffman hams it up for the media at the Cannes International Film Festival in 2008. Photograph: Pascal Le Segretain/Getty Images.

Hoffman goes on to explain that his dad travelled to Los Angeles from Chicago during the Great Depression. He dug ditches and then somehow got a job in the props department at Columbia Pictures. An aspiration to direct never flourished and he ended up selling furniture.

Hoffman had no great ambitions to act as a child. Later, while at college, he stumbled into the business largely by accident.

'People often ask, "Do you come from a dysfunctional family?" I say, I have never met a family that's functional. I had some notion of being a doctor. Then, in junior college, somebody recommended that I take some acting classes. "It's like gym," they said. "You get three credits and nobody fails." I didn't think I was any good. But it was the first thing I'd studied where the time passed. It flew by.'

He spent some time at the Pasadena Playhouse and eventually met a teacher whom 'everybody thought was a communist because he taught Stanislavski'. Unsurprisingly, the rebellious young man was impressed and took his mentor's advice to move to New York, where he ended up rooming with lifetime pals Robert Duvall and Gene Hackman.

'We were very haughty in the early days,' he says. 'I hung out with Bob and Gene and we were very serious about what we did. We looked at British actors and we thought they were very technical, but they had no emotion. That came from our training.'

Dustin had to drive cabs and toil in bars for 10 years before he got his big break. Ever the purist, he tried to talk Mike Nichols out of casting him in *The Graduate* in 1967. Now nearly 30, he was, surely, too old to play a recent graduate. He was too Jewish to convince as a preppy Wasp. Happily, Nichols rejected his advice and the movie became a smash.

Did it all go to his head?

'The truth is really the opposite,' he says. 'I really should have revelled in it a bit more. But I denied it to myself. I felt badly that I didn't deserve it. That's why I didn't do another movie for a year. I didn't like movies. You don't get to rehearse as you do in the theatre. After *The Graduate*, I was sent all this stuff in my age range and it wasn't very good. So, I just focused on theatre until *Midnight Cowboy* came along. I'd be a bit better about that now.'

Hoffman now seems to look back on his early abrasiveness with a mixture of regret and amusement. Long in therapy, he doesn't exactly endorse the young Hoffman's attitudes, but he doesn't quite reject them either. So, what about those fights with directors? It can't have been much fun wielding a megaphone at the young Hoffman.

'It was annoying because, if I look back now, I was trying to engage my skills into film-making. It's like trying to paint a canvas on a train track. You are trying to get the painting done and the train is coming closer. You eventually have to pull the painting away before the train hits. That's what making a movie is like. They can't wait for you to get it right. It's all about money.'

At any rate, Hoffman prospered in the fecund hothouse that was 1970s Hollywood. He excelled as Lenny Bruce in *Lenny* and as Carl Bernstein in *All the President's Men*. This was a time when slightly difficult actors such as Hoffman or Hackman — men who did not look like matinée idols — could headline mainstream movies. In 1979, *Kramer vs Kramer* managed the unusual feat — now only accomplished by huge event pictures such as *The Lord of the Rings* — of winning the Best Picture Oscar and becoming the most financially lucrative film of the year. Accepting his first Oscar for best actor, Dustin whinged about the competitive nature of the event.

'I have been critical of the Academy and with reason,' he said. 'I refuse to believe that I beat Jack Lemmon, that I beat Al Pacino, that I beat Peter Sellers.'

Has he softened or does he stand by those views?

'Both. I don't think art is competitive,' he says. 'That doesn't mean we're not competitive as people. There's nothing wrong with that. I want to be better than the next person. In sports, somebody comes in first. That shouldn't be true in the arts. I don't think there's an absolute "best" in that world.'

We all assume that, during these years, the average Hollywood star had to wade through cocaine and vodka to make his or her way to the set. Somehow, I can't really imagine Hoffman partying with the beautiful people at Studio 54. He seems just a little too committed. He's certainly good fun, but he doesn't look like the sort of guy who could ever have been a drug bore.

'No, no, no. I wasn't that,' he laughs. 'But I got caught up in a little of that stuff. I was getting separated from my first wife and, yes, I became a devotee of Studio 54. I smoked some weed. But I was never exactly a hardcore drug person. You know the phrase: if you can remember the 1970s, you weren't there.'

It must be tricky answering these sorts of questions when you have children. Married to attorney Lisa Gottsegen since 1980, Dustin now has four adult offspring. Growing up, the young Hoffmans must have occasionally encountered interviews during which – being an impressively frank fellow – their dad discussed his mildly wild years. I suppose one has to fall back on the classic hypocritical formulation: do as I say, not as I did.

'Well, we're lucky,' he says with a proud swell. 'There are certain things we feel strongly about. None of our kids smoke. You quickly learn that if you say "don't", then they do it behind your back. I don't say "don't smoke marijuana". You show them a bong and point out the yellow residue and say: "Do you want that in your lungs? Make up your own mind".'

Hoffman has aged well. It's been a while since he dominated a movie, but he was excellent in the recent TV series *Luck* and offered a nice supporting role in Richard J. Lewis's *Barney's Version*. Then there is his new career as a director. It's taken seven and a half decades, but he's finally wrestled complete control of the movie. To return to that analogy, nobody can force him to abandon the canvas before the train hits.

'I have never done anything like this before and it's the hardest thing I have ever done and I would be loath to do it again,' he laughs. 'When you make a movie, you get up at 6.30am, you shoot maybe 15 or 30 minutes and the rest of the day you're resting. Promoting a movie is like doing three matinées a day.'

But he still looks so lively. One can't help but think of Dustin in *Little Big Man*. For that 1970 Arthur Penn film, he allowed himself to be layered with inches of heavy makeup when playing the character as an old man. As it happens, a few sprinkles of grey and a wisp of the China pencil would have created the 75-year-old Hoffman quite effectively.

'Everyone says I've had work done. I really haven't. There are relatives of my wife who say, "You've had it done". No, sorry. Ha ha!'

I've seen him up close. He's telling the truth.

WEDNESDAY, 2 JANUARY 2013

The Making of the European Mind

Enda O'Doherty

Ireland's presidency of the European Union, which started this week, is certain to focus on tackling urgent practical problems in the economic and financial sectors, problems it has inherited from its predecessor and that it will pass on in some form to its successor.

This time of persisting anxiety for Europe is perhaps not the ideal occasion to suggest revisiting and reacquainting ourselves with the union's foundational principles, but in the face of insistent

The crowning of Charlemagne as Emperor of Europe. Getty Images.

questioning (in Britain in particular but not just there) of the value of the project, we might pause briefly to examine in what context this unlikely political construct first arose and with what hopes it was set in motion.

The international agreements that were put together in western Europe from the early 1950s onwards, and that prefigured the EU, were most obviously a response to the recent trauma of war: the initial internationalisation and pooling control of coal and steel – the essential raw materials of modern war – was intended to make a re-emergence of conflict impossible.

There was also, however, in addition to polit-ical and economic motives, a quite strongly felt notion that the six original members – Germany, France, Italy, Belgium, Netherlands and Luxembourg – had a certain culture and history in common.

The new Europeans spoke – dialects and minority languages aside – a limited number of languages, of which English was not one. Historically, the territory covered by what was known to Anglophones in the 1960s as 'the Six' was not immensely different from that occupied by the Holy Roman Empire in the ninth century, which comprised Italy only as far south as Rome and not all of eastern Germany, but included present-day Slovenia and parts of Croatia.

In the 1960s, the prosperous core of the European Economic Community was a place of refuge for poor southern Italians, Portuguese and even Yugoslavs, though not for Saxons, who were pursuing their own experiment behind the inner German border. As regards culture, the Europe of Charlemagne at the time of his death in 814 was united, more or less, under the civil and ecclesiastical power.

Whatever languages and dialects were spoken there was a single language of culture, Latin, while in terms of intellectual authority the Roman Church was dominant, almost monopolistic.

Europe after 1945 retained strong Christian features: France, Italy, Belgium, southern Holland, the Rhineland and much of southern Germany were largely Catholic or post-Catholic; northern Holland and northern Germany were Protestant or post-Protestant. But the confidence of the churches had been shaken by 18th-century enlightenment and 19th-century positivism and science.

They had not gone away, but their mode was now more defensive than magisterial. What could replace them?

Some thought that culture and what was understood as 'our common European heritage' could bind us together as religion once had (it had also of course separated us). But what did this common European heritage actually consist of? Did it even exist? The founders of the EEC were practical men and their predominant concerns were economic and political ones.

And yet there was also a feeling that Europe was a cultural entity or an entity with common values and that it should, from time to time, say something about this.

It may be that the existence of a parallel organisation, the Council of Europe, with specific responsibilities for human rights and culture, for a long time kept the European Union from seriously engaging with the dimension of values.

In fact, it was not until the Maastricht Treaty in 1992 that the union formally took on competences in the cultural field.

There has always been something uneasy about the EU's entanglement with culture, as if this field of human activity sits somewhat awkwardly with the necessarily quantitative bias of institutions based on treaties, regulations and targets. This can be seen in the clunkiness of many official statements or scripts, worthy but ponderous genuflections that seem to quickly run out of steam after the initial ritual invocation of 'the Europe of Dante, Shakespeare, Beethoven'.

Is the problem then that there is no European culture, and that the apparent desire of 'Brussels' to create one to which we might pay allegiance (along with the Ode to Joy and the European flag) is doomed to remain a somewhat pathetic failure, a pasteurised amalgam of 'the good bits' of individual national cultures that has no credibility of its own? Are national cultures the only cultures there are?

In a weekly series, which will run throughout Ireland's EU presidency, I will attempt to suggest some of the things that a European culture might be or might have been through 26 brief vignettes of historical figures who have contributed something to the continent's learning, civility, knowledge and values over perhaps 15 centuries. They will include scientists, writers, musicians, artists, philosophical and religious thinkers, and politicians and statesmen.

I do not claim that this selection can present an adequate picture of the variety of European culture; one would need to feature more than 26 people to do that. Nor am I claiming that those I have chosen are necessarily 'the greatest Europeans' in the cultural field.

What I hope to achieve through my selection is to indicate some of the currents that have moved through Europe over the centuries, currents that I think suggest we have often had, in addition to our separate national stories, significant elements of a common story shaped by a common culture: not a homogenous culture but a richly multiple one, sometimes an oppositional one, which has been based on both faith and science, driven forward by rationalism and restrained by tradition while being enriched by impulses that are variously intellectual, aesthetic and ethical.

I will also be indirectly posing the question of where Europe begins and ends. Where is 'non-Europe'? Who does not belong?

I expect to find that Europe has not always meant what it means today, that it has no particularly obvious or self-evident borders and indeed that we do not know what it will mean in the future – if we are fortunate enough to see it survive.

If it does indeed survive, that may well be because we have come to realise that retaining a sense of common purpose may require more than merely economic bonds.

Charlemagne (otherwise Carolus Magnus, Charles the Great and Karl der Grosse) was born we do not quite know where some time in the 740s and died in 814 in Aachen (otherwise Aix-la-Chapelle).

Charles was the son of the Frankish king Pepin the Short. He himself became king in 768 and was crowned Holy Roman Emperor by Pope Leo III in Rome on Christmas Day 800.

The Franks were a Germanic people who over a few centuries moved out from their central territory of Austrasia (Belgium, eastern France and Rhineland Germany) to dominate, by the late eighth century, all of France save Brittany, the northern half of Italy and much of present-day Germany and Austria.

Charlemagne's expansion of his empire met with considerable opposition in Italy, on the borders of France and Spain and, particularly, in Germany, where the pagan Saxons, resisting forcible conversion to Christianity and led by their chieftain Widukind, inflicted a costly defeat on the Franks in 782 at Süntel. Charlemagne, by way of reprisal, had 4,500 prisoners executed.

A few years later, Widukind surrendered and he and his people became Christian. When it was judged necessary to present to later generations a more perfumed account of these dramatic events, Widukind was transformed into a spiritual seeker who, as a result of a vision, came over to the light. The feast of Blessed Widukind is celebrated on 6 January.

Out for an early morning walk, at Killiney Hill in Co. Dublin. Photograph: Eric Luke.

The Saxon chief belatedly became a hero of another sort, however, to the National Socialists. In Edmund Kiss's 1934 play *Wittekind*, alien Catholics are seen as conspiring to destroy German freedom. Thousands of Teutonic maidens have been rounded up to be forced to breed with Jews, Greeks, Italians and Moors unless Widukind/Wittekind submits. It is only to avoid this horrific fate that the chieftain and his people allow themselves to become Christian.

As with the Pax Romana and the Pax Britannica, the peace that Charlemagne brought came only after opposition had been extinguished by violence. But the peace itself was genuine, and fruitful. Charlemagne promoted literacy, inviting the learned monk Alcuin of York to his palace school at Aachen. Alcuin, somewhat unusually for the time, apparently did not believe in forced conversions and may eventually have had some restraining influence over the king in this area.

Charlemagne promoted schools and scriptoria, where books were copied by teams of scribes, and endowed cathedral and monastery libraries. At a time when literacy was virtually the exclusive preserve of clerics, he also built up a state bureaucracy on the model of the church, with a corps of lay civil servants and administrators now educated to read and write in the universal language, Latin, which became the lingua franca that bound together a sprawling empire speaking scores of languages and dialects, from northern Spain to the Elbe.

The emperor himself, it seems, never mastered the skill of writing, though he could converse in Latin and Greek as well as his native language, Frankish. But what 'nationality' was Charlemagne? If you walk down the right-hand side of the long main street of the pleasant Dutch town of Vaals, you will notice, just after you pass the pizzeria La Frontiera, that the shop names have changed to German. You have, in fact, just left Vaals and entered Aachen. If you don't go quite that far along the street but swing right down Randweg, seven or eight minutes' drive will bring you into Belgium. In this corner of Europe where three countries meet, the notion of nationality can seem a little insubstantial.

Charlemagne's Frankish was a Germanic dialect that nevertheless gave many words to the French language, including the word France. One theory holds that the future emperor was born near the city of Liège, 40km west of Aachen: perhaps he was that most European of things, a Belgian.

FRIDAY, 4 JANUARY 2013

The Shocks of a January Detox

Hilary Fannin

January, the snivelling old prankster, snuck in the back door when we weren't looking. There we were, giddy with slothfulness, lolling around with warm wine and chocolate oranges, slumped and rippling like moist dough on our squeaky new couches, watching satisfyingly bleak Swedish detective programmes and scratching our sagging backsides. And there was January, blue and frosty and yellow-fanged, sliding open the patio door and slipping into the house.

January. Time to fret and fail, time to chuck out the empties, time to throw open the windows to the gales and the rain and the soul-destroying music of other people's house alarms. Time to unpack the New Year's resolutions, the fresh and the familiar and the downright cruel, and embrace the crawling shock of detox.

It's time, my friends, to check in for the long black nights of self-loathing and pound-shedding and nicotine-withdrawing; time to wade out of the lake of damn fine half-price French wines and stand, shivering, naked, fat and bruised, on the shores of our excess.

They say we fail, or rather our resolve fails, because we aim too high. We want to fly too close to the sun; we want too much too fast. We want to be perfect versions of what we are. Along with the creamy liqueurs and spongy Maltesers and cold roast potatoes, we've also ingested an unhealthy diet of airbrushed celebrity. The most common New Year resolution is not to improve our souls or cultivate our wit (though many of us would like to read more and watch less television); no, if the screaming from the magazine racks is to be believed, what most of us want is to lose weight and get fit.

Routinely, we women in particular (although by no means exclusively) say we hate ourselves, or at least bits of ourselves. We stand in front of mirrors in cafés and shops and other people's bathrooms and wail, 'Oh God, I look like an elephant.' We bump into each other in car parks and dark bars, and terrorise each other.

A friend says: 'You look fantastic! Have you lost weight?' And immediately the thought, like a tiny whip, occurs to you: 'Christ, I must have looked like a shagging house the last time she saw me.'

Some poor fool offers us a chocolate biscuit in January and we accuse them of insanity. Are you mad? Are you out of your mind? Offering me empty calories when I spent the last two hours trying to make the measuring tape I got out of the Christmas cracker actually circumnavigate my waist? Don't you recognise obesity when you see it? Don't you register the straining seams of my less-than-attractive leggings? Are you trying to sabotage my determination? Ruin my life?

We recite mantras to each other; we say that we hate our knees or our hips or our stomachs or our thighs. We say we hate the way we look on the beach or in the bath or in the neon chamber of a mirrored dressing room. We say we want Kate Middleton's upper arms and Cheryl Cole's hair extensions and Beyoncé's derrière and Daniel Craig's pectoral muscles.

We say we are going to work at it, get there, climb that mountain, smooth out those ripples, tighten those godforsaken abs. God almighty, I just want to get through a week of this brand new year

without someone encouraging me to hang out of ceiling bungees and bounce my bootie up and down in the name of fitness.

What did we do before fitness? Eh? My granny certainly never ran a half-marathon and a lunge in any direction would have been out of the question. Why can't we wear slips and nylons and big tweedy skirts again, and sit down and do the crossword and watch the birds break the ice with their beaks?

Why do we have to run around in Lycra and row to China and run to Offaly and cycle the Americas? Why do we attack ourselves like hungry piranhas at the first sign of a muffin-top?

The British minister for women and equalities, Jo Swinson, has written an open letter to magazine editors, asking them to consider the negative health implications of promoting 'miracle diets' in the post-Christmas rush to purgation. She also said in an interview that women could do more to help each other ignore the media pressure to get thin. I think she's right. We should resolve to ignore the call to skinny arms, abs and asses.

I think we should be radical, fundamental. I think we should march steadfastly against the grain and give ourselves a break. Now where's the corkscrew?

SATURDAY, 12 JANUARY 2013

A Master at Keeping the Show on the Road

Paul Cullen

Just hours after her widely praised address to the Oireachtas health committee hearing on abortion last Tuesday, Rhona Mahony was back doing what she does best in her day job at the National Maternity Hospital.

There were babies to deliver, ward rounds to complete, emails to answer and funding applications to submit.

Rhona Mahony, Master of the National Maternity Hospital. Photograph: Eric Luke.

She travelled to RTÉ for a quick interview, walked back to the hospital and was home in time to say goodnight to the children at 8.30pm.

Mahony, always outwardly calm and impeccably precise in her locutions, projects a 'business as usual' image about her busy life. 'I'm just a bog-standard person,' she insists. 'At the end of the day there's still the lunchboxes to fill and the homework to correct.'

Yet these days are anything but usual for this 42-year-old Dubliner who has been catapulted into public view since she was appointed last year as the first woman master of a Dublin maternity hospital. Mahony, for all her protestations, is anything but run of the mill.

She isn't the only obstetrician helping to keep the abortion debate on the straight and narrow; Peter Boylan (her brother-in-law) and Sam Coulter Smith have also made incisive contributions.

However, the fact that she is a woman who has broken through the glass ceiling in a traditionally male-dominated profession has added resonance to her remarks.

Mahony spoke to the hearing not just as a professional but as a woman, one who was personally offended by 'pejorative and judgemental views that women will manipulate doctors in order to obtain termination of pregnancy, on the basis of fabricated ideas of suicide ideation or intent'.

There is also a 'how does she do it?' element to the fascination about Mahony, evident this week in online discussions.

She puts in 12-hour days in a stressful job and spends the weekends on call, yet somehow juggles this with her responsibilities at home, where four children range in age from six to 14.

Belying her relative inexperience in the worlds of politics and media, she entered the Seanad chamber on Tuesday to deliver a calm, measured analysis of the abortion issue.

It was the kind of dissection of the issue that only a practitioner would make, one whose working life involves making life-and-death decisions about the women she treats and the babies they carry.

Hers is a profession charged in rare circumstances with making highly complex clinical decisions based on medical probability but without the luxury of medical certainty, she told the politicians present.

'It is imperative that we have flexibility to do so, to make decisions based on medical fact. It is imperative that we have legal protection to do this.

'What,' she asked, 'is a substantial risk to life during pregnancy – a 10 per cent risk? a 50 per cent risk? an 80 per cent risk? a 1 per cent risk of dying? The interpretation of risk is not the same for all people.'

Directly addressing the 'grey areas' doctors want the politicians to address in legislation, she added: 'I need to know I will not go to jail if in good faith I believe it is the right thing to save a woman's life to terminate a woman's pregnancy. I want to know I will not go to jail and I want to know that she will not go to jail.'

Mahony's two-minute contribution got the proceedings off to a good start and set the tone for the generally dignified three days of hearing that followed. One critic felt afterwards that the exercise amounted to 'window dressing' but was forced to admit it was 'thoughtful window dressing all the same'.

As master of Holles Street, Mahony is effectively chief executive of the hospital on a seven-year stint. With over 9,000 babies delivered each year, the hospital is one of the busiest in Europe, but its premises, which featured in *Ulysses*, are overcrowded and dilapidated.

A move to a modern building, most likely beside St Vincent's hospital, is the top priority for her term in office. In the meantime she is busy trying to raise funds, and has set up a foundation headed by former ESB head Pádraig MacManus.

Raised in Raheny, Dublin, she is not from a medical family. The decision to become a doctor was an early one, from the time she got her first Fisher Price doctor's kit for Christmas. After studying medicine in UCD, she followed the usual peripatetic route of junior doctors, with spells in many of the main Irish hospitals and a fellowship in Birmingham.

Her speciality is in foetal medicines, which means that she often deals with the kind of complex and high-risk pregnancies that are at the heart of the current debate.

Gender hasn't been an issue in her career. 'No one is bothered so long as I can do the job.'

She sees her elevation as the natural result of the rise in women studying medicine and then becoming consultants; one-third of the consultants in Holles Street are now female.

This month Dr Sharon Sheehan became the second female master when she was appointed to the post in the Coombe women's hospital.

Outside work, Mahony likes to run a few 10km a week 'to keep my head clear', and says she will read 'anything, but especially history'. She credits a supportive but publicity-shy husband, who also works in the health service, as well as helpful colleagues for helping her keep the show on the road.

Thus far she seems to have escaped the rancour that can attach to the abortion debate. Or perhaps all of that seems relatively unimportant compared with a job where, she says, 'the good days are fantastic but the bad days can be desperate'.

FRIDAY, 18 JANUARY 2013

Stage Struck

Peter Crawley

A few days ago, in circumstances that came about largely by accident, I set myself a test. Rarely do you get to the theatre without knowing something

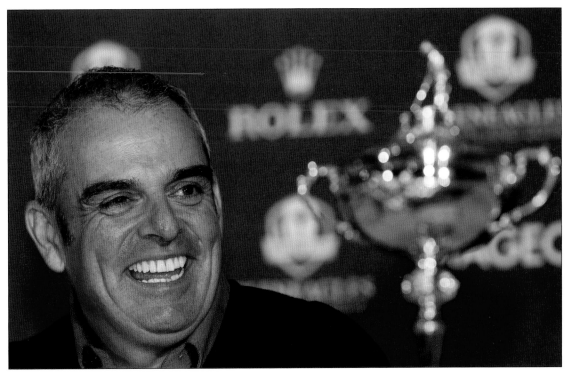

Paul McGinley of Ireland poses with the Ryder Cup trophy after being announced as the captain of the European team for the 2014 Ryder Cup. Photograph: Andrew Redington/Getty.

about the production beforehand. Maybe you've read the play. Perhaps you know the work of the company or the director. Or, at the very least, you almost always know the title of the play. I say 'almost' because last October, during the interval of *The Select (The Sun Also Rises)*, a show based on Ernest Hemmingway's novel, a woman bearing the wrong programme and a confused expression asked me why it was called *Hamlet*.

Last week, though, I was in her position. The 24 Hour Plays, staged as a fundraiser for Dublin Youth Theatre, had attracted an impressive group of professionals for its frantic exercise in accelerated theatre-making.

I took my seat without getting a programme but, I thought, the style of the six playwrights – Fiona Looney, Amy Conroy, Arthur Riordan, Michael West, Paul Mercier and Gina Moxley – ought to be as unmistakeable as a fingerprint, and

any critic ought to be able to pick the directors out of a police line-up (Garry Hynes, Louise Lowe, José Miguel Jiménez, Alan King, Annabelle Comyn and Jason Byrne).

So began the game of Spot the Playwright/ Director. In James Surowiecki's book *The Wisdom of Crowds*, a cogent argument that – among other things – groups of collaborators are smarter than any individual, he mercilessly debunks the idea of expertise.

Financial experts continually underperform in the market, lay people are better at predicting human behaviour than psychologists, and, worryingly, half the time pathologists will differ over the cause of death. All of which is a long way of admitting that I got two guesses right out of 12.

With the expertise of a non-psychologist, I know what you're probably thinking: 'Don't be so hard on yourself, Crawley! You're perfectly well qualified for your job. And, besides, the programme was probably lying.' Well, yes and thank you. But I've wondered ever since what else a blind audition approach might reveal if we arrived at a theatre stripped of expectation or prejudice. For instance, tests have shown that wine experts favoured identical wine from more expensive bottles. (Then again, those tests were run by psychologists.)

(Last week, I was surprised, at The Theatre Machine Turns You On: Vol 3 festival of new work, by how many young artists were making work about their own lives, as though inhibited by the old adage: write what you know. A better approach, for so-called experts and beginners alike, is to get a greater understanding of what you don't know and seek to fill the gaps in your knowledge.)

'Isn't it great that the theatre can still surprise you?' somebody said as I reported my score and sought whatever charity I could get. More usefully, though, I better understood the extent of my own ignorance.

SATURDAY, 19 JANUARY 2013

Obama: The Toughened Veteran of a Turbulent First Term Who Finally 'Gets It'

Lara Marlowe

As I prepare to leave Washington for Paris after four years in the US, I consider Barack Obama, the pragmatic idealist about to start his second term. Over the next three days, as Barack Obama's first term ends and his second begins, a chapter of my own life closes.

After spending virtually my entire adult life in Europe and the Middle East, I returned to the US in 2009 because I wanted to cover the Obama

presidency for *The Irish Times*. For three and a half years, he's been the central character in the narrative I wrote. When they tidy up Washington after the inaugural balls, I'll begin packing to go back to Paris.

Several Barack Obamas inhabit the American psyche. I've found elements of truth in all of them, except the paranoid, right-wing vision of a foreign-born Muslim Marxist who is hell-bent on transforming the US into 'socialist Europe'.

Jaded political observers see Obama as a cool customer whose image is fashioned by PR executives choreographing teleprompter speeches. To many of the 66 million Americans who re-elected him in November, Obama is a fundamentally wise and good leader, struggling to deliver America from its demons.

In recent days, another Obama has emerged: the toughened, street-smart veteran of a turbulent first term who finally 'gets it'. That 'make my day' Obama this week warned Republicans against taking the US economy hostage in the next round of fiscal chicken. Presenting the first serious gun control initiative since 1994, he urged the public to ask Republicans in Congress 'what's more important? Doing whatever it takes to get an A grade from the gun lobby that funds their campaigns or giving parents some peace of mind when they drop their child off for first grade?'

Ultimately, we judge our leaders by the emotions they provoke in us. I know of no other living politician who can move audiences as Obama can. For me, the speeches that stand out are Cairo in 2009, Dublin in 2011, Chicago on election night last November.

He gives us hope, which he defined in Chicago as 'that stubborn thing inside us that insists, despite all the evidence to the contrary, that something better awaits us'. He calls us to a better self, to 'a generous America, a compassionate America, a tolerant America'.

A campaign photograph of Obama hugging his wife Michelle became the most tweeted image in history. On Monday, we'll see the Obamas with

US President Barack Obama and first lady Michelle Obama wave during the inaugural parade down
Pennsylvania Avenue in Washington DC. Photograph: Doug Mills/Reuters.

their two beautiful daughters on the Capitol steps. That tightly bound family unit is part of the emotional contract that Americans have with him.

When Obama won the Nobel Peace Prize in October 2009, detractors, and even some supporters, said he won it for making speeches. His more pedantic addresses have put me to sleep. Some angered me.

He accepted the peace prize with a contorted apology for war. In September 2011, before the UN General Assembly, he acknowledged having called the previous year for 'an independent, sovereign state of Palestine' to be admitted to the UN. Then he rescinded that promise, saying, 'Peace will not come through statements and resolutions at the United Nations.'

Abandoning the Palestinians may have been necessary to secure re-election, but it was not his finest hour.

Obama saw his mother's naive idealism as weakness. An idealistic streak runs through him, but pragmatism is his default response. He addressed the tension between them in *The Audacity of Hope*. For his hero, Abraham Lincoln, 'It was never a matter of abandoning conviction for the sake of expediency. Rather, it was a matter of maintaining within himself the balance between two contradictory ideas,' he wrote.

At least the president is conscious of the compromises he makes, of the little pieces of his soul he sells off in the belief it's for the greater good.

That balance between contradictory ideas endows Obama with a rare emotional efficiency. It enables him to get angry over the Gulf oil spill and shed tears over the massacre of schoolchildren. But it also allows him to prosecute a drone war that has killed hundreds of civilians in Yemen, Afghanistan

Munster's Mike Sherry scores a try, supported by Peter O'Mahony, during his team's Heineken Cup match against Racing Metro at Thomond Park in Limerick. Photograph: Billy Stickland/Inpho.

and Pakistan. He sees the drone war as a necessary evil. He is dispassionate, not morally tortured.

Obama is daring and cautious: daring when he gambled his first term on healthcare legislation and when he ordered the assassination of Osama bin Laden; cautious in dealing with the Arab Spring, Syria and Libya.

One constant arcs through the Obama presidency. He plays the long game. If Bill Clinton craved the immediate gratification of popular adulation, Obama wants to leave a legacy. He wants to go down in history as a great president.

But as he said in his first inaugural address, 'Greatness is never a given. It must be earned.' It often takes hard times to reveal a great president. Lincoln had the War of Secession; Franklin D. Roosevelt the Great Depression and the Second

World War. One wonders what trials await Obama in his second term.

Four years ago, he said he had 'come to proclaim an end to the petty grievances and false promises, the recriminations and worn-out dogmas that for far too long have strangled our politics'.

Instead, Congressional Republicans transformed the system of checks and balances bequeathed by the Founding Fathers into a straitjacket to bind the president.

The greatest threat to America is not al-Qaeda or illegal immigrants. It's not nuclear proliferation or even the deficit. It's the inability of Republicans and Democrats to agree on the most basic tasks of governance.

Now Obama appears to be winning the war of attrition with Congressional Republicans. The

A participant gets airborne during the Red Bull Storm Chase in Bandon Bay, Co. Kerry, where they faced winds of up to 60 knots. Photograph: Sean Curtin Photo.

public places most of the blame on Congress for the polarisation and gridlock that marred his first term. In opinion surveys, Congress rates lower than root canals, cockroaches and lice.

Meanwhile, Obama enjoys his highest poll numbers in three years. Sixty-one per cent of Americans say he is a strong leader.

We're all a little older and wiser. Obama's handling of climate change shows how he has evolved. He's avoided the *sturm und drang* of an ideological debate, while quietly strengthening the Environmental Protection Agency, promoting innovation, electric cars and clean, alternative energy.

Obama has scored significant victories in the run-up to his second inauguration. On New Year's Eve, he wrested the first tax increase from Republicans since 1990.

This week, Governor Jan Brewer of Arizona, one of 25 states that challenged the Affordable Care Act in court, announced she would embrace a key component of the law by expanding Medicaid for the poor.

And yesterday, to escape blame for undermining the US economy, Republicans dropped their conditions for raising the debt ceiling.

Gun control was not an issue in last year's presidential campaign. But the 14 December massacre of 20 children and six adults in a Connecticut school profoundly altered public opinion, with 54 per cent of Americans asking for stronger gun control, compared with 39 per cent last April. Obama has seized the moment to challenge the National Rifle Association to what it calls 'the fight of the century'.

This feels like a propitious juncture in American history, a happy time to say goodbye.

On Monday, I'll watch Obama take the oath of office on the Capitol steps, with his right hand on the Bibles of Abraham Lincoln and Martin Luther King jnr. His voice will resonate down the Mall, a reminder of what he calls 'Dr King's mighty cadence'. There will be many a knotted throat and teary eye, and we'll marvel that America produced such a man, and think he is better than the country he represents.

And that is how it should be.

TUESDAY, 22 JANUARY 2013

The Tentative Beauty of Basil Blackshaw's Art

Aidan Dunne

Basil Blackshaw cleared himself a corner in Northern Irish art in the 1950s, and he has lost none of his ability when it comes to the exploration of the 'purely visual image'.

Basil Blackshaw is one of the most highly regarded Northern Irish artists to have emerged during the 20th century, and he is also one of the most brilliant. To mark his 80th birthday, the Royal Hibernian Academy and the F.E. McWilliam Gallery and Studio in Co. Down jointly invited the artist to select a retrospective exhibition. As even a cursory glance around the show at the RHA will confirm, he is a brilliant draughtsman and painter, fluently adept while never interested in showy virtuosity. In fact, a significant component of his brilliance has to do with this quality of reticence, a reticence that could even be described as evasiveness.

Blackshaw was an early developer: he was acclaimed as a precocious talent and enrolled in Belfast College of Art when he was 16. But from early on he managed to sidestep any of the things

The Gawky Cockerel *by Basil Blackshaw (1996, oil on panel). Photograph: Royal Hibernian Academy.*

that might have stereotyped him as a great, 'official' Ulster painter, or as pretty much any other kind of establishment figure. In his 1957 essay *A Portrait of a Young Man as the Artist*, John Hewitt presented a concise overview of Northern Irish art of the time and concluded that Blackshaw was 'clearly the most promising of the Northern painters of his age group. He has, in spite of his youth, cleared a corner for himself among the artists of this country'.

'Cleared a corner' strikes just the right note for a distinctly rural artist. Blackshaw's instinct has been to keep that corner consistently clear. Traditionally, artists tended to make a living by teaching part-time in the schools they have attended. In Belfast, Blackshaw found himself working as an assistant to his teacher, Romeo Toogood, whom he admired greatly and acknowledged as an important influence. But as he put it bluntly: 'I wasn't interested in teaching.'

When a heavy spell of snow prevented him

getting in to the college, he simply didn't go back once the snow had cleared. He walked away from a subsequent job in a technical school in the same way.

It has been noted that Blackshaw's work does not engage directly with the Troubles, which echoes similar criticism of Seamus Heaney. Equally, it could be said, Blackshaw did not get pointlessly diverted into mainstream modernism, gravitate towards the British art world, or relax into a provincial version of either, a fate that befell many Northern Irish artists preceding and contemporaneous.

Not that his record is unblemished. Blackshaw has owned up to being unduly swayed for a while by the 1980s vogue for neo-expressionism, an influence evident until about 1990. But in general he has not been averse to influences. There are many, some obvious, but he has usually managed to absorb them well, infusing them with what Hewitt termed his 'characteristic intensity', an intensity deriving from and 'within the circle of his experience'. It is this immediacy that comes through strongly in his best work.

Oskar Kokoschka was an early influence, but Blackshaw quickly became wary of the risk of painterly swagger underlying such a bold, expressive manner. Paul Cézanne was and perhaps is important with respect to Blackshaw's approach to landscape, but he has always made something personal and exceptional with anything taken from Cézanne. As early as 1953 his *The Field* is a superb, fully achieved, iconic painting.

Alberto Giacometti is another enduring influence, most notably in the portraits, figure paintings and nudes. In one sense Blackshaw, at home in muddy rural lanes amid dogs and hens and horses, may seem like an unlikely painter of the nude, but he was lucky enough to encounter a model, Jude Stevens, who has been an inspired collaborator in a long series of very fine paintings. Stevens has also written informatively about the experience of working with Blackshaw.

Lecturer and critic Mike Catto once referred to the 'hesitation' of Blackshaw's style, immediately pointing out that hesitation wasn't quite the right word. But it does convey Blackshaw's practice of only taking a painting as far as it needs, and of closing in on it as though he is stalking it. He never goes for an overly elaborate finish, lending a great deal of what he does a beautifully tentative, sketchy quality.

On occasion, the image as such is barely there, bringing to mind the Lacanian idea expounded by Darian Leader in his book *Stealing the Mona Lisa* that a painting is in essence a screen for what lies beyond it, a decoy designed to engage our attention.

Blackshaw's most fully achieved exposition of this idea – and there is no suggestion that he was consciously setting out to do this – is in a magnificent series of *Windows* paintings made in the early 2000s. As minimal and spare as Rothko, with a more austere palette, these works indicate how serious Blackshaw is about what he does.

The impulse to configure the painting as a screen is evident in every area of his work, including figure paintings and portraits. It should be said, though, that when he paints people and, even more so, animals, they are certainly there before us. Just look at his paintings of dogs or horses in isolation, and you can feel a direct, nervous connection with a living animal.

Blackshaw prioritises that moment of looking. He is famously uneasy about theorising. When he noted, in an interview with Brian Kennedy, that he would like to own a drawing by Joseph Beuys, he quickly elaborated: 'I think his line is beautiful. But there again talking about association, Beuys had a philosophy behind his work but I took no notice of this.

'I just love his line and love his images. I wouldn't want to know what they are about, it doesn't matter to me. People always want to know what a painting's about, but I don't as long as I enjoy the image – a purely visual image.'

SATURDAY, 26 JANUARY 2013

Farewell to the Man Who Gave Dublin Star Quality

Miriam Lord

We grew up in the shadow of Croke Park, but never knew it until Heffo arrived. We grew up in the grey shadow of Croke Park, but never really knew it.

It was the place where country people went on a Sunday. They would park their cars on our street and cut through Ballybough and up the Clonliffe Road.

Going to 'the match'. It rankled, even though we didn't have a car.

The younger boys collected English football cards, untroubled by the swelling roars from Croker as they sat out on the path swapping them.

Heighway, Bremner, Best, Giles, Osgood. These men were their sporting stars, but distant ones they could only see in a magazine.

Micheál O'Hehir provided the soundtrack for those teenage Sundays. There was always Gaelic on the radio, but it was background noise, no more.

Until Heffo came along.

And with him, these gorgeous young men with flowing hair and attitude and slacks that flared from the hip. Real football stars, not photographs from a packet of chewing gum.

They were exciting, they were sportsmen, they were winners and they were ours. This was

Kevin Heffernan, photographed in 1989 by Billy Stickland. Photograph: Inpho.

Dublin supporter Gerry Gowran with the memorial booklet for Kevin Heffernan's funeral at the Church of St Vincent de Paul, Marino, in Dublin. Photograph: Eric Luke.

Gaelic football, this was showbiz and this was DUBLIN!

Summers would never be the same.

Kevin Heffernan, the manager, gave a lot to the GAA, but he gave a lot more to his city. He gave us pride and a sense of belonging and he gave us some of the best times ever.

The team and the hysteria came from nowhere. It was 1974 and, suddenly, Dublin were in an All-Ireland final.

We went mad.

Those things that everyone takes for granted now – the hype, the hoopla, the chants, the songs, the dressing up and the painting over – it didn't really happen back then. Heffo's Army changed that forever.

We swarmed up the grassy slopes behind Hill 16, packed onto the terrace and swooned.

When it rained, the dye from our paper hats ran down our faces. When it rained, the grassy slopes turned into a swamp and you risked life and limb sliding down. It always seemed to be raining, but it didn't matter. Croke Park meant something now.

The Corpo made Kevin Heffernan a Freeman of Dublin in 2005. All they did was put an official stamp on what happened 30 years ago.

Now, the man who shaped our seventies summers is gone.

Oh the Jacks are back, the Jacks are back, let the Railway end go barmy, 'cos Hill 16 has never seen the like of Heffo's Army.

That's what we sang.

Thanks, Heffo.

'He hadn't even taken out his gun . . . when one of them let off a shot and blasted him'

Conor Lally

The raiders were waiting as the garda car arrived in the credit union car park.

The gang that shot Det. Garda Adrian Donohoe in Co. Louth continued with their planned robbery as he lay dead on the ground and eventually escaped with €4,000 from the Lordship Credit Union.

The raiders spoke with what were described as local accents. They appeared to have very good knowledge of the road network in the area and of the times for the movement of cash from the credit union at Bellurgan on the Cooley Peninsula north of Dundalk.

A gang of criminals from the north Louth and south Armagh area are the chief suspects. They raided the post office on a Friday night in 2011 and escaped with just over €60,000 as armed gardaí were about to arrive to escort the cash into a bank night safe in Dundalk.

However, the investigation into the events of last Friday night is still in the early stages and the involvement of dissident republicans is not being discounted.

Det. Garda Donohoe was shot in the head and face on the right side at close range the moment he stepped out of his unmarked garda car to check on a suspicious vehicle. He and a colleague had arrived to provide an armed escort to a credit union staff member who was just about to drive her own car the short distance into Dundalk to deposit money from the credit union into a bank night safe in the town.

Informed sources said the level of violence directed at Det. Garda Donohoe was completely disproportionate to the threat he posed to the gang.

'He hadn't even taken out his gun or challenged them properly when one of them let off a shot and blasted him in the face,' said one source.

He was a front-seat passenger of the unmarked garda car which was being driven by his colleague Det. Garda Joe Ryan.

The two armed detectives pulled into the car park of the Lordship Credit Union on the Jenkinstown Road, Bellurgan, at about 9.30pm to meet the staff member and afford her an armed escort into Dundalk.

However, when they entered the car park another car that had carried four men to the scene was waiting.

Detective Garda Adrian Donohoe, armed and on duty. Photograph: Ciara Wilkinson.

Flowers left at Dundalk Garda Station, following the shooting dead of Detective Garda Adrian Donohoe.
Photograph: Dara Mac Dónaill.

Det. Garda Donohoe thought this was unusual and the moment his car came to a standstill he alighted, intending to approach the men and ask them what they were doing there. However, he was fired at when he stepped out of his vehicle and fell to the ground. The raiders then moved towards the garda car and the credit union premises. They shouted at Det. Garda Ryan to stay back and pointed at least one firearm at him. They also shouted at credit union staff who were locking up the building at the time. They grabbed a bag containing money from a staff member, got back into their car and were driven from the scene.

Gardaí believe at least one of the gang remained in the vehicle as the getaway driver but that the other three men got out of the car during the attack. It was unclear how many were armed.

While Det. Garda Ryan was a witness to the events he did not see the full incident and the credit union staff who saw what happened were said to be 'severely traumatised'. The incident was over very quickly and it was not until the raiders had left that Det. Garda Ryan established his colleague had been fatally injured.

Det. Garda Donohoe lived in the townland where he was shot and his son and daughter, who are six and seven, attend school across the road from the location of the shooting.

The alarm was raised from the scene immediately and garda vehicles in the region sped into the area in an effort to intercept the escape of the raiders in their car.

North of the Border the PSNI reacted in a similar fashion in an effort to put in place a cordon of manpower that might frustrate the escape.

The getaway vehicle is believed to have been driven to the Ballymacscanlon roundabout within 2km of the crime scene, from where the raiders would have left the Cooley Peninsula, and the M1 could have taken them in the direction of Dublin or north over the Border.

Gardaí believe the car was driven north of the Border.

There is now a strong cross-Border element to the investigation being led from Dundalk Garda station, where Det. Garda Donohoe was based and where his wife, Caroline, also works as a member of the force. The dead man's two brothers are also gardaí and are based in Swords, north Dublin, and in Navan, Co. Meath.

The scene of the killing remained sealed off yesterday and was undergoing a forensic examination by members of the Garda Technical Bureau.

Garda search teams were cutting back undergrowth around the credit union and its car park as part of a thorough search for the murder weapon or any other items that may have been discarded.

Gardaí have also taken CCTV footage from the credit union and other commercial and residential premises in the area in the hope of piecing together the gang's movements before and after the killing.

FRIDAY, 1 FEBRUARY 2013

Rumours – Pop-rock Perfection

Brian Boyd

If you're looking for full-on drink and drugs debauchery, celebrity psychosis, über dysfunctional inter-band relationships, lashings of money and ego, and extremities of fear and loathing, you have to look past the usual suspects (Zeppelin, Mötley Crüe *et al.*) and steady your gaze on Fleetwood Mac. Going into the recording of *Rumours* – still one of the bestselling albums of all time – things weren't pretty. Bass player John McVie and keyboardist Christine McVie had just divorced and weren't on speaking terms. Singer Stevie Nicks and guitarist Lindsey Buckingham were in the middle of breaking up but still on speaking terms – if shouting at each other in ferocious rage counts as speaking terms. Drummer Mick Fleetwood had just got divorced, the group had just sacked their manager and their producer, and they were doing enough cocaine 'to turn horses into unicorns' as the saying went. For good measure, Nicks and Mick embarked on a short-lived and very drunken affair.

These five people – all of whom had been romantically/sexually engaged with another band member at some time – had to sit in a room together and come up with 11 songs for a record-company imposed deadline. The only other time this kind of situation had occurred with a major band was with Abba – and they used the adverse circumstances to record some of their biggest hits. As did the Mac. But just to give some idea of the level of tension, suspicion, hatred, insecurity and paranoia that prevailed at the song-writing sessions, Christine McVie brought a new song to the table called 'You Make Loving Fun'.

It was written about her new post-divorce boyfriend (who was also the band's lighting director) and was seen as a personal attack on her erstwhile ex-husband. At around the same time, Mick Fleetwood started going out with Stevie Nicks's best friend. The blizzard of cocaine was such that the band, seriously, wanted to give their dealer a credit on the album. The label demurred and a stand-off was only averted when said dealer was shot dead, allegedly by an organised crime gang.

Given all that went on, *Rumours* should have been a mess. The songs were recorded in a small, wooden, windowless studio with the band

Some of the more than 140 dogs recovered by the ISPCA and Leitrim Animal Welfare from a property in a rural area where they were living in deplorable conditions. Photograph: Shelley Corcoran.

arriving at 7pm each night, getting off their collective heads until the early hours and only putting down music and vocals when they were too whacked out to keep on partying. Yet it's as close to a near-perfect pop-rock artefact as you could ever hope to hear, and its appeal lies in the fact that we are listening in to love breaking down. How did the band manage to stay together to finish the album?

Stevie Nicks now recalls it was a case of 'I'm not the problem, I'm not quitting. You're the problem, you should quit'. With no one prepared to give in, they effectively stayed together out of spite. *Rumours* is 35 years old now and there's a special commemorative, expanded edition of the album just released.

Pure music reality TV.

SATURDAY, 2 FEBRUARY 2013

Apology Shows SF Leader's Convoluted Sense of Reality

Noel Whelan

'A garda has been shot,' is the breaking news headline dreaded by all with someone in the force. When we hear it we hold our breath until the newsreader reveals where it happened and then guiltily breathe a sigh of relief that it is some place other than where our loved ones are stationed. For the family of Adrian Donohoe the nightmare feared by every Garda

Sinn Féin leader Gerry Adams and his Twitter alter ego Teddy, as seen by Martyn Turner.

family became a brutal reality in Louth last Friday night.

Anyone who has attended a Garda passing-out ceremony in Templemore will confirm that it's a terrific day. The uniforms and marching routines give the event additional pomp and ceremony.

There are moments during the proceedings, however, when you realise it is no ordinary graduation. It sinks in that by choosing a policing career these graduates are putting themselves in harm's way – in the line of fire. As gardaí they are expected, and expect of themselves – even when off-duty perhaps – to be the first to rescue those in danger, assist those in distress, pursue the speeding driver and confront the aggressive perpetrator.

One of the poignant moments at a Templemore graduation is when the Gary Sheehan Memorial Medal is presented to the best all-round probationer. It is awarded to the recruit who, as

well as distinguishing him or herself in the academic field, has contributed significantly to life at the Garda College and to the stations and communities where they served during their training period.

The medal commemorates recruit Garda Gary Sheehan who, along with Private Patrick Kelly, was shot dead by the Provisional IRA in a wood in Ballinamore, Co. Leitrim, on 16 December 1983. They were part of a search operation to release kidnapped businessman Don Tidey.

I remember where I was when I heard that Gary Sheehan and Private Kelly had been shot. It had the effect of routing me from simplistic teenage notions that Provisional IRA members were in some way champions of freedom, fighting a foreign power. The Tidey kidnapping was an IRA fundraising effort and they were prepared to kill anyone who got in their way.

The IRA also killed a garda during a fundraising operation in Adare on 7 June 1996. On that morning IRA members fired 15 rounds from an AK-47 at two garda detectives. One of them, Jerry McCabe, was shot three times and killed. His partner Ben O'Sullivan was seriously injured. The IRA, and Sinn Féin on its behalf, denied involvement.

On Monday, 11 June 1996, Sinn Féin's then vice-president Pat Doherty on RTÉ's *Questions and Answers* programme refused to condemn the killing and said he believed the IRA statement, which categorically denied involvement in the Adare shootings. On the same night on the BBC *Newsnight* programme, Martin McGuinness, who was well placed to know better, expressed certainty that the IRA's statement of non-involvement was true.

In the following years, however, Sinn Féin gradually changed its position. The IRA eventually accepted one of its units was involved but claimed it had operated without authorisation. Four IRA members were arrested and put on trial for the murder of a garda. At the trial two key witnesses withdrew their intended evidence citing IRA intimidation and the Director of Public Prosecutions had no option but to accept manslaughter pleas.

Then in a further shift in position Sinn Féin representatives, and Martin Ferris in particular, became the cheerleaders in chief for their early release.

Ultimately, in the lead-in to St Patrick's Day in 2005, Sinn Féin again changed tack. Adams and others were being cold-shouldered by Senator Ted Kennedy and other leading Irish-Americans because of the IRA's involvement in crime, including the Northern Bank robbery, Robert McCartney's murder, and because of its failure to fully disarm.

That week the McCabe killers issued a statement from prison saying they did not want their release to be part of further negotiations with the Irish Government. In so doing they were seeking to make a virtue of reality since the minister for justice Michael McDowell and even Bertie Ahern had already ruled it out.

In their statement, the killers also said they deeply regretted and apologised for the hurt and grief they caused to the McCabe and O'Sullivan families. McCabe's widow Ann dismissed the IRA's apology as sickening. 'It means absolutely nothing,' she told the *Washington Post*.

This week Adams is again backed into a political corner and has sought to construct a shield of apology. The similarities between the McCabe killing and that of Garda Donohoe are chilling – although there is no suggestion the IRA is involved.

As party leaders paid Dáil tributes to Garda Donohoe, Adams, who claims he was never in the IRA, apologised on behalf of the IRA for a killing committed by members of the IRA who, although disowned by the IRA at the time, are now celebrated as IRA heroes. It illustrates how convoluted the Sinn Féin leader's version of reality has had to become.

Adams also apologised to families of 'other members of the State forces' killed by republicans. It was a revealing choice of vocabulary. The rest of us do not put that distance between us and members of the Garda Síochána. We do not see Gary Sheehan and Jerry McCabe as part of 'State forces'. To us they were like Adrian Donohoe – protectors of our peace shot down in the service of our community.

WEDNESDAY, 6 FEBRUARY 2013

Ireland 2023: The Bono Interview

Editor's note: This interview was written by Bono – questions and answers – as part of the Ireland 2023 supplement published in The Irish Times *on*

6 February 2013. The supplement was in support of Hireland, a not-for-profit social movement that aims to contribute to Ireland's recovery by helping generate one job at a time by tapping into Ireland's collective entrepreneurship, which is central to the solution of the country's current economic and social difficulties.

Irish Times: Earth calling Bono. Come in. Over.

Do you read us? (Ha ha.)

Bono: Roger that. Over.

Hello from the first band in space. Over.

Holograms galorama? President Obama just called to wish us well.

IT: You're a fan?

B: That's right. I do like President Obama. I think she's doing a great job. I loved President Clinton too. Who knew there was an even bigger job than president of the US. Though if Michelle gets a second term the Democrats will be in office for 20 years, probably not good for democracy. Marco Rubio and Chris Christie are both serious Republican candidates and with Chelsea Clinton and Governor Springsteen rumoured to be running against them. Fun to watch.

What's this interview for, by the way?

IT: *The Irish Times.*

B: Ah yes, for the annual print edition! I've kept them all. I remember around 2020 when you interviewed our President Sir Bob Lord Geldof. You asked him about the improper language he used when promoting his noble causes.

'What the fuck is fuckin' improper language?' he replied.

James Joyce didn't know what improper language was either. He and President G. both changed the world with the stories they told and the shock of the way they told them. I think that's very IRISH.

IT: How proud are you that your friend has become such a success story?

B: Like all friends, pride followed by annoyance. That, too, is very Irish. To be honest, I've got

concerns about the way he expanded his business interests while holding office. BoomTownRat Co. taking over Tullow Oil and Providence. I mean, really. Still, he brought tourism back to Dalkey. The renaming of Dalkey Island to *The Island of Bob* was a small price to pay. I was just gazing down at it this morning and trying to imagine what one of the most beautiful coastlines in the world would have looked like belching smoke and bile.

IT: Do you regret not going into politics like Sir Bob, or other musicians, for example The Pussy Riot Collective?

B: They may want to hold high office but they did still show up for our launch into space, drinking our wine and stealing our thunder. Despite their rock star excesses they are deadly serious in their attempt to slow down Tsar Putin's march into Greater Russia. One of Pussy Riot has relatives in the Ukraine who are NOT happy. We love them. They're noisy. Noisy is good. Speaking of which, I don't have much time – got to get ready for this gig. That's gonna be noisy.

IT: I thought in space no one can hear you scream.

B: That's rubbish. Edge has been screaming at me all morning. The scream is an important form of communication. The first thing we do when we are born. Lets the world know we've arrived.

My goodness. You do get high up here, breathing pure oxygen.

Is there anything more worldly, or less, than being out of this world?

First band into space.

IT: Is this just a shameless publicity stunt?

B: Yes.

IT: Why is it still important to you to make a splash? Haven't you achieved everything you wanted?

B: (Pretending to ignore the question.) Hey, how about those Rolling Stones? What a 2023 they're having. Their last few farewell tours have really been something, but this is the best one yet.

Ok, that's why we had to come up here. To top them. There, I've said it.

Did you know our little space gig is going to be broadcast all over the United States of Africa? First time ever.

IT: It's certainly the music market to crack. Bigger than China now 1.5 billion . . .

B: Indeed. We saw Kilimanjaro yesterday. I know it was a controversial decision but the fake snow looked great from here. You know, I was in Tanzania for that delegation led by Taoiseach Brian O'Driscoll to thank all the African musicians – Youssou N'Dour, Angelique Kidjo, K'Naan, Kenna – who spearheaded the 'Drop the Debt' campaign for Ireland. We went from there to the inauguration of Ngozi Okonjo-Iweala – first President of the whole of Africa.

He's canny old Brian O'. I got a lot of pressure to vote for Robbie Keane when he ran against him. But that row with the European Commissioner, Thierry Henry, did Robbie no favours. Let it go man. Let it go.

IT: You've known President Iweala for a long time?

B: She's fantastic – she was on ONE's board for many years. I first met her when she was the Nigerian Finance Minister, the 'Corruption Cop'. She was a voice of reason from the get go. People forget how tough things were, but look at the continent now. Polio gone, malaria gone, TB too; sharia law run out of town. Aids about to become a memory when this vaccine happens. Bill and Melinda got a Nobel Prize for that one – and it looks like Bill could get it again for his work on solar solutions in the Sahel. Renewable energy? No wonder all the smart people want to go to Africa. Though the air is thin up here, it's thick with possibility there.

IT: Ten years ago, in 2013, did you ever foresee what a decade this would be? Did you imagine that in only 10 years, fundamentalism – both theistic and atheistic – would be replaced by true tolerance? This telepathic thing that replaced the internet really helped, didn't it? It must have hurt you, though, when Facebook was replaced by MindRead.

B: Not at all. Some of the same people were involved. Let's not forget in their heyday Facebook could ask a question of its three-and-a-half billion users and get an answer in real time. Impressive stuff. MindRead just cuts out the typing. Wireless, handless.

IT: But didn't you lose most of what you made in the apparel sector?

B: Lost my shirt – ha ha. Ali made Edun the success it is today then she cut me out. How quickly those girl-next-door types can turn mean. A sphincter-tightening business, the fashion business.

IT: So, the last 10 years, let's take it category by category, starting with a subject you seem to enjoy pontificating about. Religion.

B: Another Irishman once said, 'We have just enough religion to hate each other but not enough to love each other.' But now that's changed.

IT: Right. Love.

B: Well I am in love. Me and Pippa have two kids now. Mercedez and Sony fit in very well with their older brothers and sisters. I didn't think I could ever love again after Ali ran off with that bollix from Ballymena, Liam Neeson. But hey, I guess 'the heart has more reasons than reason ever knows'. At any rate, people are still falling in love in Ireland. Particularly after midnight. The argument as to whether to take anything said after three in the morning seriously rages on. Particularly after three in the morning.

IT: Europe.

B: Ah that's a big subject these days, and getting much, much bigger. I began to really worry back in 2017, when Britain exited Europe and Tsar Putin took a left turn into the euro zone. I mean, just for example, Putin was utterly wrong when he claimed that the elderly and their drag on health budgets would sink us. As an Irishman it gives me immense pride that the Solas retraining scheme launched in 2015 across Europe, targeting the over-sixties, has produced some of the most unexpected tech geniuses – ironically in the new and blooming high-tech health solutions sector.

But the whole game has changed now with the New Commonwealth under Clinton. With the US, Canada, Australia and India rejoining up with the UK, and The United States of Africa – that's nearly half the world's population. I just heard the old protectorate Hong Kong is in too. That city alone adds another 57 million souls. And President Aung San Suu Kyi is seriously considering it, even though Burma – like Ireland – wasn't part of the original gang. You can imagine how tricky this is for me at home with the King in my ear every other weekend. It's very real this England–Ireland love affair – they really want us in.

IT: So do you think Ireland would be wiser to leave Europe and join the New Commonwealth?
B: This is existential stuff. As this rock star well knows, size is not – always – everything. Europe has begun to change from a thought to a feeling. You remember when all the Portuguese and Spanish turned up at that great Irish Gathering? And when then taoiseach 'Endgame' Kenny launched the 'Buy Europe' campaign? As well as the economic benefits, those things educated us about each other. Some argued it kick-started the Irish recovery. In fact, the new Irish Culture Minister Gerard Depardieu is calling for a 10th anniversary of the Gathering to be held in Moscow this year – with a reforming of Pussy Riot to headline as a one-off. He's trying to get U2 there too. Edge says he won't support 'a bunch of girls' but Adam's all for it.

Have you read Depardieu's bestseller *The Dingle Archipelago*? I think it's just messianic rambling.

IT: And you're against that? Actually, we gave it five stars.
B: It's true, one shouldn't underestimate a good messianic complex. They're great entertainment. I mean, after all, we are called to walk in His way.

IT: A couple of lighter topics. Cars – I know you're interested in cars.
B: Heavily into the new electric cars, though the silence in NY is a little unnerving, and the air in LA is beautiful. I still miss a little bit of noise and dirt but I'm old fashioned.

And these self-driving buggies have changed the whole vibe socially. Pubs packed again in rural Ireland and everyone being driven home by computers. Flann O'Brien couldn't have made it up.

IT: Sport.
B: Has changed a lot. Golf back in the Olympics and Ireland top of the medal tables. And before you ask, yes of course they should adjust for population.

To have been the winning jockey of the Grand National last year was a real highlight for me personally. 100/1 with Paddy Power. I like those odds.

IT: Movies.
B: The mother and the mirror of our dreams. This 3D thing they project into your brain is good, isn't it? And well done to Larry Mullen for winning the Oscar. First man to win for best supporting actress. Genius! What an achievement.

Look I've really got to go . . . first band in space. They are calling me.

IT: Ok, thanks for your time. Final question. What say you of the next 10 years?
B: It took from the time of Jesus to the time of Leonardo for information to double. Now it doubles every 18 months. So in ten years, who knows where we'll be doing a gig. I hear Mick and Keith are working on a time travel device. Developing it since the '60s.

Irish Coast Guard helicopter Rescue 116 visits pupils of Dunboyne Junior and Senior Primary Schools as part of Engineers' Week. Photograph: Alan Betson.

Felicidad 2023 *tout le monde*! The year of Grace. Aren't they all? Over and out.
Bono.

SATURDAY, 9 FEBRUARY 2013

Noonan Kept His Head When Things Looked Their Worst

Stephen Collins

The scale of the government's achievement in winning a meaningful deal on the promissory notes should steady nerves in the Coalition after a wobbly few weeks and today's poor opinion poll results.

The outcome of the negotiations with the European Central Bank points up the importance of keeping the political focus on the long game, and ignoring the relentless outrage and indignation generated by the Opposition and fanned by the media.

The manner in which the elder statesman of the government, Michael Noonan, has been acclaimed in recent days should be a lesson to his colleagues in the Coalition, ministers and backbenchers alike, about the importance of holding their nerve when things are looking their worst.

Noonan, who will be 70 in three months, has defied the cliché that all political careers end in failure. A successful minister for justice in the 1980s, his reputation was most unfairly tarnished during his period as minister for health in the

1990s, and his short period as leader of Fine Gael ended in political disaster.

After all that he made a return to the front rank of politics after the abortive heave against his old rival Enda Kenny in the summer of 2010 and he hasn't looked back since. He kept his head when others appeared to be losing theirs during the final tense negotiations with the ECB.

The Coalition's credibility as well as the country's vital national interest was on the line. The fact that it all came good in the end should boost morale in both government parties at a difficult time. An impressive aspect of the drama of the final 24 hours before the deal was done was the fact that the government had clearly prepared for a range of contingencies.

The complex legislation on the liquidation of the Irish Bank Resolution Corporation had been drafted some time ago and was ready to go at a moment's notice.

The leak from the ECB that triggered the all-night debate in the Oireachtas was probably fortuitous as it necessitated quick decision-making. The fact that the Irish side was ready to move was vital.

The latest *Irish Times*/Ipsos MRBI poll showing Fianna Fáil back in first place for the first time since the crash could be a timely warning to Fine Gael and Labour TDs about how things can change quickly in politics.

The steady decline in Fianna Fáil support from the autumn of 2008, leading to the catastrophic collapse in the election of February 2011, was the most dramatic change in the Irish political landscape for generations.

The recovery by the party since April of last year shows that Irish politics has taken another turn, but it should not be all that surprising. The most striking feature of Irish political history is the stability of our democracy and party system even in times of extreme stress.

At one level the election of 2011 marked an amazing turnaround. Fianna Fáil went from

78 seats in the previous election to just 20, with its vote dropping from 42 per cent to 17 per cent. It was in the top three biggest electoral changes in western Europe since 1945, with only Italy and the Netherlands experiencing such a dramatic collapse in a governing party.

What made the Irish case different from the other two, however, was that in Italy and the Netherlands the collapse of a long-established party came about due to the rise of a new political force. In Ireland it was not a new party but Fine Gael, the successor of the party that founded the State in 1922, that took over the mantle of the biggest party after a lapse of 79 years.

And to reinforce the stability of the system, the Labour Party, which was founded just over a century ago, became the second biggest party for the first time in its history.

During the 2011 campaign the Fine Gael director of elections, Phil Hogan, asked Fianna Fáil supporters to lend his party their votes for one election and many of them obliged. It seems that after two years of the Coalition a significant number of them are at least thinking of returning home.

The development is a sobering one for Fine Gael, but there is no need to press the panic button just yet. Back in June 2010 there was panic in Fine Gael when Labour pulled ahead of it in the polls, and there was a heave against Kenny's leadership. He managed to see off his rival and hasn't looked back since, so it should take more than one poor poll now to undermine his confidence.

The demonstration of competence in govern-ment, by contrast with the irresponsibility of Fianna Fáil during the boom years, will be a strong card to play at the next election as long as Fine Gael doesn't flinch from doing what is necessary to get the economy back to robust health.

Labour's drop back to 10 per cent will obviously cause some angst in that party, but it should reinforce the point that its only chance of making it out of government in good order is to

Some of the 257 participants in the TodayFM Shave or Dye 2013 charity fundraising event.
Photograph: Alan Betson.

stick it out until the end when it can hope to have some real achievements to its name.

The local and European elections next year will be the real test of where all the parties stand. The Local Electoral Area Boundary Committee is drawing up new electoral areas. The date for submissions closed at the end of January, and a report detailing the new boundaries will be published in May.

A crucial element in the committee's terms of reference is that the number of councillors representing each electoral area should typically be seven and not more than 10 or fewer than six. In a seven-seat area a quota will be 12.5 per cent, and if the committee goes for the upper limit and introduces 10-seaters across the country it will be just 9 per cent.

The elections, which will take place in June of next year, will be particularly important for Fianna Fáil. The party needs a big infusion of new blood if it is going to make a significant recovery at the next general election. Big seven-seat-plus electoral areas should give it a chance of getting new people elected, particularly in Dublin, where it badly needs new talent.

THURSDAY, 14 FEBRUARY 2013

Generation Ink Gives Way to Generation Link

Laura Slattery

The media is full of old farts who, for the sake of argument, I will now unfairly define as anyone who is old enough to remember punk but wasn't one.

In some respects, this shouldn't be too much of

a problem if your audience is also mature, as it is in the newspaper industry. We can all make merry with that exciting Boomtown Rats revival story without having to explain that Bob 'dad of Pixie' Geldof is the bloke who never actually said 'give us your f**king money' live on television, but that's the kind of crazy urban myth that used to circulate before we had YouTube and could check.

Over the past decade, the newspaper business has indulged in some natural wastage. This has nothing to do with dead trees and everything to do with reducing the number of people who work for them by not replacing retirees (including incentivised early retirees) if it can help it. So it's not really accurate to say the media is full of old farts: middle-aged farts is much more like it.

Bear in mind I'm a full six years older than my byline photograph and a bit cranky at the moment because my slippers have holes in them.

It's all relative anyway. A few years ago, a colleague, at that time approaching 40, was delighted but puzzled to be referred to as one of 'the young people' in the office by a more senior figure. As for actual young people, well, a group of them encircled me at a media event in Google Docks recently and they all worked for TheJournal.ie.

I bring this up because on Monday's *Newsnight*, Susie Boniface, aka press blogger Fleet Street Fox, told presenter Gavin Esler (who is surprisingly about to turn 60) that the newspaper's audience was not just diverging between two mediums, print and online, but between two age cohorts, which she defined as the over 35s and the under 35s. Generation Ink and Generation Link, if you will.

Then on Tuesday, figures from the Joint National Readership Survey, which is measuring the online readership of its member publications for the first time, showed that 17 per cent of people under the age of 45 consume Irish newspaper content online on at least a weekly basis. Among people aged 45-plus, that figure dropped to 8 per cent.

Other reports show that older readers are simply less likely to have the hardware. A UPC study on Ireland's digital landscape published last November suggested ownership of smartphones and laptops peaks among 25–34s and declines with age.

For iPads and other tablets, the peak was in the 35–44 age group, which is interesting, as it hints there would be an audience available to news groups pushing content that appeals to this parents-of-small-kids demographic if they invested in bespoke tablet apps and dared to whack a subscription charge on top.

In the old mono-platform days, editors who wanted to boost product appeal to a younger audience simply had to clamp their eyes on the nearest intern and commission something that, from their perspective, would adequately tick the 'young fart' box.

It was a question of balance, with that balance still inevitably tipped in favour of the kind of conservative hand-wringing and 'bogeyman in the back garden' genres that leave twentysomethings bemused, if not outright alienated.

In this multi-platform era, however, the conventional wisdom is one of differentiation between the online and print product, with the content tailored in parallel with existing demographic preferences.

In practice, this involves aiming your print edition at the middle-aged audience that it's most likely to retain, while publishing online-only content that requires prior knowledge of important cultural figures such as Kim Kardashian.

The reverse approach – online publication of grammar whinges and big print spreads on Lena Dunham and Aaron Swartz – isn't as instinctive. In theory, it could compel a mature audience to spend more time online and invite a younger audience to buy a paper out of their tight discretionary incomes, but the latter outcome, in particular, seems unlikely.

My view is that this generation gap in online consumption will soon close, perhaps even faster than the similarly pronounced chasm between Dublin and the rest of the country. This will allow news brands to return to a simpler, one-platform product (a digital one).

That still won't entirely fix the problem of an industry that's slow to embrace the knowledge and energy of the under-25s on its workforce and lets younger readers slip away. Each generation refreshes the culture that it finds. It's scary, but maybe it's the turn of those 1990s babies to start putting the 'new' in 'news'.

SATURDAY, 16 FEBRUARY 2013

New Pope. Same Church?

Paddy Agnew

Pope Benedict's resignation is the most radical move in the Catholic Church in 50 years. Could it open the doors to a wider transformation? Don't count on it.

So, ironically, Benedict XVI, a pope widely perceived as a safe pair of hands and even more conservative than his predecessor, may have provoked the greatest change in the Catholic Church's modern history. Cautious, timid, stubborn old Benedict, by stepping down from the Seat of Peter, could have initiated a process of radical rethinking not seen since the second Vatican Council in the 1960s.

The holy father's resignation is an intrinsically modern act, one that seems more temporal than spiritual, even for a man of deep faith. It makes him look less like the holy father of the universal church and more like the resigning CEO of a multinational company with a staff of 1.3 billion.

Cardinal Stanislaw Dziwisz, the former private secretary of John Paul II, said in a widely reported comment this week that popes 'do not come down off the cross'. While the cardinal of Cracow might claim that his comment was taken out of context, it nonetheless touched on a cornerstone of Catholic experience.

Canon law and theological argument suggested that a papal resignation was always a possibility, but no one has lived through one since the time of Gregory XII, who resigned in 1415. Popes, we thought, go out with their boots on. But if the idea that a modern pope never resigns was simply a question of custom and practice rather than anything to do with Christ's teachings, all sorts of possibilities present themselves.

Clerical celibacy and the ban on women priests, to name but two issues, are also expressions of custom and practice more than of any specific teaching by Christ. So can they now change, too?

Last week in St Peter's Square, this correspondent ran into the worldwide head of one of the oldest religious orders in the church, a man with a vast experience of missionary work, especially in Latin America. He was positively bubbling. He confessed that in 2005 when he saw Joseph Ratzinger step out onto the papal balcony as Benedict XVI, he was deeply depressed, adding that it took some time for him to overcome his negative feelings about the new pope.

Now he and many others hope that the resignation can change some of the ground rules, making it possible for the church to reconsider its position on myriad issues, from social justice to sexual mores.

It is equally conceivable, though, that the conservative forces that have gripped the Catholic Church for the past 35 years of Wojtyla and Ratzinger rule will continue to run the show.

A couple of months ago, at a Vatican-run ceremony in a central Rome church outside the Holy See, I ran into a distinguished Italian lawyer.

The conversation quickly turned to church affairs and in particular to the recent turbulent times experienced by the pontificate of Benedict XVI, as most dramatically illustrated by the trial last autumn of the pope's butler, Paolo Gabriele, who was convicted of stealing confidential documents from the papal apartment.

My learned friend shook his head sadly. Things

Pope Benedict XVI arrives to lead Ash Wednesday mass at the Vatican, one of his final public engagements before retiring. Photograph: Alessandro Bianchi/Reuters.

have got badly out of hand, he said. This whole mess should never have happened. 'What we need here, right now, is an Italian pope. The Italian popes know how to run the church.'

In one sense, my lawyer friend has a point. Italians know how to manoeuvre their way around a Holy See that the dissident theologian Hans Küng this week called a 'medieval/baroque court'. They are playing a home game, with the language, the fans, the media and usually the referee, the old guy in white, on their side.

When you move around the Holy See, attending news conferences and ceremonies and interviewing senior figures, one thing is clear. Without Italian, you are dead. It is not just that

the procedures, the thinking and the office culture are all Italian; it is that they are Italian in the style of the court in a 16th-century Tuscan city republic.

The issue is about more than media communication. The Holy See, seat of governance of the Catholic Church, is peculiarly Italian but it is also riven with internal power struggles, rivalries and jealousies, as the papal butler's 'Vatileaks' made clear. As Küng pointed out this week, it might matter little if the college of cardinals picks an African, an Asian or a Latin American as the next Pope; such is the 'Romanisation' of church HQ that unless radical organisational changes are introduced to the curia, the Vatican's

Clouds are seen over St Peter's Basilica on the evening Pope Benedict XVI stunned the Roman Catholic Church by announcing he was retiring, the first pope to do so in 700 years. Photograph: Alessandro Bianchi/Reuters.

Pope Benedict XVI delivers his blessing during his last Angelus noon prayer, from the window of his studio overlooking St Peter's Square in the Vatican. Photograph: L'Osservatore Romano.

administrative apparatus, the new man will simply be absorbed by its medieval ways and rendered relatively ineffective.

Küng argues that the 'medieval/baroque Vatican court' must be transformed into a 'modern, efficient central church administration'.

Is that really possible in this country? Italy does very good Chianti, extraordinary historical patrimony, wonderful fashion and many other things, but it does not do modern, efficient administration.

It is not a modern, transparent, accountable democracy. Transparency International, the body that monitors corporate and political corruption worldwide, rates Italy 72nd, just above Bosnia, Montenegro and Tunisia.

The Italian influence does not stop at linguistic advantage or curia squabbling. When the 117 or so elector cardinals, who are under 80 years of age, go into conclave to elect the new pope in the middle of next month, Italy will still be hugely over-represented with 27 cardinals, a formidable conservative rump. By comparison, Latin America will have 19 cardinals, even though 483 million Catholics, or 41.3 per cent of the world's Catholics, live in that region. Given this, and the fact that all the elector cardinals have been nominated by either John Paul II or Benedict XVI, is it unrealistic to expect radical change from the next pope? Perhaps not.

By any measure, this will be an unprecedented

conclave. For a start, the cardinals around the world have had plenty of time to prepare a strategy and avoid their mistake of 2005, when most of the cardinals arrived in Rome to find that a group of senior curia cardinals already had their candidate, Cardinal Ratzinger, up and running. And as dean of the college of cardinals, Ratzinger was so impressive in the manner in which he handled interregnum set pieces, such as the funeral of John Paul II, that many of the local cardinals simply nodded and said, 'He'll do'.

The resignation will make this conclave radically different. There will be no period of mourning; the grief that hung over Rome throughout April 2005 will be missing. Rather, this will be a state-of-the-church moment when just about everyone with something to say about the future of the church will be able to make themselves heard.

The lobby group for women priests will be burning pink smoke during the conclave, gay-rights activists are getting ready to protest in Rome, and we can expect much else besides, especially from the lobbies for the victims of clerical sex abuse. To protest when a much-loved figure such as John Paul II died seemed utterly inappropriate. To protest now, well, that's different.

Even if the conclave ran off against a background of tranquillity, many of the 'modern' issues that dogged Benedict's pontificate will have to be discussed not just in the conclave but also in the meetings the cardinals will hold in Rome beforehand.

Relations with Islam; relations with the Jews; sexual mores; the clerical sex-abuse crisis; the role of traditionalist groups such as the Lefebrvists; the fall-off in first-world vocations; ecumenism; the growth of groups such as the Association of Catholic Priests of Ireland (there are others all over Europe); the persecution of Christians in parts of Africa and the Middle East; Catholic divorcees denied the Eucharist; these and others are all issues that are sure to be in the cardinals' minds, if only because these are some of the many challenges that will face the new Pope.

As to who it will be, the field is wide open. Most church insiders say the new Pope will have to be young – that is, in his late 50s or early 60s – vigorous, in excellent health and, of course, a stout defender of the fundamental tenets of Catholic teaching. After that, the geographical question of a European or a non-European pope is secondary. First of all, he has to be able to do the job whether he comes from Milan or Manila.

What will almost certainly be debated over the next six weeks is the Eurocentric nature of Benedict's pontificate; his insistence that the traditional home of the church had to become the theatre of a new evangelisation. With the church in relative crisis in the developed world, this might seem to make sense. Yet, given that Europe now represents 277 million Catholics, or 23.7 per cent of the universal church, does it really make sense? Has the time come to radically change tack?

Another unprecedented aspect of this conclave concerns Benedict himself. He will take no physical part; that is clear. But will the fact that he is having his tea and playing his piano just a couple of hundred metres round the corner influence anyone?

In his address to the Roman priests on Thursday, for example, Benedict spoke at length about Vatican II, appearing to attribute misunder-standings and 'banalisations' of the council to the media. Was he saying that his successor would do well to prepare himself a strong PR machine, something manifestly lacking in Benedict's pontificate?

When Benedict was elected, many saw him as someone who would steer the Catholic Church through the transitionary period that would follow the 27-year pontificate of John Paul II. That time has passed. Many in the church may now be ready for change. But is the college of cardinals equally ready?

'I, as Taoiseach, on behalf of the State, the Government and our citizens, deeply regret and apologise unreservedly to all those women for the hurt that was done to them'

Miriam Lord

The Dáil was charged with strong emotion as Kenny made his apology.

It was dark when the Magdalene women left Leinster House. They joined hands and formed a line across the width of the granite plinth.

'Come into the light!' shouted the photo-graphers.

And these elderly women began to walk, and as they walked towards that light they quickened their pace and some began to cheer. All smiling – but through tears, for some.

'See ya, ladies. Night, night. Safe home now,' shouted a friendly young policeman.

This was the night the women of the Magdalene laundries thought they would never see, and a night that those who were present in the Dáil chamber will never forget.

It was an evening when our Taoiseach and national parliament did the right and decent thing by the wronged Magdalene women.

It was a powerful, compelling speech from the Taoiseach. It was riveting. And with it, he answered those people who questioned his sincerity and motives after that first, wishy-washy response to the McAleese report.

But it wasn't Enda Kenny who stole the show,

rather it was the response of the women in the wake of his address.

Who would blame them if they were to show a hint of bitterness or anger? Or if they had shrugged their shoulders at a gesture that has come years too late? Yet they didn't.

They wanted that apology and that vindication and validation. When it came, they were the epitome of grace and dignity. 'I thought it was wonderful. God bless him. Now I'm a proud woman today. God bless the Taoiseach,' said Marina Gambold, echoing the gratitude expressed by her companions-in-arms for what Enda Kenny had done for them.

They arrived at Leinster House in the late afternoon, wondering what would happen.

A few arrived early. A handful of grey-haired women with careworn faces, they settled in the gallery to watch Leaders' Questions. On both sides of them sat groups of secondary schoolgirls, spruce in their uniforms, with their laughing faces and lovely teeth.

We wondered if they felt sad, looking at the girls, for the youthful fun they never had. But, as their reaction to the speech would later show, the Magdalene women aren't like that.

Seats were reserved in the gallery for the women. Soon it was standing room only. Alan Shatter called up to talk to them before the debate began. A babble of female voices filled the Dáil. Then, on the stroke of half past six, the Taoiseach led in his Cabinet. He took his seat in total silence.

Joan Burton waved up to some of the women. Clare Daly, opposite, did the same.

Enda stood. He thanked Martin McAleese for his report and all those who assisted in its compilation. Then he quickly got down to business.

'The Government was adamant that these ageing and elderly women would get the compassion and the recognition for which they have fought for so long, deserved so deeply, and had, until now, been so abjectly denied. The reality

Kathleen Jannette and her sister Mary McManus, who were in Stanhope Street Magdalene Laundry from 1951–1954, photographed with Mary's daughter Pamela Connor and a family friend, Joan Farrelly, outside the Dáil after an apology from Enda Kenny on behalf of the State. Photograph: Alan Betson.

is that for 90 years, Ireland subjected these women and their experience to a profound and studied indifference.'

In the gallery, some of the women held hands. Some were crying. You could almost see the weight lifting from their shoulders. It was so quiet we could hear the clock ticking.

At times, the Taoiseach's voice thickened and it seemed like he might falter. He spoke of the Magdalene women having to bury and carry in their hearts the dark secrets of 'a cruel, pitiless Ireland' for all their lives. Innocents forced to carry an unjust stigma foisted on them by a pious and prim society.

The Taoiseach's voice was steady and clear: 'From this moment on, you need carry it no more. Because today . . . we take it back.' There were

gasps in the gallery. Deputies blinked and welled up. Outside the round railing, Senator Marie Maloney wept. Clare Daly wrapped her arms tightly across her chest, her eyes brimming. Billy Kelleher fought back the tears.

In the public gallery, they didn't hold back. The Taoiseach listed some of the things that happened to these dignified older women when they were young girls – some told to him by them when they met last week.

It was a long, heart-wrenching list. Things like: 'I felt all alone, nobody wanted me . . . We had to sew at night, even when we were sick . . . I heard a radio sometimes in the distance . . . I broke a cup once and had to wear it hanging around my neck for three days. I felt always tired, always wet, always humiliated . . . I never saw my mam again

– she died while I was in there . . .' Tissues were passed around, noses blown, spectacles pushed up and eyes rubbed.

Fifteen minutes into the speech came the apology. The air crackled with emotion.

'I, as Taoiseach, on behalf of the State, the Government and our citizens, deeply regret and apologise unreservedly to all those women for the hurt that was done to them, and for any stigma they suffered, as a result of the time they spent in a Magdalene Laundry.'

Enda hadn't let them down.

Hands were clapped across open mouths. Hankies appeared again. There were hugs and smiles, lots of smiles.

Arrangements would be put in place for compensation and a permanent memorial erected. Finally, the Taoiseach remembered one of his meetings with the Magdalenes. One woman sang him a song at the end of it – 'Whispering Hope' – and quoted a line which stayed with him. 'When the dark midnight is over, watch for the breaking of day.' Enda paused. 'Let me hope that this day and this debate . . .' and he stopped, fighting back the tears. 'Excuse me,' he murmured. He took a gulp of air and went on '. . . heralds . . .' and he cleared his throat and paused again, 'a new dawn for all those who feared that the dark midnight might never end'. And it was over. Enda sat down, pale and drawn.

The women started to applaud. Louder and louder, some with their hands in the air. They stood and clapped the Taoiseach and they embraced and then they applauded themselves. It was such a happy, heartbreaking scene. And then the deputies began to applaud, rising too to their feet.

Even the Ceann Comhairle knew there are times when rules just have to be broken. He stood and applauded too. Ushers were in tears. Civil servants in tears. Journalists in tears.

Later the Taoiseach went into the gallery to meet the women before they left, tired but walking taller, happy. A huge burden lifted.

There are times when the Dáil makes you want to bang your head off the wall in frustration. And there are times when our parliament can make us proud. Last night was one of those times. And Enda Kenny can feel proud too.

He made it a special night to remember for his, and our, special guests.

WEDNESDAY, 20 FEBRUARY 2013

Why Don't We Have a Perfect Bookshop?

Manchán Magan

Ireland is best known for its writers, yet do we have a bookshop worthy of that reputation? Think of the glorious Selexyz bookshop in a soaring Gothic church in Maastricht, with shelves stretching up the 800-year-old walls as if they were ivy cladding the marble columns. It's like a bookshop made in heaven, paper bricks rising towards the spire, with walkways reaching towards the frescoed ceiling – and a coffee shop right on the altar.

Or the El Ateneo bookshop in an ornate old theatre in Buenos Aires, with its original gilt carvings, painted ceiling and theatre boxes as reading rooms. It stays open all night, fuelled by a café on the stage, framed by crimson theatre curtains.

Without a bookshop that encouraged lingering, Joyce might never have got *Ulysses* published. It was at Shakespeare and Company in Paris that he got to know Sylvia Beach, its owner, who bravely decided to risk publishing his 'indecent, unpublishable' manuscript and, in doing so, changed the course of modern literature.

Beach's shop was a meeting place for Ernest Hemingway, F. Scott FitzGerald, T.S. Eliot and Ezra Pound, as well as the inspiration for the current Shakespeare and Company, founded beside Notre Dame by George Whitman. This was a

The El Ateneo bookshop in Buenos Aires. Photograph: Luis Davilla/Getty.

regular haunt of Beckett's and still provides a bed for the likes of Dervla Murphy and Jeanette Winterson on their peregrinations, and a place to perform for so many Irish writers.

Whitman's Shakespeare and Company inspired the famous City Lights bookshop in San Francisco, which became a nexus for the next generation of literary innovators – Allen Ginsberg, Jack Kerouac, William S. Burroughs, Charles Bukowski – and continued the struggle for artistic freedom when it published Ginsberg's poetry and was prosecuted for obscenity.

Its role in the cultural development of the United States was recognised in 2001 when City

Lights was declared an official historic landmark for its 'significant contribution to major developments in post-World War II literature'.

Which brings us back to Dublin and the sad lack of any such haven to cherish new writing and writers in this Unesco City of Literature. Selexyz, El Ateneo and the rest are not like Eason or Hughes & Hughes: each of them is, as City Lights describes itself, a literary meeting place.

It's what Dublin needs. Not an official, government-funded institution but a haven for literature lovers, which would give writers and readers what Whelan's gives musicians and music lovers.

The nearest we have to it now is Lilliput Press, a bookshop and publisher in a charming Edwardian house in the gradually gentrifying Dublin district of Stoneybatter. With its hand-painted signs, wooden facade and books arranged in what must once have been the front parlour, it is full of quirky panache – but it's small and sells only books published by Lilliput.

Recently it has begun to host cultural evenings, including excellent Listen at Lilliput events – platforms for musical and literary artists of all descriptions 'to showcase their work in an intimate and sympathetic environment'.

The Gutter Bookshop in Temple Bar is another impressive new Dublin store. Its staff recommendations are impeccable, and it has a rare ability to present books in a way that makes them as irresistible as fine patisserie, but it's a bit bright and clean to encourage lengthy mooching.

Ideally a bookshop needs a certain tattiness, a lived-in, homely quality, with nooks and crannies to get lost in. Great bookshops are like a wardrobe to Narnia, making browsers lose their bearings, as in Charlie Byrne's in Galway, or Strand Bookstore in Manhattan, with its almost 30km of new, used and rare books.

I have fallen through all sorts of disorientating spatial wormholes at Strand, ending up in sections on vintage pulp, etiquette and magic studies – and even in a department devoted to collating personalised libraries, where you can buy or rent books by the foot.

The nearest Dublin came to bookshops of this breed were Greene's, beside Merrion Square, and the Winding Stair bookshop, beside the Ha'penny Bridge. Greene's is long gone, and while the renovated Winding Stair has a fine restaurant, its bookshop is limited.

What we need now is a charming old building in a prime location near the Liffey – not a landmark building that needs to be venerated but an overlooked gem. It should be spacious but warren-like, with separate areas for new and old books and unusual genres. It needs to have small spaces for public readings, for book groups and for launches, plus a café that turns into a wine and Irish tapas bar at night.

Of course, no independent bookstore could afford such a space. City Lights and Shakespeare and Company exist only because the buildings were acquired aeons ago. The only way this dream can be made real is if the building is provided free, or at a peppercorn rent by the State or an ecclesiastical body. The church has always been the great patron of literature in Ireland: without it we would have no illustrated manuscripts, including Trinity College Dublin's Book of Kells cash cow.

With the right property in relatively sound condition and an ideal location, the rest is easily achievable. The shop would have a small core staff supported by a revolving team of aspiring writers and book lovers who are visiting the city and, in return for their help, would be allowed to sleep among the book stacks at night, like the Tumbleweeds at Shakespeare and Company, who get a bed during their stay in Paris in return for helping out for a few hours each day and overseeing the evening events before locking up at 11pm. Their presence in the building, reading or writing their own masterpieces, brings life to the building and adds security.

It might take a year or so for this chaotic,

idiosyncratic home of impassioned bibliophiles to develop a reputation among travellers and readers. I'd foresee a *New York Times* feature on it within a year, and some boho *Guardian* journalist would probably be sleeping on the floor before the doors even opened.

Soon there would be no difficulty attracting the best of writers to give intimate readings each evening. They would not be paid – which might encourage the writers to try to make their readings interesting for a change, to attract buyers, rather than to follow the convention that distinguished writers must imply in their manner of reading that the task is beneath them.

Suddenly tourists would have something to do each night that didn't involve alcohol.

After the first year the shop could launch a literary competition and perhaps invite one of the main literary journals – *The Dublin Review*, *The Stinging Fly* or *Irish Pages* – to share its premises. Once it has settled into itself it could start a boutique imprint, publishing a choice selection of titles it believes passionately in.

It would then be only a matter of time before the next Joyce or Beckett shuffled through its doors and the little bookshop-cum-publisher took a deep breath before daring to publish his or her brilliant but dangerous work. The rest is the history of the future, waiting to be written.

The one final question is who will be the brave, crazy, selfless, inspirational person who'll lead this Utopia? All I can say is that this vision was first described to me by Lisa Hannigan, days after she herself had sung her heart out at a tiny gig at Shakespeare and Company. Lisa, it's up to you now.

Minister for Health James Reilly (left) tries to force open jammed lift doors with the help of Adrian McLaughlin, a member of the Leinster House staff, in the new Phoenix Care Centre where they were stuck for 20 minutes along with photographer Brenda Fitzsimons.

O'Gara Synonymous with Last-ditch Feats of Escapology

Gerry Thornley

With each passing week, the 2013 Six Nations feels like the end of an era and now, with Ronan O'Gara's exclusion from an Irish squad for the first time in 13 seasons, the feeling has been reinforced. Time waits for no man indeed, and nor does it wait for a generation.

The apparent demise of O'Gara's Test career may yet prove premature, but for all the protestations to the contrary by Les Kiss and Mick Kearney yesterday, Sunday's squad announcement probably does mark the end of O'Gara's Test career.

Nor has there been a more productive Irish rugby career in terms of Test caps and Test points. O'Gara is, veritably, a legend in his own playing career. He will, fittingly, forever be remembered as the man with ice in his veins and the technical skills to deliver the match-winning drop goal in the Millennium Stadium four years ago, which delivered Ireland's only Grand Slam in the last 65 years.

O'Gara has become synonymous with last-ditch feats of escapology over his illustrious career, and understandably so, for never in the history of the game has one player won so many matches with virtually the last kick of the game. It says everything about his drive and personality that O'Gara assuredly welcomed the pressure and attention. He wanted it and thrived on it.

No Irish outhalf has ever had a better or more complete kicking game, be it off the 'tee', drop goals, long raking one-bounce touch finders, deft, perfectly-weighted grubbers (Christian Cullen and others will testify to that) or crosskicks. Shane Horgan, a beneficiary with that defining try against England at Croker when Rog also kicked 21 points, would be amongst many who would verify that.

But O'Gara possessed a wonderful all-round skills set, be it with that cultured right boot, or the great hands that could pick passes up off his shoelaces or deliver long, flat passes off either hand. Ironically, O'Gara had shown signs of a return to form with Munster in their anti-climactic draw with the Ospreys last Saturday, which suggests this decision was coming before the weekend and was the result of the Murrayfield performance.

O'Gara has been in a difficult place this season, what with hopes of a fourth Lions tour ebbing away, Munster adapting to a redesigned game under a new coaching ticket, unresolved negotiations for a new contract after the conclusion of this season and, most of all perhaps, a desire to do too much when introduced off the bench.

As ever, there has been some wild speculation as to Declan Kidney's motives for this decision, as with preferring Paddy Jackson to start at Murrayfield or passing on the captaincy baton from Brian O'Driscoll to Jamie Heaslip, such as an apparent attempt to ingratiate himself with his IRFU paymasters. Most likely, the decision is simply in response to the latest flawed display off the bench by O'Gara and Ian Madigan's continuing good form.

After their long association together through PBC, Munster and Ireland, Kidney's call to O'Gara on Sunday – when the player was apparently with his wife Jessica and their kids and so he rejected the offer to meet up – cannot have been easy for either man.

At just over 13 stone, or 83kg, for O'Gara to achieve what he has achieved in a sport that has increasingly become a land of giants is a tribute to not just his talent but also his professionalism and durability. He has made little secret over the years of his admiration for Roy Keane, and like Keane it looks like he will not be allowed to call time as he would have liked.

Participants at the Comhdháil World Irish Dancing Championships at City West Hotel in Dublin. Photograph: Cyril Byrne.

Like David Humphreys, who retired from Test rugby in 2006 aged 34 but played on with Ulster for two more seasons, O'Gara should be granted another Munster contract if he feels up to it, regardless of whether he appears in green again. He still has something to offer.

Like Keane, O'Gara has been gold dust in front of a microphone or a dictaphone. Like Keane, he is highly intelligent, thoughtful, intense and opinionated but not remotely shy about expressing his opinion. He also has a wonderful, usually dry sense of wit. When he granted an audience during Ireland's week in Queenstown, in the glassed restaurant of the team hotel with a panoramic view of Wakatipu Lake, framed by sun-kissed, snow-covered mountains, he maintained Queenstown and all its activities 'doesn't mean anything to me. The week of Test matches with my mindset I could be in Cork'.

Like Keane, you'd wonder how tolerant he could be if coaching lesser players one day but,

failing that, he would certainly make an outstanding pundit.

THURSDAY, 7 MARCH 2013

'We should explore any avenue that will help Ireland stand on its own feet'

John McManus

The managing director of the International Monetary Fund is keen to understand Ireland and the Irish people and to see this country on the road to economic success.

'We want Ireland to be a success,' exclaims Christine Lagarde five minutes into our interview

International Monetary Fund chief Christine
Lagarde in her office in Paris.
Photograph: Eric Bouvet.

in the International Monetary Fund's Paris office in advance of her visit to Dublin today.

The remark pretty much sets the tone for the interview as she swats away, or neatly sidesteps, any suggestion that Ireland might not be the triumph that everyone hopes for.

It is mid-afternoon and the Arc de Triomphe – just about visible from Lagarde's office – shines in the welcome spring sunshine. She has just come from Brussels and seems genuinely buoyed up by the outcome of the previous night's meeting of euro zone finance ministers and that morning's Ecofin assembly of the 27 member states' finance ministers, chaired by Finance Minister Michael Noonan.

'Do you know what happened?' she asks in her distinctive tone, which mixes a certain French hauteur with the clipped accent of the English upper classes in a way that can best be described as Europosh.

'Yesterday there was a particular discussion relating to one instrument – the EFSF – and then it was to be further discussed this morning to include not only the EFSF, which is of euro group competence, but the EFSM, which includes the 27 member states.'

Ireland owes the two funds – the European Financial Stabilisation Mechanism and the European Financial Stability Facility – about €30 billion and restructuring these borrowings is seen as key to a successful exit from its EU-IMF programme at the end of the year.

The troika (the IMF plus the European Commission and European Central Bank) has been told to come up with a plan and the teams have already begun work, says Lagarde. If anything, she seems more optimistic about the outcome than Noonan, who has expressed some doubt as to whether Ireland will get the additional 15 years to repay the debt that it seeks.

'I would be cautious not to limit it to an extension. I think it has really been refined yesterday during the discussions as an adjustment that might include very much an extension of the maturities but is not limited only to the extension of maturities . . .'

She is more circumspect when it comes to what else might be on the table. There is not much more that could be done on the interest rates but 'financial people can think of lots of things', she says with a smile and presumably an ironic nod to the IMF's ongoing mandate to lead reform of the financial services industry after the 2008 financial crisis.

Pushing out the repayments to the end of the term – a so-called bullet payment – is an option, she agrees, but there are many others.

'To the extent that it [a measure] is supportive

of Ireland and that it will help smooth the transition into growth and Ireland standing on its own two feet, I think we should explore any avenue,' she clarifies.

Ensuring that Ireland can stand on its own two feet come next year is the main purpose of Lagarde's visit. She describes it as 'retuning her Irish antenna', a sort of reality check on the numerous briefings and reports she receives.

She already has her own channel to Ireland. 'Ever since I was a "baby" lawyer in 1980, I have always had an assistant who was from Ireland, raised in Ireland and spoke Irish. The one that I worked with the longest was my assistant for 19 years, and that tells you something. I really like Irishwomen in particular.

'Sonia [Criseo] keeps sending extracts from the *The Irish Times*, from this, that and the other to indicate what is causing tension at the moment, what people are talking about and what is going on. She has eight brothers and sisters so she has good antennae out there,' Lagarde explains.

There is another dimension to her obvious empathy for Ireland. Lagarde worked for six years in Chicago where she rose to be the first chairwoman of the US law firm Baker McKenzie before being asked to join the French government of Dominique de Villepin in 2005.

'It was a midwestern American city and also very much an Irish one,' she says. So what is it that she likes about the Irish? She reflects momentarily before replying 'their smile' and giving one of her own.

Hostesses refresh the tea cups of Chinese leaders, President Hu Jintao (left) and Communist Party general secretary Xi Jinping (right), at the National People's Congress in the Great Hall of The People, Beijing. Photograph: Feng Li/Getty.

Victory lap

There should be plenty of smiling over the course of her visit to Dublin, which has a tinge of a victory lap about it for the IMF although no one, particularly Lagarde, wants to tempt fate.

'I want to understand where the country is – which from the reports I read is a good position – with a programme that is more than on track, with growth that has turned positive for the first time and exceptionally so in comparison with other European and euro area countries.

'I want to see how we, with the authorities, can best plan for finishing successfully the programme and to make sure that there will not be a relapse.

'That is what I am most concerned about,' says Lagarde before adding, 'I would like to clearly underline and celebrate the efforts and what has been achieved . . .' The prospect of a relapse, not just in Ireland, is one of the IMF managing director's greatest concerns at this point.

'Clearly the world economy avoided collapse last year and I am very concerned that, by moving into a semi-complacent mood, people risk a relapse.'

How real is the risk of a relapse in Ireland? 'Our sense is that it is better to plan than to get caught afterwards with a need for support down the road.'

The government is adopting 'exactly the right approach' in terms of looking at options to smooth its return to the bond market. Both in terms of renegotiating the promissory note and the bailout loans, but also in negotiating a precautionary funding line that could be called down if needed, she says.

'All of that needs to be thought through as a comprehensive package to make sure that, when the programme is over, Ireland is solid and has the tools available. The principles of comprehensiveness and anticipation are two important ones from our perspective.

'The IMF can do all sorts of things in that respect and we will discuss them with the government,' she says.

The case for such extensive international support – and the restructuring of the bailout debt in particular – is very much seen as a moral argument in Ireland: the Irish State having taken on an unbearable debt to make good the mostly European creditors of private banks.

But it's clear that Lagarde's liking for Ireland does not mean she necessarily accepts this argument. For her, the reason for giving Ireland further concessions is a pragmatic one.

'I think it [further concessions] is with a view to avoiding a bigger problem down the road.' She refuses to be drawn on whether fear of political instability along the lines seen elsewhere in Europe makes up part of this pragmatic argument.

The issue of whether the coalition might have fallen apart if the promissory note had not been renegotiated has thankfully been consigned to history. 'That has been obtained now,' she says.

'Stability is the key, actually, to the implementation of a programme and the ownership of the programme, which is why coalition governments are both strong and weak. They are stronger because they embrace a larger base when they work and they are weaker in the sense that the leader has to make sure all members of the coalition are on board,' she offers by way of a general comment.

'All I can say is that political stability is an asset for a country to deliver under a programme and for a country to take its economy forward.'

The absence of serious social unrest also marks Ireland out from the other bailout countries. Does that surprise her?

'It is difficult to diagnose. I am not an Irish political animal. The little I know about Irish people is that they have a sense of realism and pragmatism, and an understanding of what needs to be done.

'Many of them have gone through the years of exuberance – if I may say so – up until 2007 and they know that there had to be a serious correction,' she says.

Martyn Turner's take on TD Luke Flanagan's looking-glass world of garda penalty points and the Roscommon–South Leitrim TD's own driving record.

If anything, Lagarde foresees continued cohesion rather than greater unrest as long as there is continued broad political support and dialogue.

'There is a sense that everybody is engaged in the process. It is not something that is a burden for the middle class only. It is not the case that the upper middle class or upper class is not affected and the lower class completely left on their own.'

THURSDAY, 14 MARCH 2013

Joyful Welcome for Humble Pope Francis

Paddy Agnew

It has happened. People around here have been talking about it for years and years but it has finally happened.

The cardinals of the Catholic Church have chosen a non-European pope, someone whose Latin American origins, blend of doctrinal orthodoxy and concern for the poor would suggest that things might change around here, although perhaps not as much or as fast as some might want.

When the name of 76-year-old Argentine Jesuit Jorge Mario Bergoglio was proclaimed to the 100,000-strong crowd in St Peter's Square last night, there was a gasp, with many not understanding who had been elected.

When the man himself soon appeared, he did so with a humility that struck a very different note.

Given his track record as a defender of the poor, he may prove to be the Catholic Church's version of Barack Obama, in that he could well generate unrealisable hopes and expectations about the future of the Catholic Church.

The former cardinal Jorge Mario Bergoglio of Argentina waves to the waiting crowd from the central balcony of St Peter's Basilica, moments after his election as Pope Francis. Photograph: Peter Macdiarmid/Getty.

Joy

In St Peter's Square last night, there were people literally jumping for joy.

Those who would like to think that he is going to change the church's position on a whole range of issues, including Catholic teaching on homosexuality, contraception and clerical celibacy, may, however, be disappointed.

The new pope's immediate schedule makes the point. At a briefing last night, senior Vatican spokesman Fr Federico Lombardi, himself a Jesuit like the new pope, said that Pope Francis's first public outing would be to visit the Basilica of Santa Maria Maggiore this morning where he will pray to the Madonna. That hardly sounds like a radical change.

However, the fact that on Saturday he intends to hold a meeting with the media in the Paul VI Hall sends a very different message, one of openness from an organisation that, frankly, has often treated the secular media with total distrust.

Pride

Many Argentines, from ex-footballer Diego Armando Maradona to Ricardo Alfonsin, son of former Argentinian president Raul Alfonsin, last night expressed an immediate sense of understandable national pride at the election of Pope Francis. Even US president Barack Obama was much enthused, calling him a symbol for the 'poor and the vulnerable'.

To some extent, all that was inevitable. What was much less expected was that the al-Azhar Sunni university in Cairo should react positively, with sources saying that perhaps the time of the 'cold war' between Catholicism and Islam, in the wake of Benedict's 2006 Regensburg speech, may now come to an end.

For the first time ever, too, Pope Francis got to telephone his predecessor, exchanging a few words with Benedict, Roman pontiff emeritus, last night. In the coming days, he intends to meet his predecessor too. All very different, if not to say unprecedented.

Summing up the conclave's choice last night, Fr Lombardi called it a 'surprise' and a choice which demonstrated 'the cardinals' willingness to broaden their vision'.

He also called the new pope someone who represents a continuity with Pope Benedict. As of now, that remains to be seen.

THURSDAY, 14 MARCH 2013

'I think, in his own way, he's galvanised the community . . . he's taught us about the need for compassion'

Carl O'Brien

Few people knew the name of the man in the doorway – but almost everyone knew him to see.

With his wispy white hair and flowing beard, he walked the streets of Dublin's south inner city with a Dunnes Stores bag in one hand and a bundle of newspapers in the other.

For about 20 years, he used a sheltered alcove on Oliver Bond Street as a place to sleep.

He spent most of his days picking up litter, placing it in bins, or sitting for hours at a time in the local churches.

Children in the area called him 'Moses' or 'Santy'; others knew him simply as 'Dusty' or 'John'. No one knew for sure. He was an intensely private person who refused most offers of support or accommodation.

He died last January, aged 83. In temperatures of close to freezing, he was brought to St James's Hospital where he died a fortnight later. His funeral was delayed for almost two months to allow time to find relatives, although gardaí weren't able to find any.

It was a death that might ordinarily have gone unnoticed in the often harsh and hostile world of the inner city.

Ned Delahunty, also known as John Delaney. Photograph: Eddie Mallin.

The doorway on Oliver Bond Street in Dublin that was home to Ned Delahunty. Photograph: Brenda Fitzsimons.

Yesterday, however, more than 150 people – locals, shopkeepers, regular massgoers – gathered to remember a man to whom few people had ever spoken. Dozens of floral tributes and cards have been gathering in the doorway where he died over recent weeks.

'I think, in his own way, he's galvanised the community,' said Jane Forde, a local nun who stayed with him during his final days in hospital.

'You know, people say the country is banjaxed and that we're a less caring society, but the care and offers of support he got from people shows another side to society. He taught us about the need for compassion and the importance of reaching out to people in need.'

Few knew much about the man in the doorway until he was brought to hospital in January this year. For neighbours such as Teresa Hogan, his background was a mystery.

'For 20 years he was in the same spot every morning and evening, facing my flat,' she says. 'He could have been vulnerable, but everyone looked after him or kept an eye out for him.

'He always struck me as well educated or well brought up. He was so clean and so independent. He would dress neatly and tidy up after himself. I don't know, there was just something about him. And his skin – his skin was beautiful.'

Rumours swirled around about him: some speculated he was previously an academic, others were adamant his brother was a member of the judiciary or the medical establishment. In truth, no one knew.

At a distance

He kept people at a distance. Anyone who offered help or approached him out of the blue – care workers, priests or locals – could either get a gruff 'thank you' or else get drowned in a hail of expletives.

'To live on the streets, you have to be a bit tough,' Tony Geoghegan of the Merchant's Quay

Project says. 'If you're vulnerable, people will just take advantage of you. I think he learned that. You need a hard veneer to keep people away who might prey on you.'

Subtle support

People who helped him tended to offer support in subtle ways: outreach workers from various charities often left food or blankets outside his doorway; at the charity shop where he bought clothes, they would put aside items they felt he might want or need; others might leave money under his blanket if he was asleep.

Bernie Houlihan, an outreach worker with the Merchant's Quay Project, was one of those who helped arrange for him to collect his pension. It mostly seemed to go on getting his regular dinner of egg and chips at Vincenzo's, the local chipper, buying clothes from the charity shop or a few cans of beer.

No one might have known his name – until Jane Forde sat with him during the final days of his life at the intensive care unit at St James's Hospital. The doctors found he was terminally ill from cancer.

When she arrived at the hospital, she says he spoke to her for the first time. 'He said, "you're the woman who gave me a walking stick",' she recalls. 'And then he told me his name, Ned Delahunty, and that he was 83. I was shocked. I thought maybe this was a man in his 60s.'

In his final days, he took a turn. 'I held his hand – and he didn't push me away. At one point, I think he asked me, "Do you think I'm going to die?"

'I felt privileged to be able to sit and hold his hand each night, even though he had kept many of us at a distance for so long.'

Excellent care

The care from the doctors and nurses at the hospital, she says, was excellent. 'They couldn't have been kinder. If it was my own grandfather, I couldn't have been happier with the care he received.'

He died peacefully on 17 January.

The life of Ned Delahunty, the man in the doorway, remains a mystery. For locals such as Julie Howley, his life and death meant something more.

'I feel that his one story throws up the real challenge of our time,' she says. 'As a society we share a responsibility to challenge the systemic issues that stack the odds against certain people and lead to them living, and sometimes dying, in appalling conditions.

'But it is also our job to enable the individual's story to be heard so that they won't be just a statistic, but a real and full human being.'

SATURDAY, 16 MARCH 2013

John Hurt: 'I don't really look like Beckett at all. God. I should be so lucky.'

Arminta Wallace

Breakfast interviews often turn out to be a bad idea. You can easily end up with a recorded interview that you can't really hear because it's full of clanking spoons and background music, and either one or both of you hasn't fully woken up yet.

But when they said would you like to have breakfast with John Hurt, I forgot about all that. Who's going to pass up the chance to share a rack of toast with the man who has provided some of your favourite cinema moments? That heart-breaking face finally uncovered near the end of *The Elephant Man*. Max the heroin addict offering world-weary counsel to the hapless Billy in *Midnight Express*. And that fantastic scene in *Alien* when the Thing wriggles, bleeding and toothy, out of Hurt's chest.

Hurt is in town to play the shambolic hero in Samuel Beckett's one-man play *Krapp's Last Tape* at the Gate Theatre, a role with which he has been associated for 14 years and for which he has earned critical praise.

'I was living in Wicklow when Michael Colgan first asked me to do it,' he says, referring to the theatre's director. 'He came up to the Roundwood Inn. It was, shall we say, holiday time. And I wasn't exactly sober. I said, "Let me think about it." Of course I put it off. I was always a bit worried about Beckett. I thought I didn't know enough about it and that you had to be a bit of an intellectual to take it on. And I wasn't scoring myself as such. In the end I said yes.

'Six months later Michael asked me again. I said, "Michael, I said I'd do it." And he said, "I know, but you were drunk at the time." I said, "Well, I'm telling you now, and I'm drunk now." Eventually we all sobered up and put it on.'

The production – sometimes directed by Colgan, sometimes not – has since played at the Barbican and in the West End of London, as well as touring to Washington, New York and Los Angeles.

'I think – I hope – it's a better production now than it was to begin with,' Hurt says of the current incarnation, which opens at the Gate next week. 'I'm hugely fond of the play, and I'm always amazed that it reaches half as far as it does. It seems to have its own kind of magic. In fact, I get worried talking about it, because I think, Maybe it's like stardust and it will all disappear.'

Beckett being Beckett, there's very little there to begin with. The sparsest of stagings – just Krapp and his tape recorder and those precious spools of tape, really – and the minimum of dialogue. 'Yes. He takes absolutely everything away. And we keep taking more and more away, as the years go by.'

Hurt is unfazed by the mention of the great Krapps who have preceded him, such as Harold Pinter, Michael Gambon and Patrick Magee (for whom Beckett wrote the play). There's no such thing as a definitive performance in the theatre, he says – otherwise, what would be the point of going to see new productions? On the other hand, no good can come of straining to be different just for the sake of it.

'I would say, for instance, that Dame Edith Evans was definitive in the role of Lady Bracknell in *The Importance of Being Earnest*. Many people have tried to play it differently and have fallen, I think, well short – because there is a cadence. And if you don't follow that musical cadence, it won't work.'

One new thing Hurt does bring to Krapp, though, is that he actually looks a bit like Beckett. Or is that just accidental? 'I do contrive to,' he says. 'When my hair is white and it's short like this, it's very similar to his cut and so on. Let's say I can give that impression. I mean, I don't really look like Beckett at all. God. I should be so lucky.'

As food is ferried discreetly to and from our table in a quiet corner of a hotel breakfast room – Hurt has a plate of fresh fruit followed by two boiled eggs – we chat about the developments that may one day render Krapp and his tapes tech-nologically, if not emotionally, obsolete.

'Think of printing, which eliminated writing,' Hurt offers. 'Before that again, writing was regarded as such a threat to memory and the oral tradition. And now . . .' he pats his pocket. 'Mobile phones remember everything for us.'

At 73, Hurt says he has never had a problem remembering lines. 'But I'm terrible with names. This is what makes me feel old. I hate it. I find myself saying, "Who's that?" And my wife says, "Well, it's so-and-so. You saw them at such-and-such." And I don't remember. Frightening.'

Is he shy at all? Would that be why people sometimes don't register? 'I can be,' he says doubt-fully. 'Oh, but I can be bombastic as well. I'm horrible sometimes.'

His peers would beg to differ. At the 2012 Bafta awards, when he was given a lifetime-achievement award, the applause – warm and genuine – went on

John Hurt by Cyril Byrne.

and on. Was it wonderful? Embarrassing? 'More baffling than embarrassing,' he says.

Looking back on a career in which he has played Caligula in the miniseries *I, Claudius*, Jesus in Mel Brooks' irreverent *A History of the World Part One*, Control in the recent *Tinker, Tailor, Soldier, Spy* and the wonderful Jellon Lamb in the Australian film *The Proposition* – as well as creating the voices for a profusion of small-screen classics, from *Human Planet* to *The Gruffalo's Child* – clearly doesn't strike him as disturbing or threatening.

'Well, I'm so much more in the know about things that I've done than other people,' he says. 'That's one of the things when you get an award like that. You think, Do you know how conceited I was at this particular period of my life? Nobody's life is all saintly. You're such a mixture of stuff.'

Mention of saintliness prompts me to ask about the influence of his father, an Anglican vicar, on his life. 'I was brought up as an Anglican, but I went to a boarding school that was so high church it made Rome look positively puritanical,' he says. 'The Mass was in Latin, we had the sacrament in the tabernacle on the altar, the whole bit. So I don't think my prep-school upbringing was any different from that of my Catholic friends, who went through the same sort of thing – including the same sort of abuse, and all of that.'

In the autumn of 2010 Hurt spoke out about the sexual abuse to which he and other boys were subjected at their boarding school in the Kent countryside. 'It never really worried me very much,' he says. 'But I have to be careful what I say. Things can be so misconstrued nowadays, as if you're defending what happened. I'm not defending it. It was just the way things were, and I knew no other way. I just let things happen, really; things that shouldn't have happened. No question about that. What I would say is that it didn't seem

Irish women's rugby Grand Slam champion teammates Claire Molloy, Larissa Muldoon and Joy Neville celebrate their victory. Photograph: Dan Sheridan/Inpho.

to worry me as much as it worried a lot of other boys in the school.'

The happiness of his home life is what Hurt chooses to remember. 'My brother was a terrific brother. He is seven years older than me, and we used to have a game called Town, which we played all the time. We had Dinky Toys, and he built houses; there was a whole life going on there, with different people in it. All day long we would play.'

The brother, now known as Anselm, has been a Benedictine monk at Glenstal Abbey for many years. 'I brought him to Tangier for his 80th birthday. I was making a film there for Jim Jarmusch. We had a fantastic celebration.'

There was also a sister, Monica, who died from dementia some years ago. 'God, was it cruel. Horrible.'

Having come through all these life experiences, has Hurt come to any philosophical conclusions of his own? He describes himself as an atheist, the kind who asks questions rather than the kind who claims to know all the answers.

'It's what humanity has done throughout its existence, isn't it? But the subject has fascinated me hugely. All our art, throughout the centuries. All for different gods and different understandings. There's so much in religion which is constructive and so much which is destructive, and they seem to go hand in hand. I don't understand that, frankly. I just pick up the threads in what I do and how I live. But it ain't no rock, that's for sure. It's a shifting sand all the time.

'One never feels completely secure. Of course, security, to an actor, is an odd thing to try to pursue.'

A smiling waiter refreshes our cups. More toast is offered. We refuse. We sigh, full and happy. 'If we were on holidays,' Hurt says, 'we could have kippers and all sorts. Maybe next time we will.'

MONDAY, 18 MARCH 2013

Heroic Ireland Get Down and Dirty

Gavin Cummiskey

Nothing glamorous about this victory but Grand Slams never come easy. Just ask Declan Kidney. A huge dollop of luck is needed but the essential ingredient is the strength of will shown by the leaders. In this team the actions of Fiona Coghlan, Joy Neville and cool-as-ice place-kicker Niamh Briggs have been contagious.

It was a match that won't be used to promote women's rugby, but the knock-on effect – and there were plenty – will reverberate for years to come. 'We couldn't really get to play our game at all, the conditions were horrendous,' said Ireland captain Fiona Coghlan immediately after yesterday's nervy 6-3 defeat of Italy.

Of course, Coghlan now joins Karl Mullen and Brian O'Driscoll in a very elite club. 'It was ugly but we don't mind winning like that.' She's right, so what. There was plenty of pretty stuff earlier in the campaign, especially the 25-0 flailing of England in Ashbourne when Lynne Cantwell shined in midfield.

This game demanded the opposite: a punishing, brutal slog with outhalf Nora Stapleton and fullback Niamh Briggs keeping the forwards' spirits high by probing them forward with the boot. When Ireland coach Philip Doyle opened his window yesterday morning and saw the icy rain beating down, he knew there would only be one way to direct the troops.

'I didn't think the weather was going to be as bad to be honest,' said Doyle. 'We had to change our game plan and it was very hard. We played too much rugby in the first half. We just played into their hands and all they had to do was wait for us to fumble. We had to switch it around in the second half.

'If that was a dry surface we would have ran that Italian team off the park. No doubt, we would have cut them up. This is their third wet Six Nations game so they're obviously used to it. I could see it all going wrong for us. Everything was falling into their hands – but testament to our girls.'

Italy were intent on spoiling the St Patrick's Day party of 500, largely female, travelling supporters, taking the lead after just two minutes with a Veronica Schiavon penalty before Briggs levelled it up.

'We haven't played like that at all this season. I told them this was like a club game in Munster and we would have to dig really deep. I think we got the rub of the green on Paddy's Day,' said Doyle.

Briggs put Ireland ahead on 50 minutes but the moment of the match, the courageous play that ultimately stopped what seemed Italy's relentless march towards Ireland's try line, was pure Limerick. Joy Neville is a sister of long-serving Garryowen backrower Paul. In the 80th minute, the veteran number eight realised something had to be done. It was a textbook defensive steal at the breakdown. It saved Ireland. 'It was an incredible turnover from Joy, she's a wizard at the breakdown. That backrow of ours is pretty special,' said Doyle.

Everything moved in slow motion with Neville unsure how referee Claire Daniels would see it. 'I took the risk when it was offered when I saw her coming around the corner and she was isolated,' said Neville. 'I heard the whistle and was worried it might be their penalty. Was just relieved to see the arm go up for us.'

The towering Maz Reilly grabbed the next lineout and with it came the Grand Slam.

'To be fair to the union,' Doyle was keen to mention, 'they have backed me 100 per cent this season with all the funding and all the technical support I wanted. Thankfully I can bring back the silverware for them. But I'll always ask for more. I will be going back and they'll be annoyed with what I want but that's the name of the game. They are very open to suggestions, I'll say that.'

Being Jeffrey Archer

Patrick Freyn

'How many years since you stopped smoking?' Jeffrey Archer, blockbuster author, former politician, multimillionaire and ex-con, asks the young hotel receptionist who has just brought him his phone and glasses from his room.

'Three,' she says.

'You've four to go,' he says cheerfully. 'It takes seven years to clear the system.'

'My wife makes me tell beautiful women to stop smoking,' he explains to me as the young woman stands there. 'A third of the people in her hospital' – Mary Archer has just retired as chairwoman of Cambridge University Hospitals NHS Foundation Trust – 'have smoking-related diseases'.

Archer, a whirlwind of septuagenarian energy, likes to take things and people in hand. He takes the young woman from reception in hand. He takes the interview location in hand. 'This is a bit busy,' he says of the bar I'm sitting in when he arrives, before repositioning us in the bigger room next door. The chair by the table is too hot, he says, and moves seats once more.

He takes me in hand. When he hears I have aspirations to write a novel, he scolds me – 'Well, Patrick, are you going to do it or just talk about it?' – and repeatedly comes back to it. 'Don't spend the rest of your life saying, "I could have written the best novel if I hadn't been working night and day".'

As he tells it, he even took the prison system in hand during the two years he spent incarcerated, from 2001 to 2003, for perjuring himself when he sued the *Daily Star* in 1987. (It had claimed he'd paid for sex.) He ran the prison's hospital, gave prisoners advice, lobbied for changes to the system and even operated a weekly salon of sorts. 'I had teas on Sunday afternoon at the hospital,' he says. 'I used to invite people I thought were interesting, and matron would make crumpets.'

Archer's new book, *Best Kept Secret*, the latest in the *Clifton Chronicles* series, is selling very well.

'It's already sold 31,000 copies,' he says. 'They rang me at the airport. They're very happy bunnies. Number one in the *Sunday Times* this Sunday. It's number one in Smith's. It's number one in Tesco.'

He taps out each beat on his fingers. 'Thirty-one thousand puts you at the top two or three in the world . . . Last week James Patterson sold 8,000. I wiped him out.'

Figures just lodge in his brain, he says. He can tell you the sales figures for each of his books, how much everything in his art collection is worth and what he's made from theatre investments (a return of about 0.5 per cent a year). He can even tell you how much he made as an infant luggage handler in Weston-super-Mare.

'I'd take people's luggage from the station to their houses in a pram. I was seven or eight. I made 30 shillings in three weeks,' he says proudly. 'I was always a fan of free enterprise.'

This entrepreneurial spirit was why he joined the Tory party rather than Labour. It's also why he wrote his debut, *Not a Penny More, Not a Penny Less*, during a period of near bankruptcy in the mid 1970s. 'I couldn't get a job and stupidly thought writing would get me out of my problems. Fourteen publishers turned it down, and the fifteenth gave me £3,000.'

His books are psychologically light, plot-heavy narratives filled with melodramatic revelations, lavish lifestyles and dastardly villains. They are ripping yarns that sell very well. If they didn't, he's

Jeffrey Archer by Bryan O'Brien.

not sure he would write at all. He is only slightly concerned about the lack of critical acclaim, concluding that storytelling is an underestimated craft among the literati.

'I always remember in this city, years ago, I was walking down O'Connell Street and there was a tramp sitting in the corner, and he said' – Archer does a passable Irish accent – '"It's lovely to see you, Jeffrey. Is there any Irish blood in you?" I said, "Not that I'm aware of. I would love there to be, but I cannot pretend there is. Why do you ask?"

'"Because you're a seanachaí! There has to be Irish blood in you." So I rushed off to ask what a seanachaí was, and since then, when asked, I say I'm a storyteller.'

The Indians appreciate storytelling, apparently. He's a bestseller worldwide but a superstar in India. 'Three thousand people come to see me speak in India,' he says. 'The average age is 18 or 19, and they're all girls. It's like being a pop star. You walk in and they start screaming. Tell me what that's about?

'Fifty million people have read *Kane and Abel* in India. They've made two Bollywood films of my books, unofficially. Half the books are pirated. But if you asked, "Would you rather one million people had read you and you got all the money or 50 million had read you?" I'd go with the 50 million.'

The only reason he can think of for his Indian success is that, at a time when gender issues are to the fore in India, they might appreciate his 'long-time commitment to women's rights'.

Yes, you read that correctly. Archer believes this latent feminism is clear throughout his work. To be fair, he made a statement to the Indian press at the end of a recent book tour that 'there will always be stupid men who don't realise women are equal'. And they printed it in every paper.

'A 12-year-old girl came up and said, "I've

Shabnam, Wafa Nazari and Barya Shafaq from Afghanistan, wearing traditional costume and rehearsing for Nowruz, a traditional New Year celebration by over 300 million people in the Middle East and Central Asia. Dublin City Council marked Nowruz with an evening of music, dancing and poetry by members of the Afghan, Azerbaijani Baha'i, Iranian, Kazakh, Kurdish and Turkish communities. Photograph: Alan Betson.

written a novel, and I'm going to replace you." And I brought her up on stage, and I said, "Don't tell me, tell the audience," and they cheered her and cheered her.'

He doesn't think this commitment to equality should come as a surprise. 'You live with my wife, had my mother and work for Margaret Thatcher, how could you think anything else? . . . Mary once said she looked forward to the day when mediocre women took over the jobs currently held by mediocre men.'

His active political career came to an end with the perjury scandal and his stint in prison. 'I slept three weeks on a wing with 21 murderers, and when I asked why, they said, "This is the safest place. You don't want to be with the young hooligans. They scream all night and might even attack you, but the murderers won't touch you."'

He talks about this period a little as though it were a spell working with a charity. He's still in touch with two of his former prisonmates. He has just received a letter from one who has just finished a master's degree. He's a huge advocate of prison education.

Boredom led him to write his bestselling prison diaries and to volunteer in the prison hospital. 'I took over the hospital,' he says. 'The doctors came to me and said, "We don't have a manager. You be the manager!" They'd never had a manager. So I ran it for them, and they loved it.'

He got on reasonably well with his fellow prisoners, his role in the hospital earning him a

Tourists capturing images of themselves and the snow at Wicklow's Sally Gap. Photograph: Eric Luke.

certain amount of respect. 'I couldn't hit anyone, but they were terrified of my tongue.'

They opened up to him and told him stories, some of which ended up in his post-prison writings. He found most of them to be untrustworthy narrators, though, and he met only one man he felt really shouldn't have been there – apart from himself, of course. 'I thought putting me in prison was a silly waste of time.'

It's all behind him now. 'We held our champagne-and-shepherd's-pie party the year after I came out, and the press said no one would turn up. But everyone did.'

He has since had, he says, a great decade. He believes his charity work and book sales have done a lot to rehabilitate him.

He still has a vigorous writing routine. He writes for eight hours a day in two-hour bursts and produces a book a year. Three years ago he committed to writing the *Clifton Chronicles*, an entertaining century-long epic centred on a familiarly suave novelist called Harry Clifton, who at one point is jailed for a crime he did not commit.

'I committed to the series because I was terrified of drifting,' says Archer. 'I have enough money, obviously. My wife and family are stable. I have everything I want. There's nothing you can give me.' He pauses for a moment and chuckles. 'Though there are paintings I would happily steal.'

In person he is extremely confident, mildly bossy and unfailingly polite. He roots around his Kindle for the name of an author he thinks I'd like, asks the receptionist to fetch his phone to show me a painting he's bought and brings me to the lobby to look at a Paul Henry painting he's impressed by.

He's charming and likeable. He's also a convicted perjurer for whom everything has turned out quite well. 'I have had a wonderful life,' he beams.

What does he think when people say his life has mirrored the melodrama of his books?

'I think that's true,' he says.

Does he feel responsible for the ups and downs in his life?

'Sometimes, but everyone has ups and downs . . . Mine are just public.'

What does he feel about his reputation as someone untrustworthy?

'My closest friends are some of the most admired people in the world,' he says. 'Why is that? Those are the perceptions of people who've never met me or dealt with me.'

What does he think his flaws are?

He laughs. 'Mind your own business.'

'That could be my last line,' I say.

'Said with humour!' he says and grins.

Rough Justice

Keith Duggan

The bare fact of the story is chilling almost a quarter of a century on. In the dusky light of 19 April 1989, a young white woman was accosted while jogging through Central Park in Manhattan, violently attacked, dragged into a secluded green area, raped and left for dead.

The hours afterwards were a blur of swift police response, public outcry and the parading of five Harlem teenagers, who confessed to the crime as the unrepentant faces of a mob that had embarked on a gleeful spree of violence and harassment in the park that evening.

New York was a dysfunctional and ailing city in the late 1980s: period buildings were boarded-up husks; the subway system's stations were menacing and its trains and corridors a riot of graffiti; entire neighbourhoods were in the grip of a crack epidemic; and street violence, both casual and life-ending, was regarded as a consequence of daring to be a citizen of any of the five boroughs.

But this crime was the nadir. It stirred deep, unconscious fears, and the nature of the attack disturbed people in a way other violent crimes had not. As Ed Koch, as mayor of New York, said, 'Central Park was holy'.

Those tranquil green acres had been a common playground since 1857. That a mob from a district many regarded as irrevocably ghettoised were now stalking women was proof that civilisation was fragmenting. 'They' even had a term for their rampaging: 'wilding'. Overnight, the phrase became part of the lexicon of fear.

The jogger was not immediately named, and as she fought for life she became an Everywoman – the most shocking example of the fact that violent predators, in the form of young black men, could attack anyone at any time.

A desire to set the record straight was Sarah Burns' chief motivation for making *The Central Park Five*, a harrowing documentary that traces the frenzied atmosphere leading to the wrongful conviction of Kevin Richardson, Yusef Salaam, Raymond Santana, Antron McCray and Kharey Wise for the crime.

The first four, who had been 14 and 15 at the time and so been tried as juveniles, served their full sentences. Wise, who, as he had been 16, was tried as an adult and sentenced to between five and 15 years in jail. He was released in 2002, after more than 13 years in prison, only after a chance meeting with another young man from Harlem at Auburn Correctional Facility in upstate New York, where they were inmates.

Matias Reyes had also been in Central Park that night in 1989. A recidivist sexual offender, Reyes was the lone assailant; some pang of conscience at Wise's incarceration prompted him to admit to being responsible for the attack and rape. Forensic evidence confirmed this. The

Front page of the New York Daily News *of 21 April 1989 characterising the crime that led to the* *wrongful conviction of five men. Photograph:* New York Daily News/Getty.

Yusef Salaam being escorted by police. Photograph: **New York Daily News/Getty.**

convictions of the five were vacated, but in circumstances that were as subdued as those of the original convictions were incendiary.

Unfair and unjust
The lack of fairness and justice is what so offended me about this story,' Burns says when we meet on a rainy Monday afternoon in Brooklyn, near the basement office of Florentine Films. 'We actually got a little criticism for not being tougher on the NYPD and the prosecutors. But it wasn't about trying to vilify them. We simply wanted to set the record straight, because a lot of people still don't know that these men are innocent. They vaguely remember that "wilding" case.

'And the other aim was to restore some of the humanity that was taken away when the boys were lumped together as this "wolf pack" and the reaction was to lock them away. And to hopefully

bring up the debate about how we stop this happening in the future.

'The victim represented resurgent New York,' says Burns. 'She worked on Wall Street. In race and class she was the opposite to these kids. There was a widespread assumption that these kids came from depraved circumstances.

'Kharey had a difficult childhood, but for the most part they were lower middle class. Yusef's mom is a teacher. These were kids who were at school, playing sport and had caring, loving parents. These were not children raised in crack houses. Raymond Santana's dad told his son to go to Central Park that night because he felt it safer. Racial tensions were ratcheted up and the us-versus-them tension was heightened.

'Why was it so easy for people to believe that these kids committed this crime, even after it became clear that there was no evidence to

Kharey Wise (centre) during his arraignment. Photograph: **New York Daily News/Getty.**

connect them other than these hugely problematic, inconsistent statements that they gave? It is because their guilt made sense to people. And then you have this sociological image of the criminal black man, which is a hugely pervasive and really dangerous idea, and which recurs today.'

Sarah Burns was a six-year-old living in New Hampshire in 1989. She was unaware of the case until a work placement took her to the law firm representing the five men in a civil case they are taking against the city of New York, which has been dragging on for a decade.

She became fascinated by it, and a book she wrote about it laid the foundation for the film. Understandably, the men were wary at first of speaking with her; words, after all, had led to their downfall in the hours after the arrest.

As would become clear, they had invented their roles in the crime. A gang of teenagers had indeed run through the park that night, and several people had been attacked. The five boys were on the fringes of the gang, but they had attacked nobody and were simply in the wrong place at the wrong time.

They retracted their confessions as soon as they were released from custody, protesting that they were pressured and coerced, but by then they had been cast as barbarians in a legal and media drama that demanded justice. Archive footage of their pre-trial appearances show skinny black teenagers looking sullen and dressed in oversized suits.

The language and commentary swirling around the city in the days of the trial shocked Burns as she researched the case. Donald Trump

Drawing recapturing the trial of the men accused of the Central Park rape. Credit: Christine Cornell.

took out full-page advertisements in city news-papers calling for restoration of the death penalty; Pat Buchanan, a former presidential candidate, wrote an opinion piece suggesting, as Burns paraphrases, 'that the eldest of the five should be hanged in Central Park and the younger boys horsewhipped'.

Their tone matched the public mood. Archive vox-pop interviews show indignant New Yorkers agreeing that it was time to turn to capital punishment, and there was a widespread belief that the boys were products of homes that lacked moral compasses.

The film does not flinch from drawing a com-parison between the calls for 'justice' and the lynch-mob mentality of early-20th-century United States.

'When you see those adverts, you can't but think of lynching,' says Burns. 'Donald Trump calls for the death penalty in response to this case even though this was not a crime that was eligible for the death penalty, and these boys were too young anyway. They were boys.'

The film – a sombre presentation of the way lives were destroyed – does not suggest they were deliberately framed. Rather, the detectives investigating the case were convinced they had the culprits and dismissed any evidence that indicated otherwise. The film-makers tried to interview the police officers and prosecutors involved but were rebuffed.

The most compelling voices in the docu-mentary belong to the five accused – men approaching middle-age now but, because their lives were stalled, perpetually caught between being the naive teenagers they were then and the adults attempting to cope with the aftermath they are now. All are exceptionally eloquent and, as Burns says, graceful in their telling of the story.

One of five, Antron McCray, was willing to talk but couldn't face being filmed, so we hear but don't see him. 'It was a challenge,' says Burns. 'His story is so, so sad. He had this incredibly stable loving family unit. He was so close to his stepdad, and he just felt so let down by him that it ruined their relationship. The pain is right there in his mom's face. Antron and his mom are just incredibly private, and he is a very shy person.

'Also, he has moved from New York and changed his name – McCray is his stepdad's name – and he created a new life for himself. So when the convictions were vacated it didn't have any outward effect on his status. He was reluctant to speak in case he lost his job.

'And the effect of it all on the families was extreme. The family members saw the press bonfire every day and had coworkers and people on the street talking about this. The trauma for them is huge. You talk to Antron McCray's mother now and it is like all of this happened yesterday.'

It might have happened yesterday: in 2013, objectors regard New York Police Department's stop-and-frisk policy as a flagrant breach of civil liberties. Within the past fortnight, there has been heavy tension between the NYPD and residents in the Flatbush area of Brooklyn over the death of a 16-year-old black teenager named Kimani Gray on 9 March, after officers shot him seven times. Police accounts differ radically from those of witnesses.

The prevailing message of *The Central Park Five* – that for young black male New Yorkers the rules are shadier and more complex – ring as true as ever. The legal wrangle with the city continues to occupy the time and the minds of the five men, with little chance of an official admission of culpability.

But the film has brought a measure of recognition and apology. Kevin Richardson attended its screening at Toronto Film Festival last year and spoke about his experience. Five hundred people gave him a standing ovation when he was introduced, and he was too emotional to speak for several minutes.

Afterwards, he was standing outside the theatre with Burns when a member of the audience came up and said that the ovation was an apology. 'Time and time again people stand up and say, "I remember the story. I thought you were guilty. I'm sorry."'

For most people who remember it at all, any mention of the 'wilding' case evokes vague memories of a best-forgotten period. As it turns out, even the phrase was most likely the result of an inadvertent fabrication. None of the men had heard the word, let alone uttered it. The best guess is that they were singing *Wild Thing* by Tone-Loc, a hit of the day, in the holding cell before they realised the gravity of the situation.

All but Antron McCray live in New York, a city that has been re-imagined as prosperous and safe over the past two decades. Central Park, ice-coated and sparkling in winter and verdant in summer, remains a holy place and is, once again, a safe haven for joggers.

Trisha Meili, the primary victim that night, returned to full health and then chronicled what is a valorous story in her biography, *I Am the Central Park Jogger*. She ran the city marathon in 1995.

The Central Park Five will be broadcast in the US next month on PBS. The last cinema still showing it in New York last weekend was the new MIST theatre on 116th street in Harlem – the heartland of where the boys had lived before the full fury of law and order descended on them. The woman at the ticket booth smiles in greeting, but her face clouds over when I ask if she has seen it. 'Oh, I saw it all right,' she said quietly. 'Saw it with my own eyes.'

WEDNESDAY, 3 APRIL 2013

The Difference between Seán Dunne and the Little People

Colm Keena

The difference between the position of property developer Seán Dunne, whose bankruptcy move in the US could see him emerging from his debts this year, and the position of people here with distressed mortgages, who are to be told by their banks for years to come what they can spend their money on, is truly shocking.

Dunne, who owes hundreds of millions to Irish and UK banks, and who is among the largest of debtors on the books of the State-owned National Asset Management Agency, has said he may end up paying back less than 2 per cent of what he owes. Society will have to shoulder the rest.

Meanwhile, thousands of people who did nothing wilder than pay a once-standard price for a modest home, and took out loans that fell within the guidelines then being operated by the banks, find themselves being told their debts cannot be forgiven for fear of moral hazard.

It is commonplace to hear people say that no one was forced to take out loans during the boom, and that all that is being asked is that people who can afford to pay back their debts do so. That argument is only partly valid. The property boom went on for quite some time and people were in the mean time getting married, having children and so on. Their lives were moving on and decisions had to be made.

Seán Dunne as seen by Martyn Turner.

Lisa Jordan (left) from Ratoath and Maria Kelly from Enfield at Grand National at Fairyhouse Races.
Photograph: Brenda Fitzsimons.

Meanwhile, the boards of the main banks sanctioned huge borrowings from abroad to fund a lending spree that was inflating property prices and feeding into the profits they used to justify their enormous remuneration. There is something profoundly unfair about people being told in such circumstances that the responsibility for their mortgages is 100 per cent their own.

In the US some years ago, economist Joseph Stiglitz suggested a court-administered process whereby those who had borrowed to buy their homes during the bubble years should have part of their debts forgiven. The overall circumstances of the mortgage holder's position would dictate the size of the debt write-down, with ability to repay − once you'd given up on foreign holidays and subscription TV − not being a valid reason for having to repay all of the debt assumed. The suggestion has the merit of addressing the culpability of the banks for what has happened to so many people.

The arguments against such a move are well rehearsed. Such a process would transfer the burden of paying off the debt created by the banking system from the holders of bubble-era mortgages to the general population. The State could end up having to further prop up the banks and might even be pushed to having to seek debt forgiveness itself.

Some time ago, when presiding over the publication of a report by the Central Bank on the capital needs of the banks, the governor, Patrick Honohan, was asked to respond to the fact that senior bankers had been paid massive salaries and bonuses for making disastrously inept business decisions and the general public was now being asked to pay for the consequences of those decisions. Prof. Honohan, understandably, responded by pointing out that the correct policy response was the one that most efficaciously got the banks, and the economy, back to work, and that fairness was not the speciality of his institution.

The idea of focusing on what will work, as against what is fair, has great moral weight on its side. People, especially politicians and commentators, who bang on about unfairness while ignoring the complexity of the position we are in are worse than an irritating nuisance. It is distressing that after a disastrous period in our history marked by opportunism, hostility towards critical debate, and an all-pervasive lack of seriousness, examples of such attitudes continue not just to exist at leadership level in Ireland, but also to serve some people well in their chosen careers.

That said, the responses to fixing the problems besetting Ireland repeatedly throw up examples of such egregious unfairness that it can be easy to feel that our democratic model is being stretched to breaking point. The recent comments by Noam Chomsky to this newspaper, where he warned about the effect of the ECB's policies on democratic consent, are just another instance of such concern being expressed.

It has been well documented that people are hard-wired to throw self-interest aside when they feel they are being treated like mugs. The economic crisis in Ireland and Europe, which has dragged on for so long, has involved people swallowing bucketloads of unfairness in the hope that in time it will serve their best interests and the common good. But people shouldn't be pushed too far.

The failure of the previous government's plan to squeeze more revenue out of our non-resident multi-millionaires and billionaires has already illustrated how, if you are rich enough, you can evade government efforts to repair public finances. The Seán Dunne story shows that if you want quick debt forgiveness and the opportunity to get on with your life, you need to have above-ordinary levels of debt.

It is not a pretty picture. Perfection is not for this world, but the government, in implementing policies that are so offensive to people's sense of how the world should work, must not forget that when you stand back far enough, efficacy and fairness are not at odds with each other, but rather are necessary bedfellows.

On Being a Northsider

Róisín Ingle

Playing a game of 'If I won the Lotto . . .' with a friend recently, I realised that my dream of returning to my home village, specifically in one of the castellated houses on Sandymount Green, has without my quite noticing faded a bit.

In the past when I've played that game I've expressed an almost violent yen to return there. I'd immediately put an imaginary down-payment on a house I glimpsed inside once, the one that contains a surprise ballroom.

My grandfather kept pigeons down the road in Bath Avenue and I always imagined I knew how they felt, homing their way back after long journeys, their little hearts lifting at the sight of the Shelly Banks. It's as though when my mother sold the house part of me stayed in Sandymount, like an abandoned glove skewered forever on the railings of the Green. Not changing my bank, or my doctor, or my chipper for that matter was, I think now, a statement of intent: 'Sandymount. When the tide turns, I'll be back.'

Maybe everybody has this romantic attachment to where they grew up. I learnt to ride my bike by falling off it repeatedly on the path outside Ryan's pub, and I exchanged butter vouchers for everything except butter in Miss Roddy's shop. Sandymount still feels like home to me and yet my actual home for years now has been across the river in the north inner city. I can take or leave the southsider label, but I thought I'd always be a Sandymounter.

It seems I'm moving on. It seems I'm a northsider now. I was on my way home on a Dublin Bike when I got caught late at night in a mad March snow shower. I thought there was a bike stand at Connolly Station, but there isn't, and while contemplating my next move I noticed a young

The Air Corps planes fly over the Millennium Spire during the 1916 Easter Sunday Commemoration Ceremony at the GPO. Photograph: Brenda Fitzsimons.

Japanese woman with a map looking as confused as I was. I am a total sucker for a lost tourist. I always imagine them back home, telling friends about the time they were lost and about how this over-zealous person with an inane grin insisted on escorting them. Thinking of this future conversation gave me and my ego an instant Ready Brek glow.

The woman was looking for her B&B on Gardiner Street so it wasn't enough to just point her in the right direction, I walked her there, telling her all about the spire and the Gathering and, for some reason, perhaps in case she needed some emergency tights, Penneys.

Afterwards, outside the Abbey, some teenagers were keeping warm waiting for friends. Turned out they were fellow northsiders from Clontarf. When I told them I lived in North Strand, they looked at me, their faces a mix of pity and fear. And I found myself launching a defence of my adopted home. I told them about Da Mimmo's, the best Italian north of the Liffey, and about Brady's butchers and the new grocer's on the North Strand Road where you can always get fennel even if you can't find it anywhere else. Not that I find myself needing fennel much, but it's good to know it's there if I do.

I told them about my great neighbours and the lovely street we live on that my brother, when he comes to stay, says is one of the quietest houses he's ever slept in. I didn't tell them about the two times my phone was stolen from my hand as I walked and talked in my neighbourhood, because the gardaí told me it could have happened anywhere in the city. It could even have happened in Sandymount, I found myself thinking.

My late-night love letter to the North Strand told me something I hadn't realised: I'm a proud North Strander. I think my children have a lot to do with it. They come in the door after we've been away and don't say with a mix of self-pity and fear, 'Janey mac, but the north inner city's a bit grim'; they say, 'I like playing in other people's houses but I love our little house the best'.

And it strikes me that their romance with their own place is blossoming. Beautiful Fairview Park is their Sandymount Green. The railway bridge they pass under on their way home is their equivalent of Ryan's corner. When soon we swap their balance bikes for pedal bikes, this is where they'll fall off and get back on and this is where they will always feel at home, no matter where they end up. For years they will long for North Strand the way I used to long for Sandymount. And then maybe one day, they just won't anymore. Or at least not quite as much as they used to.

MONDAY, 8 APRIL 2013

Low Lie Mighty Harlequins as Munster Roll Back the Fears

Gerry Thornley

Oh ye of little faith. Rolling back the years in vintage fashion, Munster defied their own recent formline, the odds, the Gods, the tea leaves and perhaps even the fears of many of their most diehard fans in yesterday's stirring Heineken Cup quarter-final at the Stoop to eclipse Harlequins.

In the process, they saved their season and kept Irish interest alive on semi-final weekend for the 14th time in 16 years. Why do we ever doubt them?

As Paul O'Connell noted immediately afterwards, not quite licking his lips at the prospect, they'll be underdogs again three weeks hence when the tournament favourites Clermont host them on Saturday, 27 April (kick-off 6pm local time, 5pm Irish).

At least the game will be in Montpellier's Stade de la Mosson rather than their own Stade Marcel

Michelin fortress, where Clermont extended their unbeaten record to 58 matches with a ruthless demolition of Montpellier by 36-14 on Saturday – after the latter had dominated the first quarter or so.

Earlier that day, Leinster will host Biarritz in the Amlin Challenge Cup semi-final, but that would have felt like a slight anti-climax by the province's recent European standards.

A try-laden weekend was completed by a second tryless affair yesterday when Toulon beat Leicester 21-15 to earn a semi-final at Twickenham against Saracens, on Sunday, 28 April.

As a minor aside to extending their season, Munster's leading Lions candidates did themselves no harm in front of Warren Gatland and his coaching ticket. And they gave themselves another day in the shop window three days before the squad is announced.

Paul O'Connell, official man of the match, was such a towering figure that not alone has he edged closer to selection, he will have given Gatland serious thoughts of making him the tourists' captain again.

Conor Murray was facing off with Danny Care for the third scrumhalf's slot along with Mike Phillips and Ben Youngs, and thoroughly eclipsed the Englishman with his carrying, offloading, passing, kicking game and all-round work-rate.

He surely will be on the plane now, and the cases for both Peter O'Mahony and Simon Zebo can't have been harmed either.

O'Mahony was simply savage when Munster took Harlequins and the game almost literally by the scruff of the neck in the third quarter, when Zebo, in his first game for eight weeks since breaking a metatarsal bone, also shone with his chasing and catching.

'He's great, isn't he?' said Rob Penney of his captain. 'It's hard to explain what he does. Everyone speaks about him in glowing terms, and so they should.

'First and foremost, he's just a wonderful man. He's a great bloke. And you couple that with his

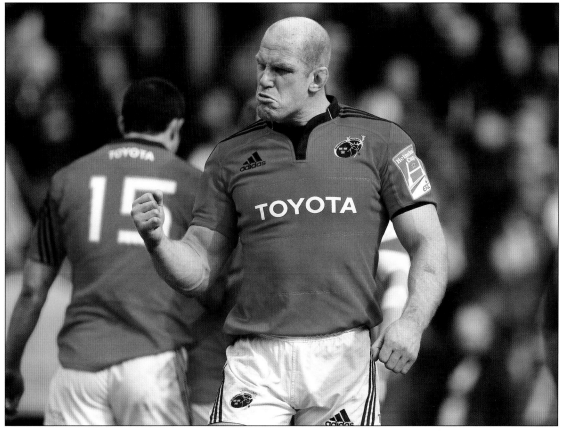

Munster captain Paul O'Connell shows his satisfaction after his team's thrilling Heineken Cup Quarter-Final win over Harlequins at the Twickenham Stoop in London. Photograph: Dan Sheridan/Inpho.

empathetic outlook on life – he sees things through other people's shoes, so he understands the trials and tribulations of what other people are going through.

'And he's just got this understanding that makes everyone feel good to be around him. You couple that with his rugby ability and he's just a really complete man, and Munster obviously have fed off him for a long period, and equally Rog today was superb. You can't speak highly enough about both of them.'

'I suppose there was a lot of doubt after last week,' admitted O'Connell. 'We probably threw a bit of a dummy against Glasgow. It wasn't our intention; we were very low during the week.

'It was a great, great performance. Some of the young guys, Peter O'Mahony and Tommy O'Donnell – it's hard to pick guys out, but I thought they were phenomenal – particularly in that 10-, 15-minute period after half-time, they really stood up.'

It was put to O'Connell that this had been traditional Munster cup rugby. 'It probably was. It's funny, I was laughing with Rob [Penney] after-wards because he probably can't win.

'We never discussed playing as we did. Our plan was to just do what was required of us at any given moment and that's what we did today.

'We did things which put them under a lot of pressure and built pressure on them. I think our maul, kick game, the carrying of some of the younger players was excellent.'

Generously saying 'well done' to a 'brilliant, brilliant Munster' performance, Harlequins head coach Conor O'Shea added: 'I thought Paul O'Connell was absolutely majestic; the whole team was physical but he was the totem the whole team rose around.

'Paul O'Connell is one of the greatest secondrows in rugby and one of the greatest secondrows Ireland have ever produced, if not the greatest. As the team rallied around him you could see that was the focus. Peter O'Mahony and Donnacha Ryan, they all gave their all but he was the man they all rallied around.'

A prospective Lions captain? 'Definitely.'

'It's going to be tough,' said O'Shea, echoing the words of O'Connell and Penney, who quipped that Clermont can only put 15 players on the pitch at one time, 'but you never, ever write Munster off'.

FRIDAY, 12 APRIL 2013

The Woman Who Fell to Earth

Tara Brady

I t's not easy being one of the most beautiful women on the planet. No, really. Just ask Olga Kurylenko. At 33, the Ukrainian-born star of incoming sci-fi extravaganza *Oblivion* can attribute at least some of her international prominence to a physical appearance that has been in no way poked at with an ugly stick.

Aged 13, she was plucked from obscurity when a modelling agent spotted her at a Moscow underground station. It was, she says, a 'crazy chance' – she just happened to be there on a day trip with her mum; within three years, she was a *Vogue* and *Marie Claire* cover star.

Actress and model Olga Kurylenko poses on the red carpet as she arrives to attend the UK premier of **Oblivion** *in central London. Photograph: Andrew Cowie/Getty.*

People try to fight back the flames at Barna in Co. Galway. Photograph: Joe O'Shaughnessy.

Still, there are certain drawbacks to being a model-turned-actor.

'Definitely,' she interjects even before I can finish the much-maligned phrase. 'Yes. It was harder. It doesn't help. You have to prove yourself a little bit more. Everything you see is the result of a complicated process of script reading, hesitating, declining and choosing. And choosing is hard. Sometimes it's hard just saying "no". You get a chance to do a movie with an actor or director you've always wanted to work with but the part is just arm candy. And it kills me. Euch! I want to work with this guy but I'm just not doing this. You have to be strong. You have to believe you'll get your chance again with a better role and on your own terms.'

She has, understandably, been keen to avoid 'Bond-girl-type roles' since she played Camille in 2008's *Quantum of Solace*. Being a Bond babe, she concedes, isn't necessarily as much fun as it looks.

'Don't get me wrong,' she says. 'The Bond film was a great experience and he [Daniel Craig]

was great to work with. All the people I worked with on Bond were lovely. And I learned skills with guns and fighting that have been useful to bring into other films. It's not a question of never doing something like that again. There are only so many genres. You will always get to a point where you are repeating yourself. But I really didn't want to get stuck in that kind of role.'

Thus far, saying no to the 'trashy stuff' seems to be paying dividends. *Oblivion* arrives on the back of appearances in Terrence Malick's *To the Wonder* and Martin McDonagh's *Seven Psychopaths*. There's also the day-job: Kurylenko is currently appearing on TV's *Magic City* alongside Jeffrey Dean Morgan and Danny Huston.

'I've had to decline a lot of parts,' she says. 'And I'm sure I'll make mistakes and have made mistakes. But I'm happy following my instincts, my gut.'

Oblivion is Kurylenko's most visible project since she left her Bond years firmly behind. The project began life as a graphic novel by *Tron: Legacy* director Joseph Kosinski and arrives in cinemas as an IMAX-ready spectacle with Tom Cruise attached. The newly appointed Irishman plays the last drone mechanic stationed on a post-apocalyptic earth. Andrea Riseborough co-stars as Her Indoors; Kurylenko is the mysterious survivor Tom brings home from work. Intergalactic insurrection and domestic strife ensues.

'We've seen post-apocalyptic films before but this is a bit different,' says Kurylenko. 'I watched *Solaris* twice in preparation for *Oblivion*. Because it felt – you know – right. They both deal with space and memory in a similar way.'

She has always loved sci-fi and recalls being scared witless by *Alien* back in her native Ukraine: 'I can see how one might not like the horror genre or certain kinds of comedy, but who doesn't like science fiction? It's so entertaining. We all want to know or guess at the future. It's a dream.'

A cheer goes up outside the hotel. Olga Kurylenko smiles and gestures towards the window of her room: 'Tom's back'.

She admits she still has to catch herself when she finds herself, as today, at the centre of considerable hoopla. It's nothing at all like her upbringing.

Olga Konstantinovna Kurylenko was born and raised in the Ukrainian port of Berdyansk. Her parents divorced shortly after her birth leaving Kurylenko's mother, an art teacher, to share child-raising duties with her grandmother, Raisa. The family's small, four-room flat was shared with an aunt, uncle, grandparents and cousins. They mostly lived on cabbage and potatoes and knew well how to darn and mend. The collapse of the Soviet Union added further financial strain.

'The times became harder for people in the country,' recalls Kurylenko. 'The shops were all empty. There was nothing to buy and nothing to spend. There were queues for everything. I was at school so my grandmother stood in those queues for hours to get a piece of bread or a sausage or a pack of sugar. Everything was deficit.'

Does she remember a corresponding cultural shift?

'Yes. I remember. I was a kid at school but there were small differences. I remember we stopped wearing uniforms and started wearing our own clothing. We were pioneers then one day – suddenly – we weren't. But day-to-day, I kept doing all the same things I had been doing. Music. Ballet. Art school.'

She laughs: 'We were doing all the same things but there was less talk about Lenin when we were doing them.'

Take out the Lenin and that all sounds like a very girlie education. Was that the case?

'Oh yes. I was a very girlie girl. As a girl – as a kid – I wanted to be more of a tomboy but my mum wouldn't let me. She really loved me being girlie. She'd put big bows in my hair and dress me in the fluffiest dresses. I liked acrobatics and I wanted to study karate, but she insisted on ballet. I liked ballet – of course – but I always wanted to do something tougher.'

By 16 – after that chance encounter on the Moscow Metro – Kurylenko had relocated to Paris and was the family's primary breadwinner. She was lonely, particularly between modelling jobs, and soon found a refuge in the French capital's many cinémathèques. It started with the collected works of David Lynch; Lars von Trier's *Breaking the Waves* sealed the deal; Olga Kurylenko was a cinephile.

'Where I grew up, it was impossible to be a big movie kid,' she says. 'We had no sources. First of all, it was Soviet Union so everything I saw growing up was a Soviet movie. They weren't movies that meant anything to my generation. Later on, when I moved to France, people would be talking to me about all these classics and were always surprised I hadn't watched them. That came later for me. I had a lot to discover. I became a total movie chick. I would see three movies a day. It was fun.'

Buoyed by her new passion, Olga presented herself to an acting agency shortly after her 2004

Health minister James Reilly launching the V for Vaccination programme at the Royal College of Physicians of Ireland. Photograph: Dara Mac Dónaill.

divorce from French photographer Cedric Van Mol. (She has since remarried − albeit briefly − to the mobile phone accessory mogul Damian Gabrielle.) Film work, she says, has allowed her to live out all her youthful tomboy dreams.

'I love doing action. I almost feel that filming action is better than watching action films. I shouldn't say it but it's true. Watching action is pretty pictures and having fun. Doing it is developing a new skill set and a rush of adrenalin.'

In this spirit, *Oblivion* sees Kurylenko riding on Tom Cruise's futuristic motorbike across the wilds of Iceland. She likes her fight craft and relishes the precision it demands.

'We had to rehearse, rehearse, rehearse,' she says. 'There's a lot of preparation on this kind of project because if something goes wrong on a movie like *Oblivion*, it could be very expensive to fix or reshoot. You're working with machines and stunts. Everything is checked and timed. Everything is perfect.'

How very unlike her time on Terrence Malick's dreamy *To the Wonder* in which an emotionally retarded Ben Affleck must choose between two perennially spinning potential mates, as played by Kurylenko and Rachel McAdams. The director only shot Kurylenko's eyes during her audition and the finished picture is ethereal even by Malickian standards. What on earth were the film-maker's instructions?

'It was like a sort of dance and choreography,' says Kurylenko. 'There was a lot of movement. Malick doesn't like his actors to stop. He was always pushing us to keep moving, whether

The iconic postcard showing children on a Connemara bog. Photograph: John Hinde Ireland.

walking or running or turning. You know what the mood of the scene is and you know what the thought of the day is and you know what the characters are doing today. After that a lot of it is teamwork.'

It sounds pretty exhausting.

'You get through a lot of material,' says Kurylenko. 'He tries to capture all versions of everything. So we try the same things over and over in different ways. That's why a lot of it gets cut out. He has so many options at the end of a shoot. But it feels natural. It's a very natural world – houses, grass, trees.'

She smiles: 'It's not like being in space with Tom Cruise.'

FRIDAY, 12 APRIL 2013

Tributes Paid to Ginger-haired Boy Immortalised in John Hinde Postcard

Lorna Siggins

Warm tributes have been paid in north Connemara to Paddy 'Red' Lydon, the ginger-haired boy immortalised in an iconic John Hinde postcard of the west of Ireland.

Lydon, who was photographed collecting turf with his younger sister Mary and a donkey half a century ago, died in Galway this week aged 65.

Millions of visitors are believed to have been drawn to Connemara from the 1960s by Hinde's depictions of a simple peasantry working an unspoilt landscape, where, naturally, it never rained.

Hinde sold millions of his 'Views of Ireland', which were printed in his factory in Cabinteely, Co. Dublin, yet Paddy Lydon often joked to friends that he was paid just half a crown for his modelling.

The Somerset-born photographer was often accused of 'manufacturing' images which were initially popular but later dismissed as the 'apogee of kitsch'.

However, Lydon's family recalls that the young boy and his sister, Mary, were out collecting turf to fill their donkey's creels near their home in Derryinver when Hinde came across them.

'All he asked them to do was to go home and change their clothes,' first cousin Pat Lydon told *The Irish Times*.

The postcard was not a feature on Lydon's mantelpiece, and he didn't talk too much about it afterwards, his cousin recalled. 'He would joke that his father, Christy, had cut the turf and had made everything in it – the kids, the creels – except for the ass!'

While the card travelled the world, the red-haired boy, who was one of five siblings, stayed at home and never married. His sister Mary moved to England. Their mother was fatally injured in a road incident in the mid-1970s, and their father died in 1979.

'He was a fine carpenter who made good currachs,' said his neighbour, Eamon Lacey.

He was also a 'quiet man' with 'close friends', who would be missed in the locality, according to Margaret Veldon of Veldon's in Letterfrack.

Hinde sold his postcard business in 1972. In 1993, he was 'rehabilitated' in artistic circles when an exhibition of his imagery was staged by the Irish Museum of Modern Art.

Interviewed in *The Irish Times,* Hinde rejected the 'kitsch' label. 'I photographed donkeys and cottages simply because you can't imagine a Connemara bog without a donkey walking across with panniers filled with peat,' he said.

'It's part of the landscape the same way the Irish cottage is like a living thing which grew out of the ground. It's true that in some cases my images were doctored and distorted, but if you photographed a beautiful scene off the west coast of Ireland, it would come out as practically mono-chrome, so we set out to create visually the impression you'd thought you'd had.'

TUESDAY, 16 APRIL 2013

Sayonara Baby, Our Marriage is a Sham

Fintan O'Toole

Sorry, wife, but it's sayonara, baby. It's been really great for the last 30 years and I thought it would last forever. But if Ireland follows France and 11 other countries and legalises gay marriage, I'm out the door. It will all have been a sham. Our sons will have to be written off as mistakes. Our whole marriage will have been fatally undermined because the institution itself will have been reduced to a paltry thing.

This, in essence, is the primary argument against gay marriage: that recognising it will diminish all marriages. And it is a stupid argument. A marriage freely entered into is a personal relationship. It stands or falls, endures or collapses, is a heaven or a hell, solely because of the way the people in that relationship treat each other.

The nature of my marriage does not change in the slightest if my neighbours are cohabiting or my workmate is in a civil partnership. And it won't change when, sooner or later, my gay and lesbian friends have the same freedom to marry (or not to marry) that I had.

Runners make their way through Joe's Water Splash at Punchestown racecourse in Naas.
Photograph: Alan Crowhurst/Getty.

I know we're all supposed to be civil and respectful about this, but let me be honest: I don't respect the arguments against gay marriage. I don't respect them because I don't think they are really arguments at all. They are a pseudo-rational veneer on irrational prejudice. They are so weak that I don't think any intelligent person would believe them unless he or she had already decided that gay men and lesbian women are not deserving of full human equality. And that decision isn't respectable – it's vile.

As well as the proposition that marriage equality would undermine all marriage, the anti-gay argument, as elaborated by the Catholic bishops in their submission to the constitutional convention, consists of two other absurdities. One is that same-sex marriage is impermissible because marriage is all about a man and a woman making

babies: 'Marriage is the community formed by a man and woman, who publicly consent to share their whole lives, in a type of relationship oriented toward the begetting, nurturing and educating of children together.'

If the church believes this, it should refuse to recognise the marriages of those who do not have children and those whose only children are adopted. For the only thing that rationally excludes same-sex couples from this definition is the begetting bit. Same-sex couples who have children, in fact, should be accorded a higher status than heterosexual couples who have no children at all.

The other argument is that opening up marriage to same-sex couples would be unjust towards other kinds of couples who cannot get married. The bishops tell us: 'An unmarried adult

Sisters Ann (left), Catherine (centre) and Maureen Pigott from Blanchardstown in Dublin at the opening day of the Punchestown Festival in Kildare. Photographer: Dara Mac Dónaill.

may share a home with an aged parent and care for them; this is a demonstration of love and commitment but is not akin to marriage. Similarly, two siblings may live together, pooling their financial resources and sharing their interests; this too demonstrates love and commitment but is not akin to marriage.'

Would it be possible to miss the obvious point by a wider margin? The adult caring for a parent and the siblings who live together are recognised by the State as belonging together in the same family. This is all that same-sex couples who want to marry are asking for – not something different, just the same right to form a family and have it recognised.

These arguments are so thin because they are mere expressions of bigotry. You can always recognise prejudice because one of its classic features is the way it places those at whom it is aimed in a double bind. They can't do anything right. If Jews got rich, it proved they were bloodsuckers; if they stayed poor, it proved that they were leeches. If blacks submitted to slavery, it proved that they were naturally servile; if they revolted, it proved that they were savages.

This is exactly what the opponents of same-sex marriage do to gay men and lesbian women. If they have sex outside marriage, they're promiscuous and a danger to society and morality. If they demand the right to be recognised as a faithful and eternal couple, they're undermining marriage and are therefore a danger to society and morality.

There is only one way out of this double bind – don't have sex at all. This is the official position of some of the Christian churches, who accept that homosexuality is natural and therefore God-given, and then insist that God did not intend it to be expressed in any physical way. This makes God a sadist, but it also makes those who hold this view bigots. For at its heart is pure revulsion.

Opposition to same-sex marriage is opposition to the proposition that all citizens are entitled to equal treatment by their state and its laws. And it's time we called that opposition what it is – not conservatism but prejudice. It is prejudice in the same sense that hatred of blacks or Jews or Catholics is prejudice. And it is no less shameful.

SATURDAY, 20 APRIL 2013

'They picked the wrong city to scare'

Simon Carswell

The bar is quiet at first. Most, except for one rowdy table, are nursing a post-work drink, engaging in a little conversation with a neighbour or having a quiet word with friends tucked away in a booth. Given the past days, particularly in Dorchester, the Boston suburb that is one of the most Irish neighbourhoods in the US, it's reasonable that few at Eire Pub, at the corner of Adams Street and Gallivan Boulevard, at 5pm on Thursday want to talk about what happened on Monday.

Suddenly, the looping television news on screens around the bar has something new to report after days of few developments and reruns of horrific images of Monday's bomb blasts near the finishing line of the Boston Marathon. The volume is turned up.

One drinker is quickly on the phone asking a person at the other end of the line to record the press conference, the first in two days updating the investigation into the worst attack on US soil since September 2001.

Rick DesLauriers, the FBI chief leading the investigation into the Boston Marathon bombings, which killed three people and injured more than 170, opens by saying that investigators have been 'working around the clock' since the bombings on Monday. 'Oh yeah, around the clock,' the loudest man in the bar shouts sarcastically at the television. But soon even he, like the rest of the bar, is silenced.

The images of the two suspected bombers caught on surveillance videos from a business on Boylston Street, the scene of Monday's devastating blasts, flash up on the screen. It is chilling to watch the images of two men carrying backpacks. Inside those bags, possibly, are the pressure-cooker bombs filled with metal shards, ball bearings and pellets that when detonated become flying debris that can maim and kill.

The youngest victim, Martin Richard, who was just eight years old, lived around the corner from this pub. The blasts also killed Krystle Campbell, a 29-year-old restaurant manager whose freckles and red hair gave away her Irish roots, and Lu Lingzi, a 23-year-old Boston University graduate student from China.

The images of the victims have been running on television screens and in newspapers for days. Now, after a blizzard of speculation and forensic analysis of amateur footage circulated online by internet sleuths, investigators have officially released photographs of people who may be the bombers. To some in the pub, knowing that investigators at least have faces to identify is comforting.

'I would expect, based on those photos, that someone will recognise them and call it in over the next couple of days. I think they'll get them. They know they are on the run now,' says Dennis Mannix, a former police chief in Natick, a town west of Boston through which the marathon passes every year.

It seems Mannix may be right: publishing the photographs could have smoked the suspects out.

*Mourners during a candlelight vigil for Martin Richard, aged 8, who was killed in the explosions near the finish line of the Boston Marathon. Photograph: Josh Haner/*The New York Times.

Late on Thursday night and early yesterday morning a shoot-out took place between two men and police, following the killing of a campus police officer at Massachusetts Institute of Technology hours earlier. The men were the suspects in the images. One of the men died after a shoot-out with police.

Sitting in the Eire Pub, Mannix is wearing a blue and yellow Boston Marathon top. Before this week runners wore them with pride to show the achievement of having run in a race they had to qualify for. This week they wore them as a sign of solidarity.

In an emotional speech in Boston on Thursday, President Obama captured the defiance that could be seen across Boston this week, drawing an analogy between the never-ending fight against violent acts and the marathon runners' spirit to keep going until they cross the finishing line.

'On that toughest mile, just when we think that we've hit a wall, someone will be there to cheer us on and pick us up if we fall – we know that,' he said.

'And that's what the perpetrators of such senseless violence – these small, stunted individuals who would destroy instead of build and think somehow that makes them important – that's what they don't understand.'

Mannix's marathon jacket is well worn. He ran only once, in 1978, finishing in 3:43:00. That time would have put him well out of danger's way this year: the first bomb exploded on Boylston Street at 4:09:00, the second 12 seconds later, about 100m away.

The bombs were timed, whether intentionally or not, at a point in the race when most novice marathon runners would be finishing, after four hours.

Police officers with their guns drawn react to the second explosion behind them at the Boston Marathon.
Photograph: John Tlumacki/The Boston Globe/Getty Images.

'It is bad, what happened, but it could have been worse,' says Joe Cruz, a 43-year-old scientist who was half a mile from finishing the race when police blocked him and thousands of others after the blasts.

Cruz is not a marathon runner; he entered the race to raise money for charity in honour of his late father. He doesn't know if he will try again to complete the annual marathon, which started in 1897 and is popular the world over. 'It is an international event,' says Mannix. 'If you are going to run one marathon, you would want to run it, because other than Athens it is the first one.'

Mannix, whose father emigrated from Castleisland in Co. Kerry, grew up on Carruth Street, where Martin Richard lived. The boy's family home is no more than a three-minute walk

away, one house up from the corner with Van Winkle Street. It is a beautifully restored family home with a driveway big enough to kick a ball in.

Blooming magnolia and cherry blossom trees dot the surrounding streets. Only a police car parked outside gives away the Richards' house and reveals a little more of the most heartbreaking story of Monday's attacks: a lost son, a badly wounded mother and a little girl who had to have a leg amputated.

Like most families in Dorchester, the Richards have strong ties with Ireland. Bill Richard is well known for his work in the community. His wife, Denise, works at a local school. Seven-year-old Jane, now badly injured, goes to Irish-dancing classes. The people of Dorchester came out in force for a candlelight vigil to mark the loss of their boy.

'Dorchester is a really tight and close community; it is so pulling together after what happened. Seeing that little boy's face is just so devastating,' says Mannix's wife, Maureen, sitting next to him in the pub.

In a week of unforgettable images of terror and tragedy, one stands out in Dorchester: the photograph of Martin holding up a poster he had made, reading 'No more hurting people – peace'.

Bostonians chose to post similar statements along the city's streets this week. On the security cordons blocking the streets around the Boylston Street bomb sites, and on walls around the city, are messages of support, 'Stay Strong Boston' and 'Boston, you're our home', matching the electronic 'Boston Strong' signs put up by the city authorities along highways.

Stories of random acts of kindness and gestures of support circulated all week: marathon runners rushing to give blood for victims, stranded visitors unable to access hotels being put up by locals and wifi password protection being removed so people could make vital contact with loved ones.

'I feel like everyone has come together,' says Shannon Dwyer, a 19-year-old student at Emerson College, just blocks from the site of the explosions. 'We were walking around today, and there was a guy walking a dog with a sign just saying, "Come pat our dog".'

Bostonians have refused to lie down in the face of the attacks on one of their city's biggest days, second only to St Patrick's Day in terms of celebrations. 'If they picked a city to scare, they picked the wrong city,' says Dan Corrigan, a 28-year-old medical student from south of the city, at a candlelight vigil on Boston Common on Tuesday.

Corrigan, who ran on Monday, says he was stopped less than a mile from the finish by the blasts. He had planned to run only once, but this week's events make him want to enter one more time. 'This is an awful thing that has happened, but people are getting ready to run again.'

Michael Lonergan, Ireland's consul general in Boston, says the attack has left the city with raw emotions. 'People have reacted in two ways: one is shock that this could happen on Marathon Monday; and that has turned to anger over how someone could plant bombs in Boston with so many people and children watching and the scale of the horrific injuries.'

At Greenhills Irish Bakery, opposite the Eire Pub, Paul Hutchinson, a plasterer from Co. Donegal who has been living in Massachusetts for 14 years, says the perpetrators 'messed with Boston's big day' when its people 'come out of hibernation', leave winter behind and mark the start of summer.

'I was in London after the docklands bombing, I was in Donegal after the Omagh bombing, and I am here. The reaction has been the same,' he says. 'There has been a sense of compassion and strength that has brought communities together.'

Even New Yorkers, bitter rivals of Bostonians in sport, put aside their differences. The normally deeply partisan fans at Yankee Stadium sang the Boston Red Sox anthem *Sweet Caroline* on Tuesday night.

'We stood by New York after 9/11 and New York stood by us,' says Randy Brooks, a 47-year-old correctional officer in Dorchester. 'We are not Bostonians: we are Americans.'

As well as being the most Irish city in the US, Boston is also one of the most proud, home to many of the famous acts of the American Revolution and the traditional heartbeat of the country's patriotism. In the absence of a clear motive or claim by a group during the week, speculation was rife that this may be a reason why the city was attacked, if this was indeed a home-grown terror act and a political statement.

The possibility of a right-wing group choosing to attack Boston because of its broad-church liberal tradition and revolutionary past could stir anger in US political circles.

'You could speculate on why they targeted it. It is a high-profile event,' says Mannix. 'Is it about

James Nesbitt. Photograph: Twofour Productions/ITV publicity.

[the marathon] being on Patriot's Day and that an anarchist would have done it? Who knows?'

Locals are quick to rubbish claims that Boston has been immune from the terror New York City and Washington have suffered. Both aircraft that were flown into the World Trade Center's towers in September 2001 left from Boston's Logan Airport, and many Bostonians were on the flights. 'So it touches home – 9/11 always touches us,' says Brooks.

But the popularity of the Boston Marathon is such that the aftershock of Monday's bombings was felt across the US and farther afield. 'This isn't just about Boston,' says Lonergan, 'but a shock and horror story across America.'

At the makeshift memorial at Boylston Street and Arlington Street, marathon runners speaking various languages and with a range of US accents pay their respects. 'I will be back again next year,'

says Steve Bramlett, who is 56, in a Mississippi drawl. 'You cannot stop living because these things happen – that is what they want you to do.'

SATURDAY, 20 APRIL 2013

Forty Shades of Blarney and Countless Stitches Add Up to a Waste of Time

Bernice Harrison

I t turns out that *James Nesbitt's Ireland* (UTV, Monday) is pretty much the same as the next man's – that's if the next man is preserved in 40 shades of green aspic and was making a publicity film for Bord Fáilte back when American tourists wore green polyester pantsuits and poured off tour buses. 'Welcome to Ireland. The Emerald Isle. Its appeal is timeless and Ireland holds something for everyone,' said the Ballymena-born actor by way of introduction to this blarneyfest, an eight-part magazine-style travelogue that features what we're supposed to believe are twinkly Nesbitt's favourite bits of Ireland.

The real puzzle is who this series is for. It's on UTV, but could anyone who lives on this island buy this misty-eyed begob-and-begorrah stuff? Nesbitt only appears in a couple of scenes in each episode; for the rest he provides the voiceover, never once faltering over such toe-curlers as 'The Irish love to celebrate love, but then they love to celebrate most things'. He must be a better actor than I've previously given him credit for.

Inevitably, there's much mention of that dread concept the 'character'; in the real world it's shorthand for a bore with questionable personal hygiene. 'Ireland is full of characters. They can be found in every corner,' Nesbitt told us.

The wild-haired Kerry matchmaker Willie Daly is 'an eccentric'; he showed Nesbitt around Lisdoonvarna during the town's matchmaking festival. 'Last year I'd say about 186 got married, related to the festival,' he said, a claim that went unchallenged.

There were items on a mobile pizza van in Dingle, the Galway races and a visit to the yard of the horse trainer Jessica Harrington: all fine ideas – RTÉ's teatime programme *Nationwide* churns them out weekly – but packaged here with such shameless codology I became convinced this was some sort of wheeze dreamed up by people connected to The Gathering who are not above shaking the odd shillelagh. But no. I stayed tuned until the end to read the credits, and, astonishingly, *James Nesbitt's Ireland* is an independent, unsponsored production.

Next week Nesbitt (or his production team) focuses on food, because, as he said, with no trace of mortification, 'We're a great big foodie nation, us Irish.' And if you can swallow that . . .

'Horrendous. Barbaric. Inhumane', Savita's Husband Gives his Verdict

Paul Cullen and Kitty Holland

Horrendous. Barbaric. Inhumane. Praveen Halappanavar, his voice full of calm fury outside the inquest into his wife Savita's death, wasted no time yesterday in delivering his verdict on the way she was 'left there to die' in an Irish hospital.

Minutes earlier, an 11-person jury had delivered a unanimous verdict of medical misadventure in relation to Ms Halappanavar's death in University Hospital Galway last October. The jury adopted the nine recommendations suggested by coroner Dr Ciaran MacLoughlin, including one that the Medical Council should revise its guidelines for doctors on the termination of pregnancies.

But Dr MacLoughlin was quick to emphasise the verdict did not mean that deficiencies or systems failures in the hospital contributed to Ms Halappanavar's death. The rules of the inquest process meant no blame could be attached to any person caring for her.

The couple should have been celebrating their fifth wedding anniversary yesterday; instead, Mr Halappanavar was once again facing a barrage of questions from reporters, again relating his story of the couple's fruitless effort to obtain a termination of her pregnancy when she was miscarrying.

'Medicine is all about preventing the natural history of the disease and improving the patient's life and health, and look what they did. She was just left there to die. We were always kept in the dark,' he said.

'If Savita would have known her life was at risk she would have jumped off the bed, straight to a different hospital. But we were never told.'

Mr Halappanavar is still considering further action through the courts in Europe, as he believes his wife's right to life was breached, he later told *The Irish Times*. 'I haven't got my answers yet why Savita died. I will get to the bottom of the truth,' he said.

Also speaking after the inquest, a hospital spokesman acknowledged there were lapses in the standards of care provided to Ms Halappanavar.

Tony Canavan, chief operating officer of Galway Roscommon Hospital Group, promised the deficiencies identified at the inquest would be rectified by the hospital and all recommendations would be taken on board. Some of the recommendations had already been acted on, he said.

The Medical Council, whose guidelines featured prominently at the inquest, said it would reconsider these rules after the government changed the legal position.

Speaking in Cork after the verdict, Minister for Health James Reilly said lessons learned from the inquest would feed into new guidelines for medical care. The Minister said he would have no issue apologising to Mr Halappanavar but wanted to read the inquest report first.

Dr Reilly said the loss of Ms Halappanavar had been desperately hard on her husband Praveen and his family and the family of the late Ms Halappanavar, and he did not want to add to this in any way by making any kind of general comment at this time.

Dr MacLoughlin led the sympathies to Mr Halappanavar. He said he had shown tremendous loyalty and love to his wife during her final days.

Addressing Mr Halappanavar, Dr MacLoughlin said 'all of Ireland had followed the story' and he offered his sympathies on behalf of the country.

But by the end of the afternoon, when the verdict had been delivered and even the journalists had run out of questions, there was nothing for Mr Halappanavar to do but return home, 'that cold and lonely place', as his barrister described it, bereft of his beloved wife.

MONDAY, 22 APRIL 2013

A Medical Conspiracy against the Public

Ann Marie Hourihane

There is a group of people in the country who are shocked but not surprised by the treatment received by the late Savita Halappanavar, whose inquest concluded last week with a verdict of misadventure, and by her husband. Praveen Halappanavar has the sympathy of the country, not only because of the tragedy of losing his wife, but because of what he himself endured in watching her avoidable death.

The group of people who are shocked but not surprised by the suffering of Praveen Halappanavar are the relatives of hospital patients all over the country. This is the group of people who not only sympathise with Praveen Halappanavar, but identify with him.

To be the relative of a patient in the hospital system is to feel at once completely powerless and yet totally responsible. It is to feel that information is being kept from you.

Above all, being the relative of a patient in the Irish hospital system is to be convinced that no one is supervising the case as closely as you are. A truly terrifying thought, yet a reasonable one in a system that can't keep or maintain its own records.

'If I had known I would have followed them up myself,' said Praveen Halappanavar of his wife's blood results. The fact that he has this to say at the end of his ordeal is not only unutterably sad, it is a national scandal.

Yet there are relatives murmuring the same thing in hospital corridors and waiting rooms every day of the week.

At the rate our hospital care is fracturing it will soon be like the care in poorer countries, where the family arrives with the patient and stays with them for the duration of their treatment in the hospital.

In fact, in the treatment of old people in Irish hospitals, we are already at that point, as the adult children of old people travel to be with their parents at hospital meal times, to make sure that they eat.

The truth is that it is needlessly traumatic to be the relative of a patient within the Irish hospital system – and that's if your loved one emerges from that system alive.

Let us say at the outset that there are parts of the Irish hospital system where staff are compassionate and efficient, communicating freely with both relatives and patients, where morale is high and outcomes positive.

And then there are the majority of Irish hospitals. As a relative of a patient in an Irish hospital, you feel confused, patronised and above all frightened about what is going to happen to your loved one when you leave their bedside to go home.

It is truly dreadful to get into your car outside a celebrated Dublin teaching hospital, convinced that you might as well be leaving your loved one on the platform of Heuston Station. Of course, you tell yourself, this could be the normal and natural separation anxiety that will occur when you have a sick relative.

But then you remember the long day you have just had. Looking for the consultant and never finding him or her. Hearing staff about to administer different doses of the drugs, and sometimes completely different drugs, as their shifts change. Finding dirty adult nappies on the counter top in the bathroom. Lying in wait close to the nurses' station to pounce on a nurse that might talk to you. Remembering that when you arrived at visiting time you had to help your relative into the second half of their pyjamas. Removing your relative's bloodstained surgical gown, which had been lying on their bed for some time, and being told by a nurse, who doesn't raise her eyes from her paperwork, 'Just put it in the bin there'.

And these are the minor matters. To complain about these things, it is strongly implied, is to be a stroppy cow. We've got people dying in here, is the implication, and there you are making a fuss about pyjamas. We've got forms to fill out and here you are asking for a light bulb. The person asking for a light bulb for her bedside lamp was told that it would be replaced in the morning.

Praveen Halappanavar after a jury ruled his wife Savita died due to 'medical misadventure'.
Photograph: Brenda Fitzsimons.

The patient pointed out that she was only staying in the hospital – a major hospital, outside Dublin – for one night. A nurse moved her to a closed and empty ward, which had full rubbish bins outside the door. The young woman did not feel safe there. She felt she was being punished for being perceived as cheeky. She had no relatives in the town.

But these are still minor matters. Let us not forget the relatives of the mentally ill in the Irish hospital system; we shudder at their suffering. Chaotic hospital care; psychiatric services run by the doctors as medieval fiefdoms; social workers whose main job seems to be keeping patients out of their hospitals and away from treatment there; housing officers who do nothing about the bullying of mentally ill people (frequently by other mentally ill people); no sharing of information about potential treatments elsewhere, and so on.

If minor matters are disdained they can snowball into a lot of pain. Our hospital system has been described as 'a conspiracy against the public'. Praveen Halappanavar's seemingly endless ordeal reminds the public how true that is.

WEDNESDAY, I MAY 2013

Yes, Amanda Knox Was Guilty. Guilty of Being Naive and Guilty of Liking Sex

Jennifer O'Connell

If you want to know the definition of the word 'vitriol', Google 'Amanda Knox'.

Do. Try it. On Tuesday, the day of the publication of her memoir, *Waiting To Be Heard*, a search for her name generated 158 million results, including 56,000 news articles.

Some of the 56,000 news articles included: 'Signs that suggest Amanda Knox is a psychopath' (theweek.co.uk); 'What is it about Amanda Knox that so chills the blood?' (dailymail.co.uk); and 'I'm proud of my one-night stands and drug use, says Foxy Knoxy' (dailymail.co.uk).

It has been almost four years since Knox and her then boyfriend Raffaele Sollecito were convicted of Meredith Kercher's murder, and 18 months since that conviction was overturned and they were released. But the public's fascination with the case – or at least with Knox – shows no sign of abating. Of course, the publication of her long-awaited and well-written memoir this week is unlikely to help Knox slip into obscurity.

By way of contrast, Google 'Rudy Guede', and you'll get a relatively modest 402,000 results, and 215 news stories. Guede, in case you've forgotten, is the only one with a conviction for Meredith Kercher's death; the only one, in fact, whose DNA evidence was at the scene. He is currently serving a 16-year sentence for her murder.

But in the eyes of many of those populating the internet sites devoted to getting to the bottom of the case, and indeed to many journalists, 'Foxy Knoxy' remains guilty – a conviction that was reinforced recently when Italy's highest court overturned her acquittal and that of Sollecito, and ordered another trial.

Rarely has a murder case attracted so much interest around the globe, so much speculation, or so much naked vitriol. On one level, it is easy to see why that might be. When a photogenic English-speaking young woman dies a bloody death in a foreign country, the story is going to be explosive.

When the accused also happens to be a photogenic English-speaking young woman, and the circumstances suggest some kind of satanic ritual or sex game, it's the equivalent of tabloid plutonium.

Never mind that the sex-game-gone-wrong storyline wasn't based on solid forensic evidence, or indeed any real evidence: 'We were able to

Amanda Knox during one of her 2008 court hearings in Italy. Photograph: Antonio Calanni/AP.

establish guilt by closely observing [Knox's] psychological and behavioural reaction during the interrogation,' said Edgardo Giobbi, the lead investigator.

According to *Rolling Stone* magazine, another police officer said that Knox 'smelled like sex'. Even a joke about how she would 'kill for a pizza' was used by police against her.

By the time the holes in the prosecution case emerged (contaminated evidence; no physical trace of Knox in Kercher's room; lack of motive), it was too late. The explanation that Kercher had been killed by Rudy Guede – who had a history of break-ins, who left a bloody handprint on Kercher's pillow and who fled the country after the killing – wasn't about to placate a mob that had its sights on Knox.

Much of the coverage that followed was vicious and misogynistic, played out first in the murkiest corners of the internet, and migrating from there into the mainstream media.

It was alarming how quickly a 'sexually active woman' became a 'sexual predator likely to be a killer'. Her nickname was Foxy Knoxy! She had sex with a stranger she met on a train! She did cartwheels in custody! She lied and blamed someone else! Of course she is guilty!

The simple, decidedly less sexy truth – that Knox was guilty of nothing more than extreme naivety – was just too dull by comparison. She didn't do cartwheels. Her nickname referred to her prowess on the football field. (The Knox who emerges in her book is so far from 'foxy' as to be almost laughable. At school, she writes: 'I was the quirky kid . . . I didn't kiss a boy until I was 17'.)

Yes, she implicated an innocent barman, Diya 'Patrick' Lumumba, and herself, but she was, by then, under extreme duress: she writes that she was

Members of the cast of the musical **The Lion King** *rehearsing before their official opening in Dublin. Photograph: Eric Luke.*

exhausted; that police interrogated her all night, mostly in Italian; they yelled at her and slapped her on the back of the head.

'I would have believed, and said, anything to end the torment . . . my mind put together incoherent images.'

The reason so much of the public was desperate to believe in her guilt (yes, I've had those conversations over dinner, too) says more about us than it does about her. We were only too happy to swallow the lurid tabloid slurs because there is a part of us that remains fascinated and repelled by the idea of beautiful women as killers.

We also suffer, en masse, from a similar delusion to that of the policemen in Perugia: a deeply held belief in our ability to infer things about people just by looking at them, or based on a few details about their past.

A girl who would sleep with a stranger she met on a train, so the collective bias goes, must be capable of pretty much anything.

The uncomfortable epilogue to this story is that Knox is now set to reap the benefits of that prurient fascination – to the tune of the $4 million she has been paid by HarperCollins for her book. Maybe that's only fair, when so many other people have made money from the case.

Whether it will help turn the tide of public opinion in her favour, as she hopes – she says she wants 'to be reconsidered as a person' – is unlikely. Those who have already made up their minds about her won't be swayed.

There are few real revelations in the book; there is nothing about the night of Kercher's death that didn't already come out in court. Meanwhile, the judge and jury of internet forums and tabloid newspapers are already seizing on lurid details about her sexual past, and the revelation that marijuana was 'as common as pasta' in the house in Perugia.

On the other hand, the day before the publication of her memoir, a Google search for 'Amanda Knox innocent' returned 1.2 million hits. By yesterday, it had climbed to more than five million.

Knox, I can't help feeling, will probably be alright. The woman who emerges in the book is resilient. She is not going to return to Italy for the trial, on the advice of her lawyers. She's back at college, she has a boyfriend and now she has some money.

The real victims in all of this are the Kercher family, who must now face up to the prospect of another trial, and who may never know with any certainty what happened to Meredith.

Ferguson: A Man for All Seasons in Soccer

Ken Early

Yesterday the BBC posted an archive video showing Sir Alex Ferguson standing on the Old Trafford touchline after his appointment as Manchester United manager in November 1986.

Behind him the stands look small and ramshackle, under a grey sky that would not be visible were the shot filmed from the same angle in the 76,000-seat monster Old Trafford that it is today.

Ferguson tells Barry Davies about his excitement at joining United, his sense of responsibility to their millions of supporters and the importance of feeling in football.

What is striking is the deep seriousness of the man, the intensity of his stare. Many other

A robin chick calling to its parents for food. Photograph: Cyril Byrne.

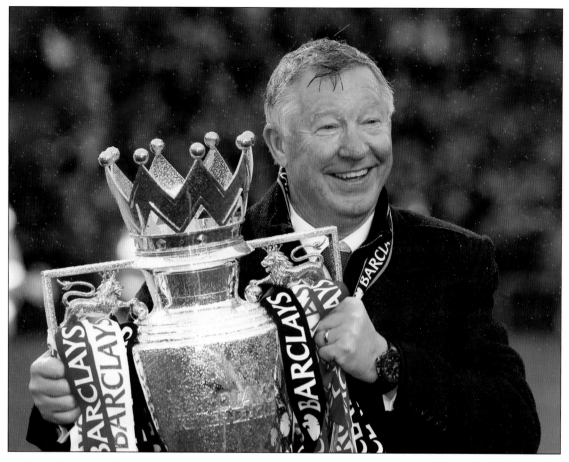

Retiring Manchester United manager Sir Alex Ferguson celebrates with the Barclays Premier League trophy following his final home match between Manchester United and Swansea City at Old Trafford. Photograph: Alex Livesey/Getty.

managers arriving in a new job would try to turn on the charm, crack a joke. Ferguson never smiles. He wears a side parting, navy blazer and tie, but looks as though he would be equally comfortable in the black coat and wide-brimmed hat of a 17th-century religious fanatic.

There was much more to Ferguson than fanaticism, as the players he didn't promptly boot out of the club were to discover. Ferguson could never have endured for so long, and won so much, if anger and intimidation were all he had to offer.

If they are the qualities most readily associated with him that may be because the angry side was the one he often showed to the media, whom he came to regard as the least important group of people he had to deal with on a regular basis.

The people who counted were those on the inside of his club – the players, staff and supporters – and insiders in the game, such as the countless other managers who will not hear a bad word said about him. These people got to see the other sides of a man for all seasons.

What is extraordinary about Ferguson is the extent to which his personality combines a palpable urge to dominate with acute emotional intelli-gence. Where many contemporary managers spend

Taoiseach Enda Kenny with European Affairs minister Lucinda Creighton (right) at the Mayo Pink Ribbon charity cycle in Castlebar, Mayo. Photograph: Keith Heneghan/Phocus.

hours analysing video footage and examining data, Ferguson has always understood that the game is about people.

He saw that the sport was constantly evolving, and his teams and methods evolved constantly to match, but he also knew that human nature was a constant in a changing sport.

Although famed as a ranter and a raver, he has never been a great phrasemaker. There have been memorable lines, like the one about 'knocking Liverpool off their f★★★ing perch' or telling a roomful of journalists 'youse are all f★★★ing idiots', but these tend to be vituperative outbursts rather than Cloughian aphorisms.

His most famous quote was on winning the Champions League in 1999: 'Football, bloody hell!' What is essentially a statement of inarticulacy endures because it captures his childlike love of the sport. Bill Shankly shared that romantic enthusiasm, as the journalist Hugh McIlvanney

wrote of him: 'How else could a manager persuade grown men that they could glory in a boys' game?'

Great talkers

Instead Ferguson is one of the great talkers. He built his empire on a million little conversations. He knew how to get into players' heads; he knew how to get what he wanted from club directors.

He portrayed his meetings with opposing managers after each game as a simple ritual of sportsmanship, but you wonder at the depth of knowledge and influence he amassed in 26 years of casual post-match chats.

Some 26 years and seven months. A reign that long would have made Ferguson the third-longest-serving Roman emperor, behind Augustus and Constantine, and the third-longest-serving pope, behind St Peter and Pius IX.

Each of these left a legacy that lasted far beyond their own time. Augustus established the

Roman Empire. Constantine founded the city now known as Istanbul. St Peter began the papacy, and Pius dreamed up papal infallibility.

Ferguson's deeds may not echo through the ages like those of St Peter, but he too is concerned for his legacy, and that may be why United look likely to appoint David Moyes as his successor, rather than the serial winner José Mourinho.

It has been claimed that Mourinho was never a serious contender because he is too arrogant, aggressive and disruptive. Yet Ferguson's contradictory personality shares many of those traits. He says he always puts the club first, yet he once sued United's largest shareholders over a racehorse.

The problem with Mourinho is that while he towers over Moyes as a trophy-winner he is no club-builder, and that appears to be what Ferguson values most.

'In my early years,' Ferguson said yesterday, 'the backing of the board, and Sir Bobby Charlton in particular, gave me the confidence and time to build a football club, rather than just a football team.'

There was Ferguson's answer to those who suggest that by allowing him to remain at the club as a director and ambassador, United risk repeating the mistakes that followed the retirement of Matt Busby, who stayed on the board to overshadow a series of unfortunate successors.

Ferguson believes that he can be more like Charlton than Busby, lending his knowledge and influence as his successor struggles to establish himself and continue the work of building the club, not just the team.

Unlike Ferguson, Moyes will not arrive at United with trophies already won to reassure the

Sister Patricia Hall, aged 75, who skydived in Galway in aid of Aware, the depression charity.
Photograph: Andrew Downes.

doubters. But he has got the stare. We'll soon see if he has got the rest.

SATURDAY, 11 MAY 2013

Hearing Father Fehily's Voice in the Back of my Head – I go, 'Ein Reich! Ein Volk! Ein Rock!'

Ross O'Carroll-Kelly

The old man asks me if I'm nervous. And, like, the weird thing is I'm not?

Seven-hundred-and-something past pupils of Castlerock College packed into the old school hall, where Father Fehily made his famous speech on the eve of the 1999 Leinster Schools Senior Cup final – the Lebensraum Speech, as it became known – and I have, like, no nerves at all. The opposite, in fact. I can't wait to stand up in front of them and say what I have to say.

We've spent the last ten minutes listening to some dope called Kelham Dolan give his reasons why *he* should be the alumni's representative on the school's Board of Governors. He's obviously McGahy's man, firstly because he was wearing Farah slacks and a jumper with leather triangles on it from Best focking Menswear – which is, like, McGahy's uniform – and secondly because his entire speech was about how state funding would allow the school to hire more staff and bring the pupil-to-teacher ratio down to a level where it's blahdy, blahdy, blah, blah.

The crowd applauds politely.

'Rugby wasn't even mentioned!' the old man goes, his jowls wobbling like a drunk on the deck of a ship. 'We've just sat through ten minutes of bloody well blather about exam results becoming the focus and rugby didn't merit so much as a bloody well mention in dispatches!'

The dude on the stage with the mic goes, 'Next, we're going to hear from our second and final candidate . . . Ross O'Carroll-Kelly.'

There ends up being an incredible reaction to my name being called. Hero worship might be too strong a word, but it's obvious from the cheer that goes up as I walk to the stage that my name means something to these people. I captained the only Castlerock College team to ever win the Leinster Schools Senior Cup and no one can take that away from me. Well, actually, they did take it away from me after I admitted taking methamphetamine, but you know what I mean. It was the school's proudest day ever until I was found guilty of a doping offence and the cup was awarded retrospectively to Newbridge College.

I step up to the mic – like I said, zero nerves. And that's despite not having even a note in front of me.

'Thank you,' I stort off by going. 'I'd like to tell you that I'd make a very good member of the Castlerock Board of Governors. But that would be a lie. I might as well tell you now, I wouldn't be capable of following what happens at meetings. I can't even follow simple movies. I still don't know who Keyzer focking Soze is and I've seen that one about seven focking times.'

Everyone laughs. People love a bit of – it's a phrase you sometimes hear – self *depreciation*?

'But there's one thing I will do – and this is, like, a *promise*? I will use my influence to stop Castlerock College becoming non-fee-paying. Because I happen to care about this school. I happen to love this school.'

The old man slaps his two big bear paws together and shouts, 'Hear, hear!'

It's incredible how I automatically know all the right shit to *say*?

'For the past few years,' I go, 'Castlerock College has been sadly going downhill fast. It storted when they pulled out of the Leinster Schools Senior Cup. Then they allowed the old rugby pitches to be used for literally Gaelic games.

Now, they want to let ordinary people into the school. And I'm here to say that it can't be allowed to happen. Because Castlerock is no ordinary school. And we shouldn't allow it to become one.'

Someone from the back shouts, 'What's the alternative? Do you have a plan?'

It's Hennessy. He's a plant. I sort of, like, laugh to myself, as if at some old memory he's stirred up. It's all port of the routine.

'When I was 15,' I go, 'I couldn't read. Father Fehily, my old rugby coach, found out and asked me why I didn't tell anyone. I said I was ashamed. He said to me, "Man's greatest invention – do you know what it is, Ross? It's the word 'help'. Never be afraid to use it."'

I look down at my old man, who's writing in an imaginary cheque-book.

I'm there, 'If the school gives up this non-fee-paying horseshit, and also returns to the Leinster Schools Senior Cup, my old man is prepared to support the school to the tune of €100,000 per year.'

There are, like, literally *gasps*? 'Not only that,' I go, 'but he has six friends who are prepared to do the same. That's, like, €600,000. Enough for this once great school not to have to go to the Deportment of Education with the begging bowl! Enough for it not to have to turn itself into a pretty much open prison where they let you sit the Leaving Cert! Put me on the Board of Governors and I will help make this school great again!' and then – hearing Father Fehily's voice in the back of my head – I go, 'Ein Reich! Ein Volk! Ein Rock!'

And the audience, in one voice, obviously remembering their own school days, responds with, 'Ein Reich! Ein Volk! Ein Rock!' except they say it, like, three or four times in a row. And suddenly I'm remembering what it was like to captain the S back in the day, because everyone is up on their feet – some of them with even, like, *tears* in their eyes?

The dude with the mic suggests a show of hands. But there's no need. He knows it. I know it.

And Kelham focking Dolan certainly knows it. I'm on the Board of Governors of Castlerock College. And it's one of the proudest days of my life.

I wonder do they pay expenses?

By the Manner of His Death, Donal Walsh Has Left a Reason to Live

Olivia O'Leary

When my mother was dying of cancer, she wanted more than anything to be outside. One day we all drove to Kennedy Park outside New Ross and wandered among the trees. We came to a hedge of conifers through which the wind blew, tossing it around like brushed velvet. My sister and myself raced across the rough grass to touch it. Then we ran back laughing to where my mother sat in her wheelchair.

'I would give anything, anything,' she said, 'just to have been able to run across and touch that hedge.'

I think of that moment whenever people talk about a hunger for life. My mother had it. Charlie Haughey had it. The day he died I was driving through north Dublin and loving how the wind and sun played in the trees and thinking how Haughey would have revelled in this wild summer's day. I was no friend of his. I spent most of my journalistic life pointing out the malign influence he had on politics, but one thing I'll grant him – he had a passion and a hunger for life.

So did Garret FitzGerald, Brian Lenihan, Maureen Potter, Maureen Toal, Luke Kelly, John McGahern. People who have that *joie de vivre*, that determination to enjoy every moment, add to life's value for the rest of us. They make us realise that life itself is the prize, that we have already won, just by existing.

Donal Walsh (front) with his family: mother Elma, sister Jema and father Fionnbar.
Photograph: Domnick Walsh/Eye Focus.

Dan Curnane from Tralee Rugby Club performs the Hakka in front of the hearse carrying the body and coffin of Donal Walsh. Photograph: Domnick Walsh/Eye Focus.

Those of us who are getting older are more likely to realise that anyway. There's nothing like a deadline to concentrate the mind, and death is the ultimate deadline, so we stop to enjoy the first chestnuts or the last blush of a June sunset. We enjoy the moment. It's called the wisdom of age.

That's why it's so extraordinary to hear that same wisdom coming from a 16-year-old – except that Donal Walsh's deadline had already been set for him by cancer. So he was old and wise in the way that those of us whose options are closing are old and wise, and yet it was with a young man's hunger that he tasted the world and yearned for it. That is why his message is so sharp, so powerful. He was already mourning not only what he knew, but also what he would never know.

There is a chance that his own generation will listen to that voice, urgent and poignant as it was, and its plea to choose life, not suicide. It is a relief

to come across people as brave as Donal and his parents, who have broken the taboo that stops us talking about death.

He laid out for us all that would be lost in all the fun that bubbles through his video: goofing with family and friends; the rugby life he once hoped for with Munster; the love of his parents and sister and friends. And then he poses the question – why would you choose to leave all that behind, if you had a choice? He had none.

Because just as those who are hungry for life make the rest of us value it more, those who die by suicide devalue it. Of course, that's not what they set out to do but that's the effect. It is a vote of no confidence in our common existence. It makes us all question what we're doing here.

There isn't one of us who hasn't been touched by the suicide of a friend or relation. We first mourn the one we have lost. We may even be angry with them, but we then start to ask whether they knew something we didn't and whether life is really all it is cracked up to be.

What Donal has left behind, on the other hand, is a reason to live, a reason to taste all the life he cannot taste. This is a gift to his own generation, scourged by suicide, a gift from a young man in his final weeks of life, to make us savour what he cannot.

Because existence itself is a privilege. The urge to achieve, or the disappointment that we haven't, ignores the fact that the most important thing to do with life is live it. I do not now belong to any church so I rarely quote scripture, except for one line from Luke which captures, I think, the spirit of what Donal Walsh was trying to say about those of us lucky enough to be alive: 'Consider the lilies, how they grow: they toil not, they spin not and yet I say unto you that Solomon in all his glory was not arrayed like one of these.'

THURSDAY, 16 MAY 2013

Damascus 'Peace Zone' at Centre of Attempts to Rebuild Syria's Tolerant Civil Society

Michael Jansen in Damascus

The Old City of Damascus, the oldest city on Earth, is a microcosm of Syria. Within its walls are Sunni and Shia Muslims, heterodox Shia Alawites, Christians of a range of denominations, Armenians, Circassians who hail from the Caucasus, Palestinians, Lebanese, Somalis, Turkomen, Kurds and Druze.

If Damascus is overtaken by the violence, chaos and anarchy inflicted by conflict on Syria's other historic cities – Aleppo, Homs and Hama – Syria could fracture and be destroyed as a geographic entity and as a home for the country's diverse 18 sectarian and ethnic communities.

It is significant that the Forum for National Harmony gathers at Maktab Anbar, a spacious traditional Damascene mansion a short walk from St Thomas's Gate (Bab Touma), the entrance to the Christian quarter.

The mansion was built in 1857 by Mahmoud Qawatli, father of Shukri Qawatli, a politician who presided over the withdrawal of French troops from Syria and over its emergence as an independent state. He served two terms as president.

In the 1880s the splendid building accommodated a secular school that not only was the font of anti-Ottoman protests but also produced many of the leading figures of free Syria. Maktab Anbar, elegant apartments built around a courtyard with a fountain, is now a cultural centre and museum.

A year ago, fighting between young men in the narrow cobbled streets of the Old City prompted a group of Muslim and Christian citizens to step in and separate the combatants.

Priest Fr Gabriel says that an area covering 12 blocks was declared a peace zone in which no fighting was allowed, though this arrangement does not prevent rebels outside the walls from intruding with mortars and attacks.

Gradually the zone 'spread to the whole of the Old City. Now we don't have problems between us. Our area is representative of the whole of Syria'.

Rafiq Lutfe adds: 'You know, we Syrians never used to consider a person's sect or ethnicity. We felt ashamed to ask about community.'

Rafiq Mardini, an agricultural engineer from Aleppo residing in Damascus, says the conflict has created divisions within families, which he tries to resolve.

'These are the most difficult,' he says.

The Forum, which also works to liberate prisoners and abductees, proclaims itself to be non-political and tries to cultivate working relationships with all sides despite hatred and bitterness among partisan factions and individuals.

A Syrian woman and her son walk in an alley in the Old City of Damascus. Photograph: Joseph Eid/AFP/Getty.

Consequently, it is seen by some on the warring sides as an 'opposition' group.

Proclaiming itself a domestic opposition organisation, Building the Syrian State seeks to promote tolerance and reconciliation through seminars and workshops. As its name suggests, the group aims to build for a post-conflict, democratic Syria.

Headed by former political prisoner Louay Hussein, it has been holding seminars and workshops for young people in Damascus with the aim of instilling respect for all communities and democratic values.

Activist Mouna Ghanem says the group is conducting workshops in Sweida, a mainly Druze city in southwest Syria, and elsewhere. 'More and more people are becoming involved in our activities.'

WEDNESDAY, 22 MAY 2013

From Spy to Governor of Mountjoy

Eoin McVey

It was the possession of three letters in January 1921 that got Sean Kavanagh arrested by the Auxiliaries in Dublin's Royal Exchange Hotel on Parliament Street.

Two years earlier, Sean, my grandfather, had moved from Waterford to Naas, Co. Kildare, to teach Irish to adults for the Gaelic League. Before that he had been active in the league, Sinn Féin and the Volunteers so naturally he made early contact with some like-minded locals in Naas. He found out from them that a local RIC sergeant was sympathetic to the cause.

On a visit to Dublin he passed this on to his friend Michael Staines (later to be first Commissioner of the Garda Síochána). A week later Staines said that Michael Collins wanted to see him. Sean told Collins that the sergeant, Jerry Maher, was confidential clerk to the inspector for Kildare and Carlow. This was of huge significance to Collins because he was anxious to get hold of the new code being used by the RIC for important telegrams. The county inspector, Kerry Supple, would have the code.

Collins instructed Sean to make contact with Maher and, typically, ordered him to say nothing of it to the local Sinn Féiners and Volunteers. Sean met Maher at least twice weekly from then on and the fruits of that (including the code) and contacts with other sources were reported back directly to Collins in Vaughan's Hotel every Saturday night.

Collins communicated with Sean by letter, passed on by friendly Great Southern Railways staff in Kingsbridge and Sallins stations. But despite his efforts, by January 1921, Sean was under suspicion by the RIC and had to go into hiding, mostly in a friend's house in Ballymore Eustace from where he continued his intelligence work and his weekly trips to Vaughan's.

On 8 January, Collins, for the first time, failed to keep his appointment. Sean decided to travel to Vaughan's the following Saturday nevertheless, and at Sallins station was given three letters.

Two of the letters, which as a lone operator he shouldn't have been given, were from the adjutant general to local Kildare battalions. The third, addressed to 'SK, Naas' was from Collins:

'Dear Sean,

I'm sorry I couldn't turn up last Saturday night. Will you meet me on next Saturday at 8? – M'

Sean didn't read the letters on the train as it was too crowded. He waited until that afternoon when he was having lunch in a quiet dining room of the Royal Exchange Hotel. Unfortunately, he had been spotted in Kingsbridge by a Black and

Tiny the Jack Russell who has become foster mother to a group of orphaned ducklings at Ballinguile farm in Rathdangan, Co. Wicklow. Photograph: Michael Kelly.

She was buried alive for 17 days in the rubble of the Dhaka clothing factory in Bangladesh but, extraordinarily, this woman survived; over 1,000 others did not. Photograph: AP.

Tan and followed. Two Auxiliaries arrested him.

He was brought to Dublin Castle where he was interrogated only about the 'M' letter because they were convinced it was from Collins. Questioning, body-blows and hair-pulling continued for two hours but he held out.

Fortunately his interrogators, Major King, OC of F Company Auxiliaries, and the notorious Capt. Hardy, decided that the meeting at eight described in the letter would be in the Royal Exchange. They brought Sean back and made him stand alone at the hotel entrance with Auxiliaries in mufti in the hotel and on both sides of the street. But Collins, who was waiting in Vaughan's, never showed up.

Sean was hauled off to Kilmainham and from there to Mountjoy, hand-cuffed to Rory O'Connor. The charge sheet accused Sean of 'having in his possession . . . a seditious document,

namely a report headed Óglaigh na hÉireann containing statements relating to road cutting' and another 'relating to the affairs of the Irish Volunteers, an unlawful association'.

Two days earlier, Ernie O'Malley and two others had escaped from Kilmainham so the ground floor of Mountjoy's Block C was turned into a fortress with Auxiliaries running it and not the usual prison warders.

Within a month, six of Sean's fellow prisoners were executed for their alleged involvement in the Bloody Sunday killings. Sean received a 12-month sentence. Collins smuggled in a letter congratulating him on his 'very light sentence'. In fact, he did just nine months, being released in December on the signing of the Treaty. On leaving, he told some (mostly hostile) warders that if the truce didn't hold, he 'would be back'.

Early in 1922 he joined the Free State Army. In August, with the rank of commandant, he was appointed governor of the Hare Park camp on the Curragh. Two years later, he left the army for the post of deputy governor of Mountjoy. He was 'back'.

He served in other prisons but spent 28 years as governor of Mountjoy, detaining many former comrades (with some difficulty), supervising executions (with great difficulty) and teaching Irish to an enthusiastic Brendan Behan. Still the teacher.

SATURDAY, 25 MAY 2013

Distraught Rigby Family Struggle to Come to Terms with Loss

Mark Hennessy

The memorial behind them recalls the men of the Lancashire Fusiliers who died in battles from the Retreat from Mons to Passchendaele in the First World War to the jungles of Burma in the Second World War.

However, the Rigby family lost their 25-year-old son, Lee, not on a foreign field that will remain glorious, if only to a few loved ones, but rather on a South London street, butchered as he walked alone.

'When [he was] in Afghanistan, you come to terms with it, you know it's dangerous. [But] you don't expect something like that on your doorstep,' said Ian Rigby, the Royal Regiment of Fusilier soldier's stepfather said, in between tears.

And the tears came in crushing torrents from his mother, Lyn; his sister, Sara McClure; his mother-in-law, Susan Metcalfe; along with his wife, Rebecca. His three youngest step-sisters, Chelsea and Courtney, both 11, and Amy (8), did not attend.

Lyn Rigby, mother of murdered off-duty soldier, Lee Rigby. Photograph: Dave Thompson/PA.

Drummer Rigby had married Rebecca Metcalfe in 2007, but they later separated, though the two were making efforts to get back together.

'I love Lee and always will. He was due to come up this weekend so we could continue our future together as a family,' she said.

On the night before he died, Rigby had sent what turned out to be his final mobile telephone text to his mother – one that will now be treasured in the way old cards and letters were treasured a century ago by the families of the fusiliers listed on the board behind them.

'Goodnight Mum, I hope you had a fantastic day today because you are the most fantastic and one in a million mum that anyone could ever wish

Michael Adebolajo speaks to a member of the public who had a camera in this video grab, taken from ITV News, following the hacking to death in Woolwich, east London, of Drummer Lee Rigby, an off-duty soldier. Photograph: **ITV News.**

for. Thank you for supporting me all these years, you're not just my mum you're my best friend. So goodnight, love you loads,' it read.

Lyn (46) sat quietly, her eyes filled to the brim with tears as the text was read out, silently gripping a teddy bear dressed in khaki and displaying the regiment's hackle – one of a collection Rigby was building for his son.

The family's nightmare began with the first confused reports from Woolwich that a man had been killed, followed moments later by reports that the victim was a soldier going to or leaving the east London army barracks.

'Really, as soon as it came on the news on television, obviously we didn't know it was Lee but your heart skips a beat when you see something like that on TV, you know your son is in that area,' Ian Rigby said.

The family had been no stranger to worry.

In 2009, Rigby served as a machine-gun gunner in Sangin in Helmand province in Afghanistan during some of the heaviest Taliban attacks upon the British army.

That year alone, the British lost 108 men – a quarter of all of the losses sustained during the conflict. Rigby's unit lost six, including one of his best friends who was killed in a roadside bomb blast.

Reading from a prepared statement, Ian Rigby, who had to break off at times, said: 'What can we say about Lee, our hero, we are so, so proud of Lee. When Lee was born the family adored him, he was a precious gift given to us.

'Lee had a fiery temper when he was younger; I used to sit on him to calm him down till he got too big at 15, then he used to sit on me.

'Lee's dream growing up was always to join

the army, which he succeeded in doing. He was dedicated and loved his job. Lee adored and cared a lot for his family; he was very much a family man, looking out for his wife, young son Jack, younger sisters, whom in turn looked up to him. He always had a banter with them but would never ever let any harm come to them.

'He was over the moon being a dad and uncle, he adored them all,' his stepfather went on, adding, 'Lee was a man who loved people. He believed life was for living and he will be sorely missed by all who knew him.'

THURSDAY, 30 MAY 2013

Prime Time Programme Puts Doubt in Minds of Parents

Anna Kenny

As a full-time working mother of three, I found the *Breach of Trust* broadcast deeply upsetting and disturbing.

I have three children under seven and am fortunate enough to have always been in a position to be able to have a childminder come to our home. However, my daughter is two years old, the same age as many of the children who were manhandled, shouted at and abused in the crèches featured on the *Prime Time* programme on Tuesday night. It was difficult viewing, imagining that it could so easily be my little girl who was forced to sit strapped into a high chair for over two hours, or cry herself to sleep on a hard floor.

Over breakfast yesterday morning I found myself questioning my four-year-old on all aspects of his Montessori. How much he liked it? What exactly happens at snack time? What happens when someone has an accident? I know he loves going every morning and have never had any doubts about the quality of care he receives, but the

programme upset me so much I felt the need to double-check.

Like a lot of working mothers I feel guilty about leaving my children in someone else's care and constantly question whether I am doing the best for them. But most working parents have no choice and pay a lot of money for what they presume is the best care they can get for their children. The doubt that *Prime Time* has sown in parents' minds is deeply worrying. It is simply wrong that children are mistreated, regardless of funding or resources, and extraordinary that, until now, this ill-treatment of our most vulnerable has not been publicised.

I found the panel's discussions about resources and training bewildering. Some people are suited to certain careers and some aren't. This is definitely the case with childcare. It is hard to imagine that more training would enable someone capable of pushing a toddler to the ground and shouting at the child to become a more suitable person to take care of that child. It is time for discussion about the quality of childcare in this State to include debate on the suitability of those providing that care.

Surely, the question to ask is not only why were these workers under so much pressure that they were forced into these actions, but how could any person treat a small child in such a way? And if the staff felt underpaid and overworked, why didn't they go to their employers and raise these issues instead of taking out their frustrations on a toddler who is totally dependent on the care they provide? Surely the blame ultimately lies with management, who should have been aware that these staff members were unsuitable.

It seemed the appalling behaviour shown was not unusual as they made no attempt to hide it from a new member of staff.

Every parent knows how difficult it can be taking care of young children and how much they can test your patience. But every person who loves children also knows how much fun it can be with the right approach and how fulfilling it is to see a

Enjoying the late May sunshine and high temperatures on the bank of the Grand Canal at Portobello in Dublin. Photograph: Eric Luke.

child develop and flourish under your care. Is this enjoyment something that we can train people to feel? I have my doubts.

Despite this, it is essential that staff get adequate training. It is hard to believe 25 per cent of those working in childcare in Ireland have no training at all. Even the kindest childcare worker needs the skills to deal with a room full of toddlers.

It was nauseating to hear lack of resources being blamed for the abuse. My anger rose as the profits of some of the businesses were revealed. Maybe it's a case that big business and childcare don't mix. It would seem overregulation makes it difficult for smaller operations to survive. And yet these regulations seem to be largely meaningless, as so many of the childcare centres featured had been found to be in breach of these regulations by the

HSE and yet they were awarded significant amounts of State funding.

Parents, as well as the HSE, need to be the inspectors of their children's well-being. They need to raise their concerns with management and report these breaches of regulations to the HSE.

One crèche featured had CCTV in every room. This footage should be viewable by all parents online as is the case in so many countries. In this way there is total supervision as parents can constantly monitor the care their children are receiving.

Trusting someone else to take care of your child is a very difficult thing to do. It won't be any easier now.

SATURDAY, 1 JUNE 2013

Post-Potter: Daniel Radcliffe Goes from Hogwarts to Inishmaan

Mark Hennessy

'It is almost a problem how much I love my job,' says Daniel Radcliffe. 'I have been thinking I have to find some outside interests. I went rock-climbing a few weeks ago. I need to find other stuff that I enjoy, because I will never take a break.'

Earlier he had bustled into a room in the building where he and other actors have been rehearsing Martin McDonagh's play *The Cripple of Inishmaan*, which is soon to open in the West End of London. Radcliffe seems unaffected by fame, despite being globally famous for more than a decade for playing Harry Potter. He apologises profusely for being late, then matches a politeness and interest in the people around him with, apparently, a curious insecurity – or, at least, a realisation of the frailties of stardom.

Nearly everything about the 23-year-old works at speed, and his enthusiasm for acting shows no sign of abating, 14 years since he was first noticed in a 1999 TV version of *David Copperfield*.

The opportunity to play the lead in *The Cripple of Inishmaan* was unbelievably fortunate, he says, following an offer from the theatre producer Michael Grandage to appear in any one of three or four plays given to him to read.

'I read *Cripple* last because as soon as I saw Martin's name on it I thought, I will probably want to do that one. And if I read that one first I won't pay proper attention to the other plays. And as soon as I read it . . .'

Radcliffe's interest in McDonagh dates back to *In Bruges,* the playwright's cult film from 2008 about two Irish hitmen, played by Brendan Gleeson and Colin Farrell, hiding in the Belgian city after a job goes wrong.

It is one of his favourite films, 'an obsession of mine for a period', he says, his words tumbling out. 'I loved that kind of dialogue, that kind of economical dialogue where there is a real joy taken in every character having their own rhythm. I think that is always a sign of great writing.

'If you took the script for *Cripple* and covered up the names on the left you would still be able to work out who is talking every time, because every character is so distinct. I have always loved that.'

Radcliffe plays Billy, a disabled 17-year-old living on Inis Meáin, who desperately wants to escape his dull life by travelling to the largest of the Aran Islands, Inis Mór, to win a role in the 1934 film *Man of Aran.*

An explanation for Billy's disability is never given in the play. Radcliffe has chosen to play him as a man with cerebral palsy, helped by a coach who has the condition. 'It has been amazing to learn from her the mechanics and what causes it. It is just another thing that I know about that I didn't know about before.

'Really, I don't want to say how amazingly hard people's lives are. I recommend that you watch [the documentary] *Don't Drop the Baby*. It's about a couple with cerebral palsy who are getting ready to have their second child. They want to have it by natural birth. That really showed me. Our perception is that their lives must be an incredible struggle all the time, but actually it is just their life. They don't particularly think about it on a day-to-day basis,' he says.

'One of the things that was important for me to get across with Billy is that he is a 17-year-old boy, so there's disability on one side, [but] it is important that his other side, a side that is incredibly strong and incredibly adept, also gets across.

'Because that is what one notices: that people are so skilful at coming up with solutions. That is one of the things that I have taken away from it,' says Radcliffe, who enthuses about the performance

Studies of actor Daniel Radcliffe by Larry Busacca of Getty Images.

in rehearsals of Pat Shortt, who plays Johnnypateenmike.

'I knew him from *Father Ted*. He is going to be amazing in this show. His work is brilliant, hysterical, inventive. I am very grateful for working with him.'

Born to a Northern Irish father and a Jewish mother, Radcliffe grew up listening to stories of his father's life in Banbridge, Co. Down, before he left for England – 'The music they listened to, the Troubles, everything'. 'My dad, rather wonderfully, was the All-Ulster Latin-American dance champion when he was in his late teens, and when all his peers were joining the territorial army my dad was leaping about in a *Strictly Come Dancing* costume.

'It is one of the things that I love about him,' he says, adding that his father's accent was 'beaten out of him' at drama schools in England. 'It was just before having a regional accent was a boon to your career. He now sounds more middle class than I do.'

Radcliffe enjoys both of his tribal identities. 'It surprises people about me. When you say either of those things, people go, "Oh, I didn't know that." I take pride in it, but I wouldn't be one of those annoying British people who say that they are Irish on St Patrick's Day.'

His Irish connections are strengthened by his regular appearances on *The Graham Norton Show* on BBC One. 'He has created something very unusual. It is special. It is the one we all want to do. It is so relaxed, and not because there is booze on the table but because you are all out there together,' Radcliffe says.

'He's like a host in the true sense of the word. He is just like a host at a dinner party, making sure the conversation bounces along. He will take the piss, but he comes at you from such a good place.'

Even before the *Harry Potter* films ended, two years ago, Radcliffe seemed to choose roles that would take him as far from Hogwarts as possible – although, he says, 'they weren't chosen because one was a horror and the other was a historical drama. It was that the scripts were brilliant.'

He is keen not to become another child actor to fall by the wayside. 'None of us wanted to let that happen. I fell into something that I adored and that gave me a sense of identity and purpose and a sense of community. That is not the wrong word to use.

'I want to work hard enough so that I can always be a part of it. One of the things that leads to people fizzling out or getting forgotten is when complacency or laziness sets in, rather than challenging themselves consistently.'

Playing Potter was 'an incredible stroke of luck'. The price is the nagging feeling that the world will never be convinced he earned his position. 'I don't want anybody to be able to say that of me. People say things like, "*Potter* will be the biggest thing that I will ever do". And that is absolutely true, but nor do I think that it is going to be the best work I ever do – and that absolutely satisfies me.

'It is amazing how well *Potter* did and how many people saw it, and that is fantastic, but it's not the end goal. What I want to do at this point is get better and better as an actor and keep learning. And I think I am.

'I never want to settle for where I am and go, "I'm happy with this, I can stop challenging myself, I have done it all". I don't think that is my make-up.'

This year Radcliffe will appear in a number of films, including *Kill Your Darlings*. It helps that he enjoys being on film sets. 'I love working with film crews, and I love technicians. I got to work with some amazing crews on *Potter*, and I have been able to work with more since.

'I was very worried about working in the US, because I had always heard that the crew are not allowed to talk to the actors and stuff like that. That's completely untrue. There are some actors who won't talk to the crew, so that is how those rumours get started.

'For me there is no point doing it unless you are going to enjoy it. I don't know how people go to work on film sets and come in grumpy every day, especially people who do my job.' What's more, he says, he has never worked with a horrible director.

'I am of the belief – I am not sure if I can swear in your newspaper – that life's too short to work with a★★★holes.'

FRIDAY, 7 JUNE 2013

Poverty Levels in Washington Are Food for Thought

Simon Carswell

Near the seat of power in the US, one out of every two children is at risk of hunger. A staggering 680,000 people in the Washington DC metropolitan area, out of a population of 4 million, are vulnerable to hunger, according to the city's Capital Area Food Bank. That includes 200,000 children. Many live across the Potomac River in the seventh and eighth wards in the Anacostia area in the southeast of the city.

'Washington is really a city of the haves and the have-nots,' says Page Dahl Crosland, the food bank's communications director. 'Most visitors to the city do not go to the other side of the river into Anacostia.'

The food bank distributes 35 million pounds of food a year – the equivalent of 27.5 million meals – to 700 food pantries, including 300 in Washington DC, which pass the food on to the hungry.

While these figures appear significant, the food is only getting to 478,000 people, leaving more than 200,000 of those at risk of hunger without food support.

The city's poverty levels are in line with the average in the country. US census data shows that almost 50 million Americans were living in poverty in 2011, more than 16 per cent of the population.

Located in the north of the city, the food bank also covers areas within the DC metropolitan area, into northern Virginia and counties in Maryland.

Everything from fresh fruit and vegetables to canned goods and even bicycles have been distributed to the poor from the food bank since it was established in 1980.

Last Wednesday afternoon, volunteers from the World Bank in central Washington were helping the food bank's staff pack bags of groceries for distribution.

Marian Barton-Peele, the food bank's senior director of partner relations, who liaises with food pantries around the city, says the number of people receiving food has increased three-fold over the past 20 years 'because the need has increased and we have done a good job of identifying where the need is'.

The typical people in receipt of food parcels are people working two or three jobs 'trying to make ends meet', she says. The average person has a monthly income of $500 and can only afford to pay rent, so they must cut back somewhere.

The food bank is trying to improve the quality of food people eat, showing people how to cook nutritionally and on a budget in a purpose-built training kitchen. There is an urban garden to teach people how to grow vegetables.

Nancy Roman, president and chief executive of the food bank, says the poor in the Washington DC area are not just underfed but poorly fed. Many people can only afford fast-food 'dollar meals', which, with their high levels of fat and sugar, lead to an increase in cases of diabetes and heart disease.

Not only do wards seven and eight have the highest poverty rates in the district of Columbia but they are also home to the city's highest obesity rates and large 'food deserts' – areas that are poorly served by full-service grocery stores.

In 2010, the two wards had seven supermarkets between them compared with 11 in ward three, the highest-income area of the city,

Fran Kane and her son J.J. Kane, from Tallaght in Dublin, with Carolyn Akintola (right), who cares for her mother Elsie, who is on Peretoneal Dialysis three times a day, at a Carers Association protest against cuts outside Leinster House. Photograph: Dara Mac Dónaill.

according to the anti-hunger group Food Research and Action Centre.

Over in Anacostia, Hannah Hawkins travels to the Capital Area Food Bank every Tuesday morning. When she returns, there are queues of almost 100 people at her centre waiting for food. 'I never have enough,' she says.

She feeds hot nutritional meals of vegetables to about 60 children ranging in age from four to 18 after school every day at the Children of Mine Youth Centre, which she founded and runs.

Each child leaves well fed and with a package of food to keep them going overnight and for their younger siblings. Some of the food includes tomatoes, kale and collard greens grown in the vegetable garden at the back of the centre.

'I have been doing this for 30 years and it is getting worse,' she says, blaming the cuts in the government's food stamps programme for bringing more young adults through her door.

When she moved into the run-down housing project that is now home to her centre, there were animals living inside and homeless people outside on the back porch. She is trying to raise money to build a new centre where people could sleep overnight.

Many of the elderly people visiting Hawkins' centre take milk and yoghurt, which they cannot afford to buy because of the high cost of their medicine.

It is a well-equipped centre but underequipped to deal with the scale of the problem.

'People who are confronted with this don't believe that in these United States of America we are going through this agony,' she says.

Cyclists Need to Get Over Themselves

Fintan O'Toole

Here is my contribution to National Bike Week, which starts on Saturday: cyclists are the spawn of the devil. This statement may contain the tiniest tincture of unfair generalisation, but given the widespread tendency to mistake a cycling helmet for a halo, it needs to be said that not all of Hell's angels ride Harleys. Cyclists like to see themselves as the great oppressed minority of the streets. The truth that dare not speak its name is that the worst oppression is inflicted on the defenceless pedestrian, and that the two-wheeled yobs do most of the oppressing.

Cyclists have issues with self-esteem: they have far too much of it. It is hard to blame them. Cycling is indeed a many-splendored thing. It is good for the environment. It shows personal responsibility in the fight against ill-health and obesity. It affords the rest of us images of heroic perseverance: an old lady pedalling up a hill against a rain-sodden West of Ireland winter wind is the visual epitome of human doggedness in the face of the innate cruelty of an absurd universe. The cyclist is Christ on a bike, martyr and saviour all in one.

The problem with all this goodness is that it creates a sense of rectitude entirely divorced from actual behaviour. Being on a bike is itself irrefutable proof of your decency, care and civic worth. You don't have to do anything else – like show a modicum of concern for those with whom you share public space.

What's happened with cycling is a classic case of the 'and the office boy kicked the dog' syndrome. On the road, trucks bully cars and cars bully cyclists. So what happens? The cyclists move onto the footpath (hint: the clue is in the name) and bully the pedestrians. Those on foot are the lowest of the low. Their space can be invaded with impunity; their safety is of no account whatsoever. W.B. Yeats wrote satirically of the revolution after which 'a beggar on horseback lashes a beggar on foot'. In the great cycling revolution, the new master of the footpath is in a smaller saddle, but for the poor beggar on foot the lash goes on.

Most weekday mornings, I do a circuit on foot (the activity might be called running if that word did not suggest notions of velocity and alacrity) around the area of north Dublin where I live. A long stretch of it has a very good cycle lane. Maybe once a month, I might see a single person on a bike in the cycle lane. This is not because there are no cyclists – there are dozens of them at any given time – it's because the cyclists simply decided at some point that they would all use the narrow footpath. They wheel along it like a panzer division while the red surface of the cycle lane glows in stark, staring nakedness.

This might be tolerable if the invaders showed even a glimmer of awareness that they are on someone else's territory and should behave with respect and caution. But, glowing as they are with that impregnable aura of goodness, most of them act as if it is the pedestrians who are the trespassers. They hurtle round corners without looking. They freewheel down hills. They ride three abreast – I've seen elderly people and parents pushing prams forced out into traffic. And when they crash into people, as they do, their usual reaction is to curse at the stupid pedestrian who was too slow or too thick to get out of their way.

The independent TD Finian McGrath, whom I often see on my morning circuit, got dog's abuse recently when he accused many cyclists of 'arrogance and bad behaviour'. But it was interesting that he got a lot of support from people who actually have to watch the streets from day to day: school wardens and lollipop ladies who reported that while motorists generally obey their signs, significant numbers of cyclists simply ignore them and plough on regardless of the safety of children. Anyone who keeps an eye on busy suburban streets can see this kind of thing happening all the time. That presumably includes the gardaí. But I've never once seen a cyclist warned, let alone arrested, for the reckless endangerment of pedestrians.

And yes of course there are many highly responsible cyclists. And yes of course cycling should be encouraged and protected and made central to all plans for sustainable transport. But walking on the footpath is sustainable transport too and it's time pedestrians stood up for their rights. Why are cyclists immune from the law? Why does the Road Safety Authority's guide for cyclists contain just a single sentence on this issue – 'Never cycle on a footpath' – which refuses to engage at all with the flagrant daily reality that they do? Why do the bike lobby groups use phrases like 'duty of care to the more vulnerable' to mean only the duty of motorists to cyclists?

And cyclists need to get over themselves. Yes, you're wonderful – thanks. Now, is there any chance you might share a bit of that beneficence with the rest of us?

WEDNESDAY, 12 JUNE 2013

'Neoliberalism' is Being Used as a Straw Man to Close Down Reasonable Debate on Policies

Dan O'Brien

In the US, reactionaries on the right of the political spectrum frequently label as 'socialists' those espousing policies, such as Obamacare in health, which are government led. Their knee-jerk description of proposals, such as higher taxes for those on the highest incomes, is simply to call them a form of 'socialism'.

These reactionaries seek to close down debate by tarnishing policies that involve a role for government with something that is ill-defined but supposedly pernicious. In the American case, that is socialism. These reactionaries do this despite there being almost no individuals or organisations in the US who describe themselves as socialists. Straw men are easy to knock down.

In Ireland, a similar unhealthy trend in political debate is emerging. Reactionaries on the left of the political spectrum increasingly describe others very critically as 'neoliberals' and policy proposals that are not state led as forms of 'neoliberalism'. The private crèche scandal revealed by RTÉ is the most recent example of this sort of name-calling, and it happens even though no political party, grouping or individual in Ireland describes itself/himself/herself as 'neoliberal'.

Just as socialism is rarely if ever defined when Americans sling mud, those who bandy about the term 'neoliberalism' here feel little need to define it. And just as socialism in American debate is portrayed as a self-evident evil, so too is neo-liberalism in the Irish context.

Both varieties of reactionaries make the most outlandish claims. Some opponents of Obamacare in the US say with great certainty that under the plan 'death panels' are being created that will result in the sick being allowed to die. Here, the neo-liberal agenda is, apparently, designed to crush the majority into some form of serfdom, or, as one angry letter-writer to this newspaper last week wrote, its objective is the 'impoverishment of many and the enrichment of a few'.

Reactionaries cannot resist resorting to such black and white characterisations. They do not like nuance and complexity. They prefer political prejudice over reason and evidence.

But in a world that is increasingly complex, reason and evidence are, thankfully, triumphing. In universities, think tanks and ministries around the world, policy-thinkers and policy-makers are generating a vast and ever growing body of literature on how best to combine the state, its agencies, market mechanisms and private business in the provision of services and much else besides. In most cases, some mix of public and private works best. At times, more private involvement is preferable; in other cases, a greater public role will deliver the best outcomes.

Healthcare in America provides a perfect example of the latter. The US spends considerably more on health as a proportion of its gross domestic product (GDP) than any other country in the world. Despite this it achieves relatively poor outcomes. The comparatively limited role of government explains this.

A bigger role for the government in the US in healthcare provision, along the lines of most other developed countries, will not only give more Americans access to affordable healthcare, it will lower costs, because massive economies of scale can be exploited when the state plays a co-ordinating and regulatory role.

In Ireland, as elsewhere, there is a case for more state involvement in some areas and less in others. That is what is happening and has happened. Talk of so-called neoliberals dictating the policy agenda has simply no supporting evidence.

In every single country in the developed world, public spending in real terms has been rising over many decades. In the decade leading up to the crash, it rose more rapidly in Ireland than in any other peer country.

If the redistributive role of government is not on the wane here or across the western world, nor is its regulatory role. State regulation is rolling forward in some areas and back in others. Over the decades there have been examples of a lessening of regulation (successfully in the cases of air travel and telecoms; unsuccessfully in the case of finance) and examples of increased regulation – in environmental protection, equality, and health and safety.

Given the evidence, one might have expected leadership in the debate from the more cerebral members of the political class. Unfortunately, that has not happened. Indeed, one of the more cerebral career politicians who is perhaps best positioned to encourage real debate – the first citizen of the State – has done the opposite.

In a recent speech, President Michael D. Higgins stated that 'the neoliberal model of unregulated markets, the privatising of the public space and the redirection of active participating citizens with rights to an existence of passive consumers with unlimited needs has exacted a terrible price on our economy and society'.

This is not only a highly politicised statement – made despite the constitutional obligation on heads of State to remain above the political fray – it runs counter to Michael D. Higgins' own objective for his presidency of encouraging questioning and opening up debate. Such a crude and politicised characterisation of Ireland's current woes will give succour to reactionaries and do nothing to raise the quality of intellectual life in Ireland.

THURSDAY, 13 JUNE 2013

Country before Crozier for Catholic Kenny

Miriam Lord

They don't make croziers like they used to. Never mind the belt of one – just the cold draught from an upward swing was once enough to cow entire governments. Not any more.

In recent months, Enda Kenny has been at the business end of a severe bludgeoning, but he hasn't flinched. If anything, pressure from the bishops – which they are entitled to exert – has merely served to strengthen his resolve.

People talk about the Taoiseach's capacity to surprise, yesterday's remarks from him in the Dáil

Fungie the Dingle dolphin leaps out of the water alongside Cork racing yacht **Antix** *at the finish of the Dún Laoghaire to Dingle race. The dolphin met the yacht at the mouth of Dingle harbour and performed a series of leaps from the water to the delight of the crew, who were first to the finish. Photograph: Youen Jacob/Provision.*

being an apparent example of this. Yet Enda has been nothing if not consistent in his approach to dealing with the highly contentious Protection of Human Life during Pregnancy Bill.

There are times when he delegates, times when he infuriates and times when he steps up to the mark and leads.

His determination to uphold the separation between church and State had already become a feature of his tenure before the abortion question became centre stage.

There was no change in Enda's attitude when Mattie McGrath tried to convince him to rethink his commitment to stewarding through this long overdue piece of legislation.

We shouldn't have been surprised. In a little over two years as Taoiseach, Enda Kenny has notched up an impressive number of 'defining' moments and 'finest hours', the latest one coming out of the blue during Leaders' Questions yesterday morning.

The political nerds went scurrying for their history books when the Taoiseach uttered a phrase destined for the history books of the future.

'I am proud to stand here as a public representative, as a Taoiseach who happens to be a Catholic, but not a Catholic Taoiseach,' he told the Dáil, invoking the shades of devout leaders past who pledged allegiance to faith first and country second.

On an otherwise uneventful Wednesday morning in Leinster House, Kenny, without any fuss, laid down a milestone in Irish political history.

Furthermore, a Taoiseach stood in the Dáil

chamber and called out the despicable behaviour of a small section of Irish society that deems it acceptable to threaten and intimidate elected representatives who do not cleave to their world view.

The House listened in silence as Enda put on the record the sort of treatment he and many of his Coalition colleagues have been subjected to ever since his government resolved to legislate for the X case.

'I am now being branded by personnel around the country as being a murderer; that I'm going to have on my soul the death of 20 million babies. I am getting medals, scapulars, plastic foetuses, letters written in blood, telephone calls all over the system, and it's not confined to me . . .'

Many of the deputies behind him nodded in agreement. Enda was speaking for them too. 'We're all getting those too,' said Independent TD Finian McGrath, who had very pointedly left his seat beside Mattie McGrath and moved to another place before Mattie began to read his script.

A number of Fine Gael deputies who have expressed their reservations about the Bill looked on in dismay. But what was most noticeable was the reaction of most of Enda's backbenchers, the majority of whom have maintained an uncomfortable public silence in the face of a vocal cohort of colleagues shouting long and loudly against the Bill.

'I am a Taoiseach for all of the people – that is my job, while I have it. I am proud to lead the government in governing for all our people – all our people – irrespective of the sector of society that they come from,' declared their leader.

'Hear, hear!' they shouted. 'Well said.' This was quite a departure for the Dáil.

And was it the first time – we think it was – when certain women's voices were raised in the House on the issue, as deputy McGrath pressed his charge that the Taoiseach is legislating for the introduction of abortion.

'The right of the unborn is a basic human right. It is the most fundamental right of all,' said McGrath.

'What about the woman?' shouted Mary Mitchell O'Connor – a question repeated by Marcella Corcoran Kennedy and Heather Humphreys, among others.

Mattie urged him to put the question to the people in a referendum. Enda replied that the government had to legislate for the X case and that is what they would do. The nation had already voted twice on the issue and 'confirmed and re-endorsed the constitutional rights of women in this country to have a termination of a pregnancy in specific circumstances'.

Do it again, urged Mattie, drawing snorts of derision with his speculative 'third time lucky'.

It was as if the Taoiseach's sense of duty to his office had emboldened those TDs who previously appeared reluctant to publicly express their views.

'Who wrote your script?' they asked McGrath.

'Circulate it!' bellowed Bernard Durkan, resplendent in his seasonal cream summer suit. And like the sound of the first cuckoo of spring, the Opposition gave forth that familiar cry that heralds the onset of a Dáil summer: 'It's the man from Del Monte!' This briefly lifted the mood.

But not for a despondent Mattie McGrath, who was getting no comfort from Enda. The conservative Catholic schoolteacher from Mayo stood by his sense of duty and doing his duty on behalf of all the people.

There was spontaneous applause from many on the Fine Gael side, most of the Labour deputies and a large majority in Sinn Féin and Independent ranks.

Another departure for a cautious Dáil. Yet no real surprise from consistent Kenny. From what we've come to know of the man, yesterday's performance was par for the course.

Could it be that after all these years, the novelty value of a Taoiseach taking a stand and sticking to it is still a wonder to behold?

Cartoon by Martyn Turner.

Midges Make the Most of Obamas at Glendalough

Miriam Lord

Glendalough – a wondrous place of myth and mystic beauty where the 'midgets' are the size of horses and would ate ya alive without salt.

We were warned about them in advance. 'They'll be going down to see the Deer's Stone, but we'll be pulling everyone out if the midgets start causing problems,' said a garda.

It's no wonder the CIA men looked so nervous, with all this talk from their Irish counterparts of ferocious 'midgets' descending the Wickla mountains and feasting on the blood of innocents.

How were they supposed to know there is a major problem with the pronunciation of the word 'midges' in Ireland? It must have been very confusing for them.

Under the circumstances, it was very brave of the Obama women to venture into the open at all. In the end, the vicious 'midgets' caused havoc and sent them running for cover.

Young Sasha and Malia, behaving as any teenage girls would, pulled faces and told their mother they wanted to go.

'Bloody midgets,' cursed one of the guards, 'they're a menace.' But the photographers were delighted. At least they got a reaction.

Oh, but Michelle Obama's second day in Ireland was great fun. From the 'midgets' in Glendalough to Bono in Dalkey, a sort of madness took over in the summer sun.

The tone was set in Wicklow. 'Have a good day!' said smiling local gardaí stopping the cars.

Appearing more than a little fed up, Michelle Obama's two teenage daughters, Sasha and Malia, also had to cope with a plague of midges during the visit to Glendalough in Co. Wicklow. Photo: Julien Behal/Press Association.

At the venue, bags were sniffed by dogs and everyone was told to line up so they could be 'wanded'.

'I beg your pardon!' shrieked the ladies of a certain age. A metal detector 'wand' was then flourished about their persons, setting off all manner of alarms. 'That would be the wiring in your bras, ladies.'

We wandered down to the stalls beside the Glendalough Hotel. Stallholder Mick Quinn was hoping Michelle and her girls might call down for a browse of his jumpers and tea-towels. If they did, he was confident of making a sale.

'I'd sell prams to nuns,' he said confidently.

It was a beautiful day, as Bono might have sung were he present, but he was waiting in his Dalkey local for the arrival of his pals from the White House.

Finally, the motorcade arrived. With a battalion of security suits in tow, the media was led along a forest path and positioned on a mucky knoll from where there was an excellent view of the ancient graveyard, round tower and St Kevin's Kitchen.

The first lady and her daughters, with George McClafferty of the Glendalough Visitor Centre acting as their guide, ambled into view. It was a beautiful, tranquil scene among the ferns and scented summer honeysuckle. There was a hush in our little glade. Birdsong provided background music. The small group came closer to the mythical Deer's Stone.

They looked on as George explained the lore behind it, Michelle in rapt attention, the two girls flapping their arms and pulling their sleeves over their hands.

Suddenly, into the sylvan stillness rose a familiar voice from a hummock of bracken. 'They're being eaten alive, Myles, eaten alive!' It was Valerie Cox, broadcasting to the *Pat Kenny Show*. She wasn't wrong either.

The scratching entourage gathered for the retreat. They hightailed it to the Upper Lake, where we hope the girls found some respite.

Then it was off to Dalkey. We had to rely on Mary Mitchell O'Connor for updates. She was ensconced in Finnegan's and tweeting to the world. The Fine Gael TD for Dún Laoghaire is a friend of the owners and taught most of the part-time lounge staff who were looking after the Obamas for lunch.

She tweeted pictures of Bono chatting with the regulars and then pictures of Michelle and Bono. This was the shot everyone wanted. Mary got a photographer's credit on the front page of this newspaper's website and the BBC and CNN rang for permission to use her work.

'I went viral,' she said later, making it sound like she'd been bitten by 'midgets' too.

Donal Finnegan, who runs the establishment with his father Dan and brothers Paul, Alan and Neil, said later that the Obamas just wanted 'the Irish pub lunch experience'.

Michelle had lobster and fresh local fish and real chips. The children sat at a separate table with Bono's two boys.

There was a carnival atmosphere outside, with a heady closing time atmosphere inside – dark and giddy – but their guests were allowed their space. They were two hours inside having lunch. Bono mustn't have had much to say.

Then it was time to go. Michelle got straight into her people carrier, smiling and giving a special wave to the primary schoolgirls from Loreto with their posies of sweet pea and freesia.

Then the media – hysterical from 'midget' bites and sunburn – rushed the pub, pinning chef Paul Finnegan up against a wall until he told them about the menu.

Afterwards, Bono and his wife had to be rescued by the local constabulary after the crowd surged inside and journalists lost the plot. The Hewsons squeezed into their Maserati and were engulfed by well-wishers.

'That's ridiculous. Sure he's in here all the time and nobody minds him,' harrumphed a neighbour.

'Great for Dalkey, great for Dublin and great for Ireland,' said Donal Finnegan.

FRIDAY, 21 JUNE 2013

The Don is Dead, Long Live the Don

Donald Clarke

If James Gandolfini, who has died in Italy at the age of 51, had lived for another few decades, then when writing an appreciation we would have found it a great deal easier to avoid focusing on his most famous role.

A bulky man, whose face always seemed to telegraph approaching rage, he was the sort of actor the entertainment industry savours. Pretty-faced leading men drift in and out of fashion – this year's Biff gives way to next year's Cory – but Hollywood always needs charismatic character actors.

Just watch Gandolfini scowling as the permanently aggrieved general in Armando Iannucci's satirical gem *In the Loop*. Catch his boozy hit-man in Andrew Dominik's recent, undervalued *Killing Them Softly*. No contemporary actor was better at combining menace with existential depression.

All of which brings us neatly to *The Sopranos*. It is strange to recall that when the HBO series premiered in 1999, the main hook was that it focused on a mobster who was undergoing psycho-analysis. The show sounded like the high concept for a low-brow comic movie. In fact, it *was* the high concept for a low-brow comic movie: *Analyse This*, starring Robert De Niro and Billy Crystal, emerged the same year.

It didn't take long for viewers to realise that David Chase, the series creator, had considerably loftier ambitions. Using enormously long story arcs, allowing minor characters to gradually drift upstage, the series changed how studios and the public thought about television drama. At the heart of it all was one of the medium's great characters.

More particularly, Tony Soprano, chief of a colourful New Jersey mob dynasty, was one of television's most interesting and influential fathers. For decades, the 'head of the family' was represented as an upstanding fellow in a hat who patiently suffered the chattering of his silly wife and the comic mishaps of his adorable children.

Homer Simpson – flawed, frustrated, lovable – hacked away at the template in the early 1990s. At the turn of the century, Tony Soprano – flawed, frustrated, psychopathic – trampled the classic model into the dust.

The notion of millennial anxiety may have been an unconvincing media invention, but Gandolfini's performance as Tony went some way towards convincing us that those pontificating columnists were on to something.

Feminists could regard him as a manifestation of male aggression. Self-pitying middle-aged men could sympathise with his inability to escape the imagined restrictions of suburban conformity. Red-meat eaters understood his resistance to all this psychoanalytic mumbo-jumbo.

The left detected comments on the corruption at the heart of late capitalism but, more than anything else, he carried the massed anxieties of modern parenthood on his enormous shoulders. Which dad wouldn't want the power to murder his teenage daughter's unsuitable boyfriend?

Appropriately for somebody who went on to play the era's most famous New Jerseyite, James Gandolfini, from an impeccably Italian, working-class background, grew up in the Garden State. He worked as a bouncer, a truck driver and a nightclub manager before drifting into the world of acting.

'I dabbled a little bit in acting in high school and then I forgot about it completely,' he later said. 'And then, at about 25, I went to a class. I don't think anybody in my family thought it was an intelligent choice. I don't think anybody thought I'd succeed, which is understandable. I think they were just happy that I was doing something.'

He did not exactly explode onto the scene, but director Tony Scott found him a tiny role in *The Last Boy Scout* and then cast him as a memorable thug in *True Romance*.

By the time *The Sopranos* came around, he had established a reputation as an essential background heavy. Seek him out in (for Tony Scott again) *Crimson Tide* and Barry Sonnenfeld's *Get Shorty*. If Chase and his team hadn't circled his name, Gandolfini would, like Warren Oates and Ward Bond before him, surely have remained a key supporting player of his time.

Like those earlier actors, he was not the most versatile of performers – try to imagine him frolicking with Jennifer Aniston in a light comedy – but he was a master at his specialist field: the lumbering wad of confused middle-aged testosterone. When *The Sopranos* broke, he achieved a rare class of fame for a character performer. He was no longer 'that bloke'. He now had a name. For all the supposed emasculation of the American chap – something Tony Soprano occasionally acknowledged – film and television still needed the wheezing, snorting, beer-drinking bloke. Gandolfini may have secured few leads in the years after *The Sopranos*, but he was a prince among attendant courtiers.

In the last year, he turned up to good effect as a CIA supremo in *Zero Dark Thirty*. In 2014, he appears opposite Tom Hardy and Noomi Rapace in Michaël R. Roskam's take on Dennis Lehane's story *Animal Rescue*. A glance at Roskam's *Bullhead* or at Lehane's *Gone Baby Gone* (or at any of Hardy's work) will confirm that the project looks likely to sweat like a manly man after some very manly work.

Character actors don't age like leading men. Had his heart not stopped so soon, Gandolfini

Families (and their vehicles) crowd onto Rossnowlagh Beach in Co. Donegal on a day when temperatures reached 25 degrees. Photograph: Alan Lewis.

could have kept working into his twilight years and Tony Soprano might have ended up being just another role on a busy CV.

As things stand, it towers over everything else he achieved.

FRIDAY, 28 JUNE 2013

Anglo Bankers Believed They Could Force an Outcome at Expense of State

Simon Carswell

The aggressive stance taken by Anglo Irish Bank chief executive David Drumm with regulators, which emerges in the latest tape recordings of conversations within Anglo at the time of the 2008 bank guarantee, shows a banker under increasing pressure to save his institution and resorting to desperate tactics as the bank edged towards collapse.

Drumm's conversations with the bank's head of capital markets John Bowe, recorded on Bowe's telephone line in Anglo's treasury department, took place against the background of a run on the bank's deposits and almost daily meetings with the regulator to respond to the deepening crisis of September 2008.

US bank Lehman Brothers had just gone bankrupt sending the financial markets into a tailspin as corporate depositors – big companies spreading large cash deposits around various banks – decided that Anglo was too risky a bet and sought the return of their money as the deposit terms matured.

The conversation between Drumm and Bowe on 19 September 2008 is focused on how, at

Cartoon by Martyn Turner.

Anglo's next meeting with the Central Bank and financial regulator, the bank can increase the pressure on regulators to agree to lend €7 billion to cover the amount of deposits lost, though – as Bowe himself acknowledged in a telephone call the previous day – the amount was likely to be higher.

One aspect of the detail within the conversations that has been lost in the coverage of these new recordings is that during the telephone conversations, the Anglo bankers were discussing a €7 billion liquidity bailout to help the bank fund itself; they did not consider at the time – either due to incompetence or self-delusion or both – that a capital bailout to cover losses on loans was necessary. As far as the bankers were concerned they were just dealing with a run on their deposits, not a black hole in their loan book, and were trying to get the regulators to act.

The €29 billion bailout of public money that the government is pumping into the bank

was eventually provided for bad customer loans.

The 19 September call shows the 'Drummer' acknowledging that it was just a matter of days before the bank would run out of money.

Meetings between all of the Irish banks and the regulators became more intense following the collapse of Lehman Brothers on the weekend of 14–15 September.

That week's discussions between Anglo and the regulator marked a turning point as the crisis deepened for Anglo in particular.

For the first time, Anglo had requested a specific sum of cash in liquidity support from the Central Bank – backed by loans on the bank's books and a promissory note as collateral. This, the bank believed privately at the time as the tapes show, would turn the tables on the regulator forcing the Central Bank and financial regulator to consider making a big call. 'Get into the f***ing simple speak: "We need the moolah, you have it,

Cartoon by Martyn Turner.

so you're going to give it to us and when would that be?" We'll start there,' Drumm tells Bowe about the strategy that they would pursue in their next meeting with the Central Bank and the financial regulator.

The strategy was to hit the ball back into the regulator's court. 'The game has changed now because really the problem now is at their door,' Drumm told Bowe. 'Because if they don't give it to us on Monday they have a bank collapse.'

In the end the strategy failed, forcing Anglo chairman Seán FitzPatrick and chief executive Drumm out of desperation to doorstep Central Bank director, economist Alan Gray – who they knew had the ear of taoiseach Brian Cowen as an adviser – at his offices in Dublin the following week to impress upon him the seriousness of the crisis and the need for an urgent solution to save the bank.

The Central Bank procrastinated for more than a week but did eventually provide some short-term

support to Anglo – in the order of a loan of about €1 billion – to tide the bank over on Monday, 29 September when it ran out of cash. Ultimately, the government stepped in with the blunderbuss approach to try to stem the run on Anglo with the €440 billion guarantee for the wider banking system, a gamble the government lost.

Patrick Honohan, now governor of the Central Bank, explored the reasons why the Central Bank chose not to provide a large emergency loan to Anglo in late September 2008 – a possible short-term solution to the banking crisis – when he investigated the causes of the banking crisis in his May 2010 report.

He concluded that if an emergency loan was given to Anglo, the Central Bank may have been forced to provide emergency loans to the entire banking system, which would have been damaging for the entire system, and that the Central Bank was uncertain whether an emergency loan to

Anglo, whether publicly disclosed or detected, would 'boost or detract' from market confidence.

The Central Bank was also seriously concerned about the potential open-ended size of emergency loans and the associated risks for the regulators, he said. So the regulator may well have been aware of the potential outcome in the bank's strategy devised by Bowe in the earlier call – that Anglo could demand a certain amount of support from the Central Bank, namely €7 billion, get the State on the hook and then 'creep up' the amount demanded from the Central Bank as the bank required it.

The most revealing aspect of the series of leaked telephone recordings, published in the *Irish Independent* this week, is the belligerent tone and expletive-ridden aggression of the conversations and what they say about Anglo's culture – that these bankers believed they could play with the regulators and pull the wool over their eyes to force an outcome at the expense of the State. The tenor of Drumm's conversations and his behaviour also show how the chief executive sets the tone in the bank and this is reflected in how his underlings spoke.

Drumm's salty language, Bowe's mischievous reciting of the German national anthem, the disregard for the government and the regulator's wishes that the bank guarantee not be abused, and the ribbing of regulators Pat Neary and Con Horan during the telephone calls was typical of the gallows humour and desperation within Anglo during its final weeks and months. Two months earlier when Rabobank in the Netherlands declined a frantic request from Anglo to take it over, Drumm disparaged the Dutch bankers in a private email to a colleague, describing them as 'windmill-lovin' clog-wearin' MOFOs'. Two weeks before the September telephone calls, Drumm sent an email out to staff inviting them to his 'Back to School Doombuster Party' early that month to try to lift their spirits and put up a brave front. 'The stock markets are down,' he wrote in

the invite to staff. 'They say the economy is in recession. It rained most of the "summer". The holidays are over. This is Anglo so there is only one thing to do – party!' A hefty bill was incurred on food, drinks and entertainment for a party reminiscent of the last days of Rome.

Almost five years putting €29 billion of public money into Anglo and biting austerity later, the sick jokes still emerging in this painful tragicomedy are very much on the Irish people.

MONDAY, 1 JULY 2013

Federer Doesn't Need to Worry About His Legacy, Just His Tennis

Brian O'Connor

Pondering your legacy is usually only for those too far up themselves to realise they are unlikely ever to have one anyway. As for getting into a sweat about someone else's, the only saving grace against accusations of having already disappeared past the point of no-return is at least it isn't a first-person lather. But even allowing for all that, and wholly irrational as it might be, here's hoping Roger Federer's declaration after his Wimbledon second-round defeat that he intends to play for years to come doesn't happen.

As one of millions worldwide who for the last decade has thrilled to the great man's virtuosity, that sounds a bit like arguing McCartney should have hung up the guitar after *Abbey Road,* or that Hemingway should have hung everything up after the war. We'd have missed out on some great stuff. But that doesn't disguise how it's still strictly down-slope stuff. And there doesn't seem to be any doubt now that Federer is on a remorseless slide from the Alpine peaks that have made him a benchmark figure in the history of sport.

Craig Coughlan, Paul O'Connor and Richie Ryan of Ringsend in Dublin take to the water at Grand Canal Dock to cool off. Photograph: Alan Betson.

Yachts Venuesworld.com, Seriously Bonkers 3, Odin, BomChickaWahWah, Shockwave *and* Alert Packaging, *competitors in the SB20 Class racing on the second day of the Volvo Dún Laoghaire regatta.* *Photograph: Alan Betson.*

Fearing for the impact on Federer's sporting legacy should he continue to incrementally slip towards also-ran status is a luxury that bears no relation to the individual's need to get up in the morning with a purpose beyond the preservation of a fortune that makes ever working for a living again irrelevant.

There is also the not-insignificant factor that the Swiss kinda likes playing tennis. And there's always statistical proof already in the book of an incomparably successful Grand Slam career, the true barometer of tennis greatness. But even 17 Grand Slam titles don't quite sum up what Federer has come to represent to sport in general and tennis in particular. In the sphere of sporting competition, no one has ever better amalgamated the principles of style and substance. With Federer, they really are two sides of the same coin. And the effect has been intoxicating.

Arguing about whether or not he's the best

ever to walk on court is futile since such things are immune to definitiveness anyway; and it's doubly hard to argue in the face of head-to-head evidence that Rafa Nadal holds an undeniable edge over his great rival. But great a player as he is, the Spaniard holds no claims to any kind of aestheticism on court, embodying instead a bludgeoning, near-manic desire to win. It's mesmerising in its own way, but no one is ever going to mistake it for beauty.

There have been times though in the past decade when Federer has effortlessly criss-crossed the bridge between performing and performance, all the while blending an incomparable array of natural gifts into a ruthlessly focused desire to win. If the substance is a prerequisite, the style has been a glorious bonus that only those chronically short of imagination can fail to warm to.

His movement on court has been routinely described as balletic by men who would usually presume a corps de ballet is a Foreign Legion regiment. And the overall impact has provoked a deeply visceral affection for an iconic figure that for good measure gives every indication of being a balanced, decent man, aware of a world beyond the next point.

Now, worrying about whether or not a dip below those exalted standards will tarnish how his career is remembered is obviously proof of having nothing much to really worry about at all. But Federer has come to personify sporting grace to so many people that the idea of him slipping in terms of performance is a genuinely sore one. Is that based on anything bar sentiment? Of course not, but take sentiment out of sport and you're left with little except movement. Is it a pressing problem? Of course it isn't. We're not talking here about some skint boxer taking way too many shots to the head. But trivial and irrelevant are not the same thing.

The vital question for any sports person approaching the end of their career is whether they have squeezed the most out of their talent. Federer can already answer that in the affirmative. When he eventually winds up, there will be none of the 'if only' anguish that plagued Björn Borg's retirement after he cried enough at 26. But everything we have seen so far this year suggests 2012's Wimbledon triumph and return to world number one status was a wonderfully defiant but final rage against time's remorseless tick.

In his pomp, even on his worst day, Federer would have found a way to beat the world No. 116. The fact that pomp is gone is reflected in how the 'shock-horror' headlines that greeted his defeat last week didn't quite ring true.

During the match, the great man's timing, normally a thing of beauty, looked dreadfully out. Routine shots that should have been put away were being swatted at with a depressing lack of conviction. There was a poignancy to it, one added to by the post-match defiance which was admirable in a way, yet sad in another.

Deciding when to pull the plug on your career is always a tough call for any sportsperson. Timing it right can often be a luxury. A lot of us are hoping Federer gets his timing right again.

And if he wins the US Open in a couple of months, there will be a massive, sheepish and hugely happy frog chorus on the sidelines wondering if time really can be turned back.

MONDAY, I JULY 2013

Post-war Food Donations Led to Album of Thanks from Starving German Children to 'You Irelanders'

Derek Scally in Berlin

Saarbrücken was in ruins when Roswitha Hemmerling returned as an 11-year-old in the summer of 1945. The war was over but, in her hometown on Germany's border to France, she still remembers how she and her six siblings were permanently hungry.

'Our ration was two slices of bread each, that was all,' she told *The Irish Times*. 'My mother didn't eat a thing so us children would have more. She was very haggard then.'

In late 1945, Roswitha and many of her friends were classified as malnourished and put on a special meal donation programme. Thanks to emergency food donations from Ireland, worth about €191 million in today's money, Roswitha and countless other children around Germany weren't hungry any more.

'In break-time we would form a queue and get extra food – sometimes it was pea soup with bacon in it, or a kind of porridge made out of milk and sweet biscuits,' she said. 'It tasted so good, particularly the taste of sugar.'

Roswitha remembers her art teacher suggesting they create an album of thanks for their Irish benefactors.

'The German women and children could scarcely believe there are countries that, out of sheer humanity, tried to help. Their hearts were full of thanks,' writes one unnamed schoolgirl, concluding her letter with a flower-bedecked red heart for 'Den Iren', 'to the Irish people'.

Another pupil called Rosemary wrote: 'The children are particularly happy when there is cocoa: you should see it. Perhaps a time will come when we can speak to you.'

It has taken 66 years, but now the Saarbrücken schoolgirls have said thanks in person. A year ago a local newspaper ran an article about how a small album had come into the possession of an Irishman, who was hunting for the schoolgirls who had made it.

'The phone didn't stop ringing for days,' said Roswitha (78). 'We were all so surprised and delighted to hear about the album again.'

Over 20 women, now in their seventies and eighties, came together to welcome Tony O'Herlihy – an energetic, retired architect – and their album, with its brown speckled cover and 90 pages yellow with age. Each woman found the drawing or rhymes she had written, in careful cursive script, as a child who had seen the horrors of war and was barely surviving its terrible aftermath.

Mr O'Herlihy told them the album had found its way to Ireland and into the hands of an eight-year-old Mary Walshe from Crumlin, who later became his wife. The story goes that her father Jack Walshe, a plumbing supervisor at the Guinness brewery in Dublin, told a friend how his daughter Mary liked drawing and had won a prize in the Texaco art competition.

Hearing this, Jack's friend gave Mary the

album as a present. Sensing it was something special, she kept it safe over the years, showing it to Tony O'Herlihy when they married in 1973.

'We would often take down the book over our 37 years together and wonder where the girls were who'd made it,' said Mr O'Herlihy. 'We often thought we must do something about it, but we always said "we'll do that tomorrow". Mary's death in 2011 made me decide that tomorrow is now.'

He brought the album to the German embassy in Dublin where staff made contact with Saarbrücken. A year later, he has pieced together much of the detail, recalling a little-known chapter of German–Irish history.

On 23 May 1945, two weeks after Victory in Europe day, taoiseach Éamon de Valera outlined a food donation programme to help counter the 'terrible conditions prevailing over most of the European Continent'.

'Millions of people are already starving and many millions more are threatened with starvation [and] I am reliably informed that the danger of even more widespread distress and famine is very grave indeed,' said Mr de Valera.

'Our people are ready to provide those necessities of life. It will involve a reduction in our ration of some commodities, but the sacrifice involved will, I am sure, be readily accepted by our people to help fellow-beings in dire distress.'

The proposal met with approval across party lines – James Dillon, Fine Gael TD for Monaghan and later minister for agriculture, saying 'a hungry German is as much deserving of pity as a hungry Pole'. Mr O'Herlihy is still piecing together details of the programme, though one

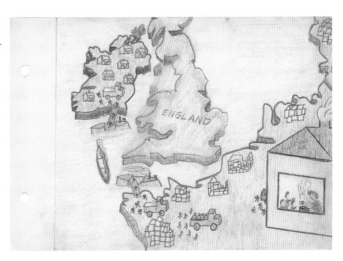

picture in the album suggests Irish food reached the western German cities of Cologne, Frankfurt, Düsseldorf, Essen, Mannheim and Ludwigsburg. His feeling is that the Red Cross and Catholic charities were involved in the programme that, thanks to his efforts, is now receiving belated recognition in Germany.

'Many of the women have told me the food from Ireland is what helped them survive,' said Birgit Kollet, a cultural officer in Saarbrücken, who helped co-ordinate the search.

Mr O'Herlihy is still searching for information about how the album came to Ireland and who gave it to his late wife. He hopes to eventually tell the full story in a book and, if sponsors can be found, present all the former Saarbrücken schoolgirls with a facsimile of their album. What began for them as a labour of love in 1946 has, since his wife's passing, become the same for him today.

'It is a story that needs to be told and reminds us of ties between our countries,' said Mr O'Herlihy. 'It is also a tribute to Mary: she very carefully looked after that book because she knew of its significance.'

SATURDAY, 6 JULY 2013

Inside Ireland's Supreme Court

Ruadhán Mac Cormaic

Thousands of protesters were on the streets of Dublin, demonstrations were taking place at Irish embassies abroad, and newspapers around the world were running daily updates on the case. France's *Libération* said it put Ireland's continued membership of the EU in doubt. In Sweden, the king and queen were under pressure to cancel a planned visit to Dublin.

It was against this backdrop that, on a midweek morning in February 1992, five judges stood up from their walnut dais in the high-ceilinged courtroom and made their way down the corridor to the Supreme Court conference room.

In keeping with the tradition of the court, the most junior member, Séamus Egan, spoke first. Then, in reverse order of seniority, came Hugh O'Flaherty, Niall McCarthy, Anthony Hederman and, finally, the chief justice, Tom Finlay. All were middle-aged or approaching retirement. They were an experienced and clever group, and the court to which they belonged was seen as a steady, conservative place. The mood was solemn. A lengthy discussion began.

The judges faced a profound dilemma. At the request of the then attorney general, Harry Whelehan, the High Court had granted an injunction preventing a 14-year-old girl, pregnant after being raped by a neighbour, travelling to Britain for an abortion. She was suicidal. After a three-day hearing, the five judges had to decide whether to uphold the High Court's decision or allow 'Miss X' to travel.

The Constitution had been amended nine years previous, in part out of fear that the Supreme Court would follow the example of its US counterpart and allow abortion, so as to expressly equate two rights to life: that of the mother and the unborn. Beyond that, the court had no legislation to guide it.

The judges met more than once to pore over the arguments, but it was clear that a majority view had formed. By four to one, the court was in favour of allowing Miss X to travel. The press corps received just a few minutes' notice before the judges – wigged, grave and dressed in black robes – retook their seats. The crowd was three-deep at the back of the court.

The then taoiseach, Albert Reynolds, was on his way to Downing Street for a meeting with his British counterpart, John Major. A call came through on the car phone from Seán Duignan, Reynolds's press adviser, who had news from the Four Courts. The line went silent: Duignan thought Reynolds hadn't heard him. Eventually the taoiseach spoke up: 'We're up to our necks in it now, Diggy. They're all out to get us.'

The X case, perhaps the most controversial ever to come before an Irish court, thrust the Supreme Court into the largely unaccustomed glare of the public gaze. But within a few days, the spotlight had moved elsewhere. The abortion debate shifted back to the streets and the airwaves, where it remains divisive 21 years later, and the court got on with the decidedly more mundane matters that land at its door every week.

It's a striking paradox. An institution that has helped shaped some of the biggest debates of the past 50 years goes about its work without impinging much on the public consciousness, save for the rare occasions when it strikes down a piece of legislation or gives a landmark judgment.

Its members tend not to be recognised on the street, and much of their time is spent dealing with technical questions of fairly limited significance. That's partly due to its status – unusual among equivalent courts – as the final court of appeal not only for Constitutional issues, but for all types of cases thrown up by the lower courts.

On a Monday, it might be asked to interpret what the Constitution has to say about when life begins. On Tuesday, it might spend the morning listening to an irate pensioner complaining that her neighbour's extension is blocking her light.

Yet few doubt the influence of the court. Under a Constitution that gave the courts unusually strong powers and left the legislature relatively weak, the Supreme Court has a key position at the apex of the courts system. The list of its judgments and its controversies are essential to understanding how the State has developed.

'I was always of the view that these fellas could crush us,' says a former long-serving minister. 'They're very powerful.'

At the Four Courts in Dublin, at the end of a narrow corridor lined with portraits of each of the supreme courts since the foundation of the State, is the conference room where the court's private meetings take place. The blue-green bookshelves are filled with statutes, law reports, textbooks and dictionaries, and in the middle of the room, on a red carpet, is a dark wooden table with eight chairs.

At the head sits the chief justice, Susan Denham. Around her, the ordinary judges of the court: John Murray, Adrian Hardiman, Nial Fennelly, Donal O'Donnell, Liam McKechnie, Frank Clarke and John Mac Menamin. The window is opaque so passers-by cannot see in.

Stories of bitter enmities on previous courts are the stuff of legend. It was said that two of the dominant figures of the 1960s and 1970s, Brian Walsh and Séamus Henchy, weren't on speaking terms, but on the current court the mood is friendly and collegiate. Views and approaches can differ sharply, but the judges have known each other for decades and there's an easy familiarity between them.

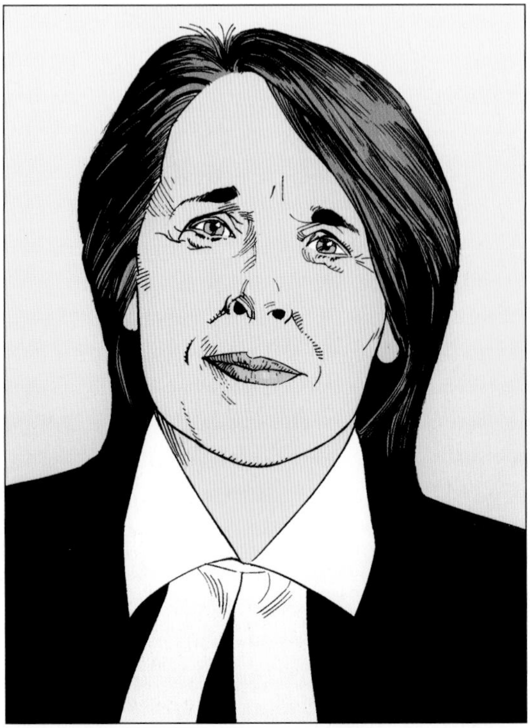

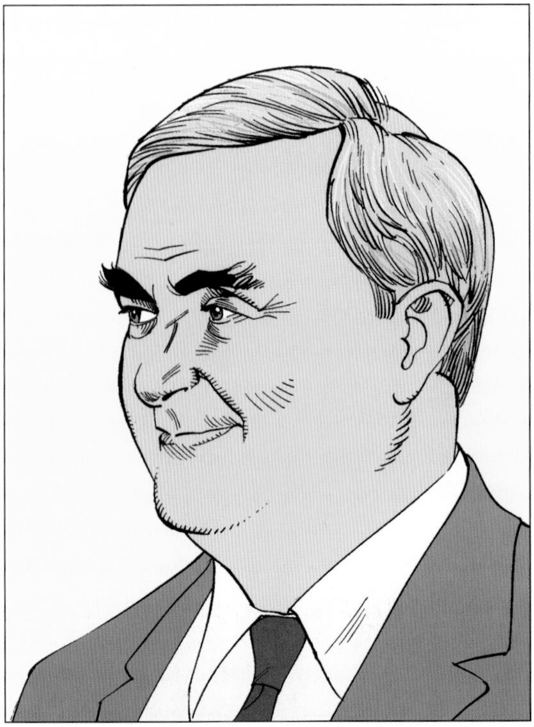

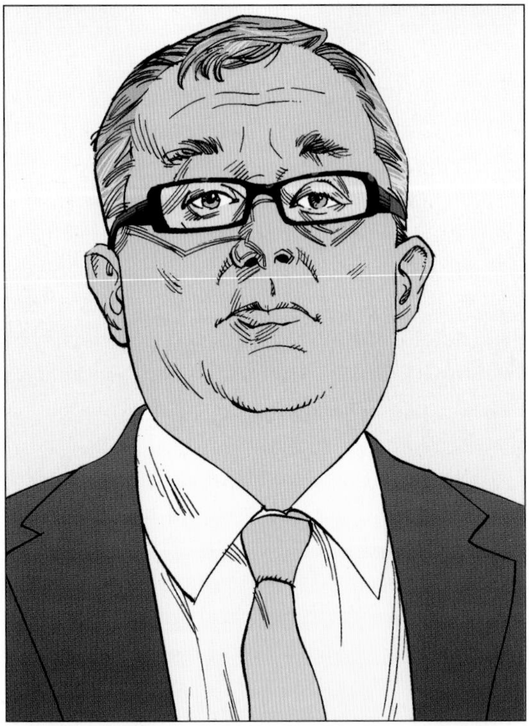

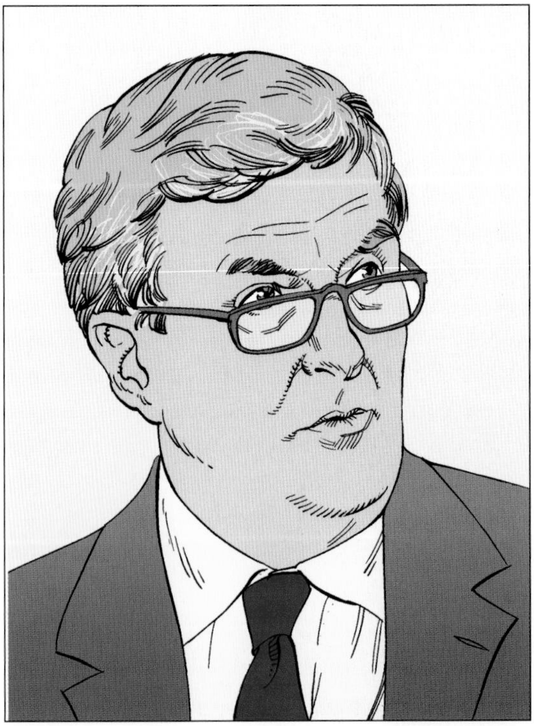

Susan Denham, John Murray, Adrian Hardiman, Nial Fennelly, Donal O'Donnell, Liam McKechnie, Frank Clarke and John Mac Menamin of the Supreme Court. Illustrated by Eoin Coveney.

In 1983, 98 lawyers wrote to *The Irish Times* to protest against the government's abortion amendment. It included the names of young barristers Frank Clarke, John Mac Menamin, Adrian Hardiman and Nial Fennelly. Today, all four sit on the Supreme Court, as does John Murray, who as Charles Haughey's attorney general helped draft that amendment.

The current group of eight have been together since March 2012, when Clarke and Mac Menamin were appointed. The court, steered by Denham for the past two years, is considered a pleasant, fair but formidable environment.

'There have always been a couple of very intelligent judges on the court, but right now there's an unusual amount of extremely smart people up there,' says one senior counsel who practises regularly in the court.

The atmosphere in public sittings varies with the composition of the court. Three judges sit for routine cases, five for those with a Constitutional element and seven for major cases with potentially wide implications. Even for the most experienced barristers, a court of seven judges peering down sceptically from the bench can be a daunting prospect.

'It doesn't matter, losing your case, but what really stings is being kicked on the way down,' says one.

Each judge has a courtroom persona. Murray and Hardiman can be pugnacious and blunt. O'Donnell is surgical and succinct. Fennelly, McKechnie, Clarke and Mac Menamin are courteous, smart and understated. When the judges see weakness in a barrister's argument, everyone will join in, and Denham will customarily find herself cast as the voice of reason keeping her colleagues in check.

At private conference, by contrast, discussions are low-key and polite. One judge can recall voices being raised only once, and that was over 'an obscure point of European law'.

'You've nowhere to go if you have a row, because you're there together in this conference room and sitting on the bench together,' says a former judge. 'There's actually great camaraderie.'

A consensus usually emerges at the first discussion immediately after a hearing, but if a judgment is particularly difficult, the group will hold several conferences. In between those meetings, paragraphs will be circulated and debated between them by email. Occasionally, position papers will be sent around, and a writer might cast their judgment in such a way that it might persuade a waverer to concur.

Nearly all judges resist labels such as liberal or conservative, pro-State or pro-plaintiff and dismiss attempts to extrapolate from their background a predisposition to decide a case a certain way.

To an extent, they have a point. While six of the current eight would be considered in the Law Library to be socially liberal and two, Murray and O'Donnell, relatively conservative, it's hard to point to a judgment where that configuration comes out. 'The characterisation is meaningful if you can feel it and touch it empirically,' says a judge. For the most part, voting records are a jumble of overlapping patterns.

Yet the court's record reveals some clear trends and internal intellectual differences. In two key cases in 2001, *Sinnott v Minister for Education* and *TD v Minister for Education,* the court pushed back against what the majority saw as attempts to cross a red line into the legislative domain.

In the Sinnott case, a seven-judge court overturned a High Court ruling that 23-year-old Jamie Sinnott, an autistic man, had an entitlement to education for as long as it was beneficial, irrespective of age. According to the Supreme Court, the right to primary education ended at the age of 18. Just a few months later, in the TD case, the court overturned, by a majority of four to one, a High Court order directing the State to build and open a number of high-support and secure units for children at risk, as it had pledged to do.

Those two decisions marked a pivotal moment in a debate, inside and outside the court, about

Taking the exceptional summer sunshine from the vantage point of the Blackrock diving tower in Galway as **The World**, *the largest residential liner in the world, is moored in the Bay. Photograph: Joe O'Shaughnessy.*

how legitimate it was for the courts to protect the implied socioeconomic rights of marginalised individuals and groups. In both cases, the majority (but not Denham, who dissented in the TD case) in effect rejected the idea that a court could issue mandatory orders telling the government how it should spend taxpayers' money.

The judgments were seen as the Supreme Court putting a brake on expansionist inclinations within the judiciary and cleaving to a strict view of the separation of powers, a stance that continues to stir considerable debate.

In some areas, however, the court has shown itself to be a more assertive voice. Its decisions place a strong emphasis on the rights of the individual and show concern about too much power being concentrated in one area.

The 'Abbeylara judgment' blocked the

Oireachtas from holding inquiries that could lead to adverse findings of fact against people who weren't TDs or senators. In *Damache v DPP* in 2011, the court ruled that a key section on search warrants in the Offences Against the State Act was unconstitutional, a ruling that infuriated gardaí and government officials.

Of all the issues preoccupying the current court, however, one of the most urgent concerns its own future. As the volume of litigation going through the High Court has increased dramatically in recent decades, a bottleneck has developed farther up the chain. There is now a four-year waiting list at the Supreme Court, a situation Denham has described as 'overwhelming' and 'damaging to Irish society and the economy'.

In an attempt to deal with the crisis, the government has pledged to hold a referendum this autumn to create a new Court of Appeal, which would hear routine or non-Constitutional appeals, and to increase the number of judges on the Supreme Court from eight to 10. Given that two judges on the current court, Murray and Fennelly, are due to retire within two years, it means the profile of the court will alter considerably over the next two years.

Taken together, these changes will bring about the biggest transformation of the Supreme Court since it was established. If the referendum is passed, it will become a true Constitutional court, with the power to pick and choose its cases and with more time to deliberate them.

Some believe the change will liberate the court and allow it the space to develop its thinking on the Constitution, perhaps in time reviving the debate, inside and out, between advocates of a more expansionist court and those who would draw clearer lines of separation between Leinster House and the Four Courts.

'Neither the law nor the Constitution is frozen in 1937,' wrote Denham in a judgment in 2006. 'The Constitution is a living instrument.' It may soon have more room to breathe.

THURSDAY, 11 JULY 2013

The More Things Change, the More They Stay the Same in Egypt

Michael Jansen in Cairo

Sitting on the balcony of his family's elegant flat watching pleasure boats strung with coloured lights and blaring loud music pass on the Nile, analyst Khairi Abaza readily acknowledges reports of the return of the *feloul*, the remnants of the 30-year regime of ousted Egyptian president Hosni Mubarak.

'Of course, they are returning,' he chuckles. 'Everyone is *feloul*. Now we have also the *feloul* of the Brotherhood.'

He says that in his village a former member of parliament from Mubarak's National Democratic Party (NDP) – which used patronage to cultivate a grass-roots following – may not stand for elections again but will secure the candidacy for his son or cousin.

The Muslim Brotherhood – which grew its own grass roots by providing the poor with clinics, schools and food – could be expected to promote its *feloul* with the aim of maintaining a presence on the political scene and preserving a role for itself.

Even in revolutionary Egypt, the more things seem to change, the more they stay the same. Figures of the Mubarak regime filled cabinets appointed by the armed forces that succeeded him and were assigned portfolios and jobs by the Muslim Brotherhood, which won parliamentary and presidential elections and, last summer, took over the running of the State from the military.

Feloul are assuming positions in the caretaker administration that overthrew the Brotherhood and president Mohamed Morsi, proclaiming they are determined to pave the way for pluralistic, multi-party democracy.

Feloul cannot be eliminated or escaped. They are prominent, influential and experienced in the ways of ruling this unruly and now rebellious country. Figures such as Gen. Abdel Fattah al-Sisi, military chief and defence minister; former chief justice Adly Mansour, now interim president; and caretaker prime minister Hazem Beblawi all served during the Mubarak era. There has been – and will be – no clean sweep of veteran members of the political, business, professional and military elite who co-operated with and were co-opted by the 'old regime'. Individuals, however, could be held accountable for their actions.

The military, police, judiciary, bureaucracy and intelligence services are accused by Morsi and the Brotherhood of constituting Egypt's 'deep state', a term associated with the military in Turkey.

The Brotherhood argues Egypt's 'deep state' is collaborating with Mubarak's crony capitalists to

An Egyptian man holds aloft pictures of ousted Egyptian president Hosni Mubarak and sports a photo on his chest of military chief General Abdel Fattah al-Sisi as Mubarak's supporters gather outside the police academy in Cairo. Photograph: Gianluigi Guercia/AFP.

overthrow the country's first freely elected president and the Brotherhood's election-won majorities in the dissolved lower and upper houses of parliament.

While some State institutions – notably the judiciary – attempted to impede Brotherhood rule, the situation is far more complex than the movement is prepared to admit. In the view of analyst Abaza, it brought about its own downfall by failing to 'rule by consensus', even though Morsi won the presidency only because he won the votes of millions of secular Egyptians who were determined to block the return of the ultimate *feloul*, Ahmed Shafiq, Mubarak's last prime minister.

Abaza, who is writing a history of Egyptian governance, believes Egypt can be ruled effectively only by rulers who 'build consensus'. The Brotherhood's old-guard leadership thought it could rule on its own while inserting its appointees into senior positions and sidelining people at all levels in State institutions. This created resentment and prompted non-cooperation.

Abaza gave an example of civil servants at local level who seem to have obstructed the delivery of fuel and provision of electricity to the countryside, undermining the Brotherhood's standing with villagers. Now that the Brotherhood has fallen, Abaza says there are no electricity cuts or fuel shortages in villages he has contacted.

If the caretaker regime is to win the confidence of the revolutionaries who have shown they can mobilise millions of Egyptians across the country, Abaza says it must 'create a new consensus' involving the military, bureaucracy, business community, academics, farmers and labourers.

To build a 'revolutionary' consensus, activists argue that the interim regime must secure progress on tasks set by the 2011 uprising. The caretaker government needs to make an early end to military trials for civilians, purge Egyptian institutions of corrupt and repressive *feloul* in power under Mubarak, and conduct public trials of those responsible for the deaths of 846 activists during the 18-day uprising.

In coming months, revolutionaries say the interim government must stem the country's economic collapse, draft a constitution acceptable to the entire society, and conduct free and fair elections.

If this effort falters and fails, Egyptians who, in Abaza's view, over the past two years have come to understand the meaning of consensus can be expected to return to the streets and squares to make certain they achieve their goal of inclusive rule by consensus: democracy.

THURSDAY, 11 JULY 2013

Taking Flight from the Ryanair Baggage Blues

Conor Pope

You won't get anything out of me this time O'Leary. Oh no. This time I'm gonna waltz past your surly check-in staff with a smirk on my face. Because today, O'Leary, I am wearing a suitcase coat.

Under your rules, I am allowed 10kg of carry-on luggage plus a jacket or coat. If I want to bring

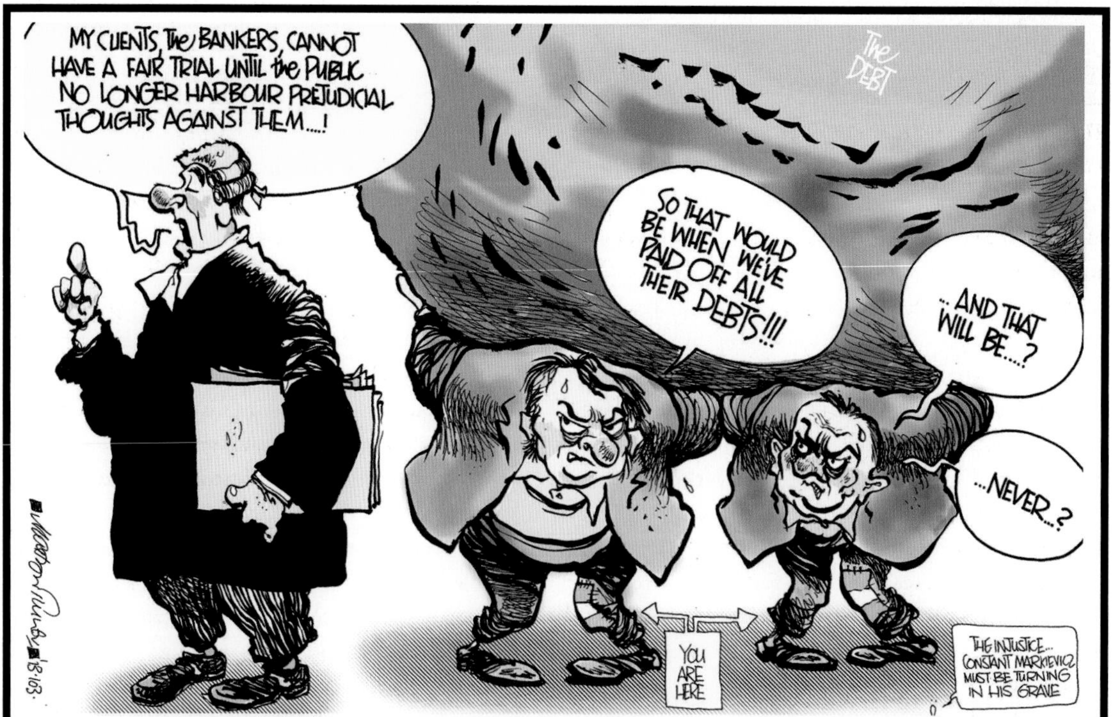
MY CLIENTS, THE BANKERS, CANNOT HAVE A FAIR TRIAL UNTIL THE PUBLIC NO LONGER HARBOUR PREJUDICIAL THOUGHTS AGAINST THEM....!
THE DEBT
SO THAT WOULD BE WHEN WE'VE PAID OFF ALL THEIR DEBTS!!!
...AND THAT WILL BE....?
...NEVER...?
YOU ARE HERE
THE INJUSTICE... CONSTANT MARKIEVICZ MUST BE TURNING IN HIS GRAVE

Martyn Turner's take on justice and the bankers.

The author dons his 'beat O'Leary' jacket.
Photograph: **The Irish Times.**

more than that you're going to hit me with charges aren't you? But you made a mistake. You left the definition of coat pretty loose didn't you? Yes, yes you did.

Who's laughing now, eh? What? Everyone?

I know. I look ridiculous, and with 9 kilos of clothes, toiletries, books, keys, passports and sun cream in the six pockets of my shiny black nylon coat, I am sweating like a drug mule at a Turkish airport, but who cares?

In my suitcase coat I have everything I need for a week in the sun. In pocket one there are three pairs of trousers, two pairs of shoes and swimming trunks. Pocket two is stuffed with flip flops, a hoodie and socks and jocks. In pocket three I have a toothbrush, deodorant and some hangover remedies.

Pocket four has two books and copies of both *Heat* and *VIP*. The two little pockets at the bottom of the jacket have my phone, keys, chewing gum, chocolate – so I don't have to spend money on sweaty airline sandwiches in their plastic coffins – and my passport.

If my passport is where I think it is, I will be able to pass my coat through security scanners and I'll be off. This Rufus Roo jacket costs €40 at www.rufusroo.com. After just two trips I'll be quids in and you, O'Leary, will be the loser.

I'll just look like one.

WEDNESDAY, 17 JULY 2013

'For once they have the power in the room'

Peter Crawley

A young couple, unable to escape the watchful eyes of their family, friends or guardians, decide that they would like some time alone together. They book a hotel room and settle in for some privacy. What can happen when no one is watching? A story of young love and romantic seclusion wouldn't ordinarily make for an unusual drama, but the couple at the centre of Christian O'Reilly's recent play *Sanctuary* are special: Sophie has epilepsy and Larry has Down syndrome. For the characters and the audience there is a curious contradiction: here are two people whose desire is to be unwatched, yet such a depiction of the agency, sexuality and desire of people with intellectual disability is very rarely seen.

O'Reilly's play, staged by Blue Teapot Theatre Company, is a romantic comedy written for the Galway-based ensemble of actors with intellectual disability. As it shears this couple away from a group of their peers – some bitter and jealous, some with romantic designs of their own – it cracks open a political quandary about the sexuality of people with special needs and asks intriguing questions of the theatre. For both reasons, Blue Teapot, in operation for 17 years now, is finally gaining wide attention.

Last year, when *Sanctuary* was first produced, a psychologist in the audience was moved to tears. 'They have the power,' he told the company's director Petal Pilley of her ensemble. 'For once they have the power in the room.' It has taken the company some time to achieve that level of control, since its formation as a charity and a creative outlet for people with disability in 1996. Pilley, who joined seven years ago, saw the opportunity to create an ensemble and introduced an acting school to develop the company as a professional outlet.

Pilley agrees that turning Blue Teapot into a professional company has involved challenging her ensemble while respecting its limits. 'It's to absolutely acknowledge intellectual disability, and to create the support for actors with ID. For example, this play has a lot of text in it and sometimes the actors need a prompt . . . It requires a little bit of sensitivity. At the same time, I'm constantly astounded by their level of emoting, the drive and the depth of understanding for the characters and the play itself.'

Sanctuary is the company's first specially commissioned work, and O'Reilly developed it in consultation with the ensemble. 'Through our working relationship over the years, I realised they had very little opportunity for romantic and sexual fulfilment in their lives because of the nature of dependency,' says Pilley. 'They live at home or in a group setting, and yet they're adult men and women. They're sassy and flirty – and the theatre's full of that.'

O'Reilly drew details and perspective from interviews with the cast and wove it into his material. 'So it's their play and their story,' says Pilley. 'Most of us know very little about the lives of people with disability. It's exciting subject matter to explore in the theatre.'

O'Reilly's play raises another vexed issue: under Irish law it is illegal for 'mentally impaired' people to have sex before marriage. The law is designed to protect the vulnerable from exploitation, but the condition of marriage seems archaic and denies adult status to people with ID. It is a law that Pilley finds shockingly outdated; something that must be looked at.

Looking, though, is not something that society is particularly primed to do when it comes to disability. Like curious children instructed not to stare at people with physical differences, we are discouraged from treating disabled people as a spectacle. When a performer with special needs takes to the stage, such reticence is automatically challenged. 'That's absolutely part of it,' says Claire Hodgson, the chief executive of the Dorset company Diverse City. 'The issue here is that the disabled people want to be looked at, as a spectacle, as a performer, which does challenge the whole thing of "looking away". Inside every performer is the desire to be watched, to be seen. I think it's about becoming visible.'

Diverse City was set up to create integrated performances. 'I've always been interested in making casts and companies that represent the world as it actually is,' Hodgson says, 'and not just a small slice of human existence.'

Hodgson will soon come to Kildare for the Performance Corporation's Big House Festival in August to work on *Come Dance with Me*. Inspired by ballroom dance, the competitive display of TV's *Strictly Come Dancing* and the subversive charm of the Baz Luhrmann film *Strictly Ballroom,* it is a collaboration with the choreographer Emma Martin and participants from St Raphael's, a Kildare care facility for people with intellectual disability.

'For people with disabilities, and particularly intellectual disabilities, it's rare to be part of a high-profile public performance,' says Hodgson. 'It isn't a community performance for friends and family – this is at the centre of a festival and will be judged

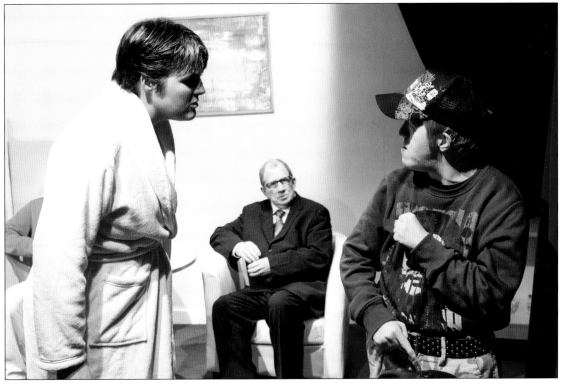

Charlene Kelly (Sophie), Frank Butcher (William) and Patrick Becker (Andrew) in Sanctuary, *staged by the Blue Teapot Theatre Company during the Galway Arts Festival. Photograph: Galway Arts Festival.*

alongside professional work. For them that's important, because they want to be seen by a wide range of people, to perform in front of big audiences and to participate in culture on a level playing field.'

As Hodgson sees it, we may be at a tipping point for a broader integration of disabled and non-disabled performers. During last year's Olympic Games, her company staged a performance, *Breathe*, a collaboration between young disabled performers from Dorset and Brazil, which launched the sailing competition. 'We're in a particular historical moment when things are really changing,' says Hodgson.

The Irish scene is burgeoning, from Blue Teapot's recent nomination for the Judge's Special Award at *The Irish Times* Irish Theatre Awards 'for giving a voice in theatre to actors with intellectual disabilities' and the forthcoming appearances of *Sanctuary* at the Galway Arts Festival and Dublin Fringe Festival, to Ignite, a new platform managed by Arts & Disability Ireland and supported by the Arts Council to commission and tour new works by artists with disabilities.

'I think the Paralympics last year changed a lot of people's minds about what disabled people could achieve,' says Hodgson. 'I think we've got a window in terms of creating work and supporting disabled artists to make work that is seen by a greater amount of people.'

Hodgson is currently developing an integrated circus company in the UK called Extraordinary Bodies, reconceiving the aesthetic of circus performance and redefining the bodies of acrobats. The agenda of *Come Dance with Me* is similar, challenging the exclusions and rigid conformity of

THE IRISH TIMES BOOK OF THE YEAR

The ghostly wreck of the tall ship **SS Astrid,** *which sank between Oysterhaven and Kinsale off the southern coast.*
Photograph: Michael Prior.

the ballroom. 'Show me your best moves, show me your best steps' is how she describes it. 'We can all learn steps, but in life, and in dance, the most important thing is that you have your own moves.'

Like Hodgson, who aspires to a culture where integration in performance is the norm and her company's interventions are no longer needed ('It would be the best outcome to work towards extinction'), Petal Pilley would like to see theatre in general become more inclusive on the stage.

Theatre can be tough, she knows, 'but it can express far more enlightened aspects of humanity as well. I think it's exciting to challenge it.' That, ultimately, is what the theatre is for, to honour the talent and ambitions of its performers, to realise their agency in collaboration with others, and to explore under-represented issues by bringing them sharply into view.

TUESDAY, 23 JULY 2013

Some of Us Aren't Too Proud to Say We Enjoyed it Immensely

Ann Marie Hourihane

Well, some of us aren't too proud to say we enjoyed it immensely. If Kate wasn't Too Posh To Push – she didn't opt for the celebrity Caesarean – then we weren't Too Posh To Watch.

What the heck, it wasn't compulsory and in this life and in this media there's always a shortage of happy drama.

From the moment the text came at 8.45am yesterday – 'Kate's in labour!' – until Michael Wolff of *Vanity Fair* explained on *Newsnight* that this story

Britain's Prince William and his wife Catherine, Duchess of Cambridge, appear outside the Lindo Wing of St Mary's Hospital in central London with their first born, a boy they later named George. Photograph: Andrew Winning/Reuters.

has the two things most loved by American women – 'a celebrity baby and the British royal family' – we were reassured, even in this country, that we were not alone on this earth in finding the latest royal birth fascinating, funny and, in fact, a weird fiesta.

If you find this attitude offensive then try thinking of the Windsors as Manchester United . . . there, that feels better, doesn't it?

Of course, birth is the other great leveller. It was pretty painful to watch Kay Burley sweating it out in front of the Lindo wing of St Mary's Hospital, Paddington. Kay's privacy was effectively breached from 1pm yesterday afternoon.

She laboured all day, delivering constantly in the sweltering heat. She stomped around talking to the general public. She got her producer to look up the new baby's stars in the *Evening Standard* (the producer couldn't find them; Kay said he wasn't used to looking up his stars. Carole Middleton had told someone the baby was going to be a Leo. In fact, he was born on the cusp).

Meanwhile, Sky's beautiful Rhiannon Mills was in Bucklebury in Berkshire, outside the Middletons' house. Rhiannon was there all day. And the even more beautiful Becky Johnson was up at a maternity hospital in Liverpool, where

Wayne and Colleen Rooney's new baby, Anthony Klay, was born recently.

All Becky could find were shell-shocked young fathers advising William to do what his wife said.

It was a day for Sky News and for the tabloids, the media that makes the British royals a global soap opera and which, although no one says so, has saved it several times.

Much was made of the fact that the royal birth was going to be announced on an easel outside Buckingham Palace. Alastair Bruce, Sky's royal commentator – as distinct from royal correspondent – got a good hour of air time out of that easel. Jeremy Thompson came out of retirement – or wherever it is he has been – to take over at Buckingham Palace. No one took over from Kay.

What is it about a royal birth that interests (some) people so much? It seems to send us feudal in some way, back to the reassurance of an unshakeable hierarchy. Back to the illusion that someone, somewhere, is living the perfect life. It is irrational, politically incorrect and probably pretty dumb.

But the people who criticise it are often superior in an unbecoming way – party poopers, in other words – who aren't that worried about other social inequalities – although Joan Smith, an English republican, was terrific on *Newsnight*.

In Ireland, royal-watchers are still in the closet – there are quite a lot of corporate lawyers who relaxed in front of the recent documentary on Diana's dresses, who have discussed whether William was right in giving Kate Diana's engage-ment ring. 'We decided he was right,' said the corporate lawyer's friend, herself a tough professional. 'Better than having it stuck in a safe somewhere.'

The rest of us have had to accustom ourselves to startling realities – like the fact that this baby had its own Wikipedia page before he was born. Even if we never signed the baby guestbook, started online by ABC News in the United States, we know about it and how it has been signed not just by Americans, but by Kenyans, Singaporeans and Indonesians.

Even Niagara Falls has been dyed blue.

Meanwhile, in another example of misleading the general public, and of a general public just gagging to be misled, film star Kate Winslet, who is expecting her third child, earlier this month shared with *OK!* readers a brief exchange she had with the Queen when she went to Buckingham Palace to collect her CBE last year.

'The Queen asked her if she likes her job. Kate reveals: "I told her that I loved it but I love being a mum even more. The Queen said: "Yes, that's the only job which matters".'

Which is a bit rich coming from two such over-achievers; particularly from the Queen, who has been working non-stop since she was 20 and pretty much refuses to retire.

Whether this child, poor little thing, is indeed the saviour of the British monarchy, very much remains to be seen. He was already a money-spinner in the womb – he generated £260 million before he was born, according to media reports.

But even the most enthusiastic royal-watchers must acknowledge that, unfortunately for the new prince, the lives of the rich and famous are not terribly child-friendly. They are rich in nannies but poor in the things that children actually like, for example, routine, living in one house all the time, and resembling your friends as much as possible.

It is fairly obvious that the British royal family, even in the last 60 years, has not been a pleasant place in which to grow up. Prince Charles's childhood seems to have been miserable and damaging. Even Princess Diana, who was always going on about how much she loved children, sent Prince William off to be a weekly boarder at the Ludgrove prep school in Berkshire when he was eight.

We can acknowledge that whilst also acknowledging that interest in this new baby reaches far beyond the shores of the UK.

Riders and horses round the bend during the Omey Derby at the Omey Races in Connemara.
Photograph: Joe O'Shaughnessy.

The joy at his birth is truly unconfined. It makes you question whether modern humans, for all our technology and sophistication, are really that different from our ancestors, who lived centuries ago and loved to worship their kings.

THURSDAY, 25 JULY 2013

Comment: Our Culture of Impunity Lives On

Frank McDonald

Given Ireland's notoriously weak laws on white-collar crime, it was probably inevitable that the Director of Public Prosecutions would withdraw corruption charges against five defendants, including a serving councillor and three former councillors, when the chief witness against them proved unable to continue giving his evidence.

With no other former councillors facing charges for taking payments from developers to have land zoned in the early 1990s, the upshot is that only Frank Dunlop himself – the 'bagman' for many of these disreputable transactions – has served a prison sentence. Those who took bribes, as the Mahon tribunal found, have not.

For anyone who saw what was going on in Dublin County Council's makeshift council chamber on Upper O'Connell Street – as I did – the outcome confirms the culture of impunity. The building is now gone, but we are still living with the consequences of decisions made at the behest of developers.

As I wrote after the tribunal published its final

James Kennedy (centre) with his wife Antoinette, family and his legal team leaving Dublin Circuit Criminal Court after corruption charges against him were dropped. Photograph: Collins.

report in March 2012, some people are living in floodplains as a result, while others have no option but to get into their cars to travel to a shopping centre because the one that was planned nearer wasn't built, because councillors persistently ignored the advice they got from professional planners.

'Corrupt and bad planning decisions have a significant impact upon people's lives,' said Jerry Barnes, of the Royal Town Planning Institute (Southern Ireland). And he cited as a prime example the 1991 rezoning of Quarryvale – tainted by widespread bribery – as a 'town centre' for the Lucan/Clondalkin agglomeration in west Dublin. It didn't matter that an actual town centre had been planned for 20 years in a central location to serve the area. What happened was that the town centre was relocated to the northeastern extremity of this

burgeoning 'new town', at the edge of the M50 – because that's where developer Owen O'Callaghan wanted to build it.

Those who championed the radical change of plan, notably the late Liam Lawlor and former Fianna Fáil councillor Colm McGrath, were paid handsomely for their support by Dunlop from his ample 'war chest'. Many other councillors also received smaller sums for voting for the Cork-based developer's daring scheme.

Just last month, the Liffey Valley shopping centre at Quarryvale was consolidated by a Bord Pleanála decision to grant permission for a Tesco 'anchor store' with 551 parking spaces – on the basis that the 180-acre site had been zoned for 'town centre' use. Senior planning inspector Robert Ryan had recommended a refusal.

Mayo man Taoiseach Enda Kenny high-fives a young Donegal fan in Croke Park after Mayo beat the northern county in the All-Ireland Senior Football Championship quarter final. Photograph: Morgan Treach/Inpho.

As he noted, Liffey Valley 'represents an almost classic "American style" shopping mall very much dependent on the private car and relatively remote from existing long-established urban centres'. Indeed, even South Dublin County Council's local area plan describes it as 'off-centre' in relation to the communities it is meant to serve.

The blame for this state of affairs lies with the councillors who took money from Dunlop and voted to discard the original plan, in favour of adopting the new one put forward by a developer. The decision they made in 1991, setting the stage for this 'off-centre' shopping mall, was undoubtedly the most corrupt in the history of Irish planning.

It wasn't only county councillors who were shaking down developers for money; the corruption reached into the corridors of power in Leinster House. The original Quarryvale developer, Tom Gilmartin, faced what the tribunal called an 'undeniably corrupt' demand for £5 million after meeting then taoiseach Charles Haughey and ministers.

As recounted in the tribunal's final report, the shocked Sligo-born developer told the still unidentified individual who demanded that this sum be lodged in an Isle of Man bank account that he made 'the Mafia look like monks' and was then warned by him that he could 'wind up in the Liffey for that statement'. In concrete shoes, presumably.

'The heart of the Mahon findings is that the system was manipulated to serve certain private interests rather than the common good,' as Barnes said. As a result, there had been 'a vast and damaging overzoning of lands throughout the country, much of it in the wrong location' – and generations will be left living with the consequences.

'I cannot imagine how we are going to cope'

Joanne Hunt

'It's an absolute nightmare. I cannot imagine how we are going to cope,' says Moira Skelly.

Ms Skelly's daughter, Ciara (18), a young woman with profound disabilities, has attended day care services at Stewarts Hospital in Palmerstown, a centre for people with intellectual disabilities, since the age of four. Ms Skelly, along with the parents of Ciara's 10 classmates, has been told by the HSE that come September, full-time day care places for their highly dependent children will no longer be available.

'When we signed up with Stewarts, we were told she'd be there from cradle to grave, that we need never worry and that the State would always look after her. It was a complete shock to us when we were told this wouldn't happen.'

Having developed normally up to the age of six months, Ciara's epileptic seizures became uncontrollable. Her ability to sit up and to interact, along with the sounds she had started to make, stopped.

'Because she had seizures from such a young age, her brain became more damaged. She developed a form of cerebral palsy and now her right arm doesn't work at all, she has quite a pronounced limp and curvature of the spine,' says her mother.

Ciara also has autism. 'Her behaviour is very challenging. Her psychological assessments say that mentally she is about the age of a two-year-old.'

From September to June, five days a week, Ciara has attended Stewarts where she has benefited from physiotherapy, occupational therapy, one-to-one training and social activities. Last year, Ms Skelly said, those turning 18 continued to be cared for by the service, but not any more. The service is being cut to 10 days a month of community-based care with no transport.

With Ciara currently on her school holidays, Ms Skelly knows what the lack of service will do to Ciara, and to her. 'Her behaviour is a huge problem when she doesn't have her day service because she gets so bored. I'm finding it more and more difficult to cope. My worry is that I won't be able to cope.'

She has to wash, dress and feed her daughter and change her nappies. 'I have to hoist her into the bath, I have to lift her to wash and dress her. She's the same weight and height as I am. I'm finding it very difficult to cope.'

She says that when parents can't cope, the government will end up putting children like Ciara into more costly institutional care.

'And that's the very last thing any parent wants to do. It's the very last resort,' she says, her voice cracking with emotion.

'I can't believe the government could ignore these children. It's like they are second-class citizens and have no rights.'

Will Newstalk Walk the Plank with Pat Kenny?

Shane Hegarty

An irony about Pat Kenny's move to an independent broadcaster is that if, in a parallel Ireland, he had forged his career in the unforgiving world of a privately owned broadcaster, and if *The Late Late Show* had been the flagship of an independent RTÉ, his career would most likely be dead by now.

Kenny took the big gig. It chewed him up, spat him out, Friday after Friday, year after year. So did the critics (I was one of them at the time). So did the public. So, even, did some of the guests –

Moira Skelly from Walkinstown in Dublin with her 18-year-old daughter, Ciara, who due to cut backs cannot continue in full-time care in Stuarts Hospital in Palmerstown because she has reached the age of 18. Photograph: Aidan Crawley.

comedians chiefly – who came to subvert the stilted nature of the interviews. No one, it seemed, believed in Pat Kenny. Except for Pat Kenny.

Even while being cut up, torn apart, he appeared never to waver in his self-belief. Many saw it more as a lack of self-awareness, but, whatever the truth, that confidence – a necessary arrogance – protected him.

It wasn't all that did. That he was in the protective environs of the slow-moving, forgiving national broadcaster meant he was paid generously and treated mercifully during professionally painful years. He kept the radio show, was given further television work. He returned to the more solid ground of television current affairs.

He endured, but rather than evolve he reverted to what made him a success in the first place. For a broadcaster so often accused of being unable to engage the brake when his mind careens off in the wrong direction, he managed to right his career in a way that even his detractors must admit was impressive.

And if you were to be extra kind, the flailing of his successor on *The Late Late Show* cast Kenny's stewardship in a slightly better light. He is now only one of a majority of *Late Late* presenters unable to live up to the needs of a show – while that show itself is dying horribly.

It was a long and winding (and lucrative) road that led him to Newstalk. Kenny will have no

Five-year-old Shauna Mahony from Kilkenny taking part in a world record attempt for the largest ever potato sack race at the Tullamore Show. Photograph: Mark Stedman/Photocall Ireland.

doubt about what he is bringing to it. Denis O'Brien's station will know what it is getting. But together they must now answer a more fundamental, bigger question: what is Newstalk for?

The station is a decade old, but it is still crawling by the standards of its rivals. Its national audience share is under 5 per cent, and it has repeatedly struggled to establish itself in most of its slots.

This, though, suggests a strategy that shouldn't be unfamiliar to O'Brien, because it is the one that, before he bought the station, brought Today FM success. In 1998, having tried and, with the exception of Eamon Dunphy's *The Last Word*, largely failed to build its own shows, its own brands, its own personalities, it reverted to the wallet and poached from RTÉ.

Ian Dempsey's switch in 1998 was a crucial moment in Irish radio, enough that his moving his breakfast show to Today FM kick-started that station's revival while causing years of subsequent angst at 2FM.

Ray D'Arcy followed from RTÉ, and a station that had teetered on the brink in its early years began to lay solid foundations through big names, an enlightened music policy and a solid team of producers who became voices in their own right.

Kenny arrives at a Newstalk that craves momentum. It has had big names before. David McWilliams was an original voice. Dunphy came and (kicking and screaming) went. Ivan Yates had his troubles, although word is that he will be back, thanks to the UK's bankruptcy process. Its other breakfast presenters seem to run low as regularly as cereal packets.

It has some decent names now, but only George Hook is a threat to his rivals. Although likeable, Tom Dunne's ratings have been low. Sean Moncrieff is underrated, but he's in the uncared-for midafternoons. It had an excellent *Off the Ball* team but ran them over in a game of chicken.

There are a myriad number of ways in which Pat Kenny's move to Newstalk could be mutually destructive. Fail on this and neither station nor presenter might recover.

There are several examples, in print media in particular, of big names leaving one organisation for another but losing their magic ingredients en route.

Besides, Kenny will be reliant on a production team that knows what it's doing and that can hang in through the early storms that are sure to buffet them.

But they are locked together now, Kenny and Newstalk, either hauling each other upwards or dragging each other down. Kenny is bringing self-certainty to a station that lacks it. Quite where the centre of gravity settles will be entertaining in itself.

MONDAY, 5 AUGUST 2013

I Survived Celebrity MasterChef but Got my Fingers Burnt

Conor Pope

It's four in the morning and I'm sitting on my kitchen floor in bits. Just like my shortbread. Until this evening I'd never baked so much as a single biscuit but now I am on my sixth batch of shortbread and it's still not coming together. Too much butter? Too little? Too much heat? Too little? I've no idea and have stopped caring. I know now that winning *Celebrity MasterChef* is beyond me and I want it to be over.

Just 12 hours later, it is.

I agreed to take part last April on a whim despite being neither a celebrity nor a chef and without having watched a full episode of the programme. When I said yes, the relief in the voice of the woman who had popped the question was as gratifying as it was clear. It was only later I realised her gratitude didn't stem from her securing a much sought-after star, but because so many proper celebs had rejected her advances and she was running out of time to fill her kitchen with faces.

Ray D'Arcy, who likes to cook, said no, as did George Hook, who doesn't. At least two other *Irish Times* writers also turned their noses up at the chance to go toe to toe with Dylan McGrath and Nick Munier. By the time they got to me, I suspect they were kind of desperate.

Conor Pope tries his hand in the kitchen. Photographs: RTÉ.

When I breezily tell friends and colleagues what I've done – breaking at least six confidentiality clauses in my contract – there is universal agreement that I will not be okay. I will, instead, be filleted by Dylan McGrath, the fiercest chef in Ireland. It is only at this point I start to worry.

I don't give a rashers about Dylan – how scary could he be? – but I don't want to disgrace myself in front of 400,000 viewers. When recording starts I am up to high dough. Sorry.

Day one in the *Celebrity MasterChef* kitchen and I meet my fellow chefs. It doesn't go well. Gary Cooke greets me with an affable 'You're a sports journalist, right?' Eh, no. A silent hour passed before he tries again. 'Oh, that's you right, you write about politics?' No.

From the off I worry about Tracy Piggott. She seems to know what she's about. She uses French terms when talking about food and got five stars in *The Restaurant*. Maia Dunphy talks down her chances but I reckon she's spinning me a yarn, like the girl outside the exam hall who insists she's done no study before coming out with straight As.

Aengus Mac Grianna is harder to read than a news bulletin about moon landings while Yvonne Keating frets about the syringe she needs for a feast of molecular gastronomy she has planned. David Gillick looks focused and fearful and Kamal Ibrahim is supremely confident.

Putting ourselves on a plate is the first task. Maia Dunphy goes for 'cheap and fun' Asian street food, Yvonne for a boozed-up bloody lamb. The rest of us cook fish. I tart mine up with basil chiffonades, not because they look or taste nice or say anything about me but because I learned what chiffonades were overnight and can pronounce the word. It sounds posh.

But before chiffonades, we have to meet the men who will judge us. They have a mean reputation, Dylan and Nick, but they are pussycats, really. Dylan with his shaved head and stubble looks awfully menacing. He has a great line in

withering stares and can be a grumpy auld bollix when the mood takes him, but he is mostly lovely and always helpful – except when you've messed up your work station. He also knows food and really cares about it.

Nick looks friendlier, with his hipster-geek glasses and his big, broad smile. It's all about the food for him too. He has very high standards. They make for a great double act.

War has been described as long periods of boredom punctuated by moments of sheer terror. That's what *MasterChef* is like.

On day two, we arrive on set before 9am and are sent to the green room where the producers tell us we have to perform just one task but we must do it in isolation. Once we leave the green room we will not be allowed return. They even sequester our phones. So we all sit around wondering what lies ahead when the radio belonging to the young researcher guarding us crackles into life.

'The hens are in position, the hens are in position,' it says clear as anything. She flees the room, desperately clawing at the radio, trying to silence it.

Sorry, what? Did that disembodied voice say 'hens'? The producers have messed up and given us a lead! Amazing. But what hens? Jesus, we are going to have to kill, gut and cook them? On television? The researcher comes back and begs us not to reveal how she has given the game away. We promise to keep her secret secret – because we are sound and we want the edge.

Gary is taken away to the hen house and, after 30 minutes, so is Maia. I am last to go. Time spent fretting about killing hens passes slowly and, after five hours, I'm climbing the walls. Eventually I am led through the dark, musty factory that houses the *MasterChef* kitchen and made wait behind double doors.

They open. I look for the chickens. There are none, just Dylan and Nick glowering at me and a producer laughing hysterically because I, like everyone else, had fallen for his hilarious joke. 'We just like messing with your heads,' he says.

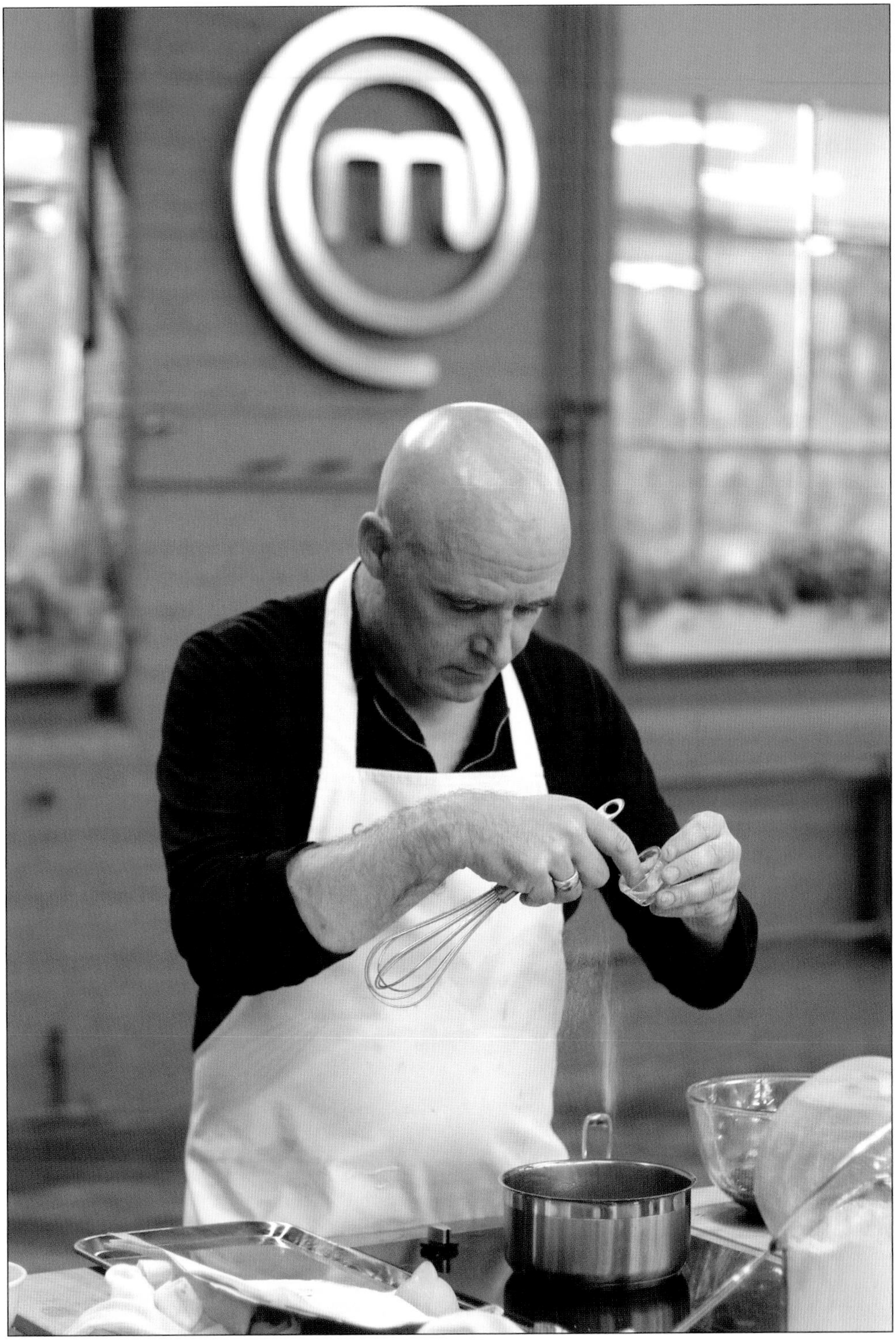

Thanks, Anthony.

I make a *crêpe suzette* – badly – but not as badly as Gary so he was sent home.

Round two sees us travel to Gavin Duffy's house in Co. Meath. Calling it a house sells it short. It is a country pile and we all pile into his kitchen to make lunch for him and his friends – or a bunch of random Americans pulled off the street.

David and Yvonne get crabs (titter) and Tracy and Kamal – whom you might recognise as 'that guy off the telly' or Mr World – were given dessert. Me, Maia and Aengus are on mains – pork belly, colcannon, beetroot, fondant potatoes.

Dylan helps. By help I mean he changes the whole menu plan at the last second and causes untold grief with his shouting and impatience. My favourite moment comes when he calls for a chinois. Me, Maia and Aengus shout 'yes chef' and run to get the chinois. But none of us knows what a chinois is. Aengus picks up a brass implement and waves it hopefully at Dylan. But that's not a chinois.

Cute as a hoor, I run into another part of the kitchen where desserts and starters are being made and I shout urgently. 'A chinois. Dylan needs the chinois. Will someone get me the chinois?' It doesn't work. Everyone stares blankly at me. They don't know what a chinois is either. Then Dylan roars. 'A sieve. I need a f**king sieve.'

So that's what a chinois is.

David and Yvonne's crabs are deemed to be most impressive so they get the next day off and miss the mystery box. I can't tell you how jealous this makes the rest of us. The self-explanatory mystery box is *MasterChef*'s blue-ribbon event.

Straight out of the blocks, I am getting it wrong. I think I have to use every ingredient, but as I stand there slack-jawed wondering how I am going to make brioche, pork, sea bass, cherries, chocolate, cabbage, pine nuts, truffles and bourbon work together in just an hour, Dylan explains the rules to me. I can pick and choose.

I decided to marinate the pork. Then I decide not to. The clock ticks. So I fry the pancetta, pine nuts and shredded cabbage, dust the sea bass in flour and ta-da! Done. It is not complex but it tastes okay. I am safe.

I work alongside Kamal. He is not safe but doesn't know it. He is one of the most confident people I have ever met and even his inability to tell lettuce and cabbage apart or understand why plastic might melt in an oven doesn't shake his faith in his own ability. It is rather sweet. The judges are not impressed. They send him home. He takes his dismissal hard and it is hard not to feel sorry for him.

Soon I am feeling sorry for myself. Episode three marks the start of Dessert Storm. I told the producers repeatedly that I was shocking at baking. I don't have a sweet tooth and have never made a dessert in my life. The only time I made pancakes, I made my four-year-old daughter cry.

For the fourth task, we are introduced to Clare Clarke. She is a legend. I have never heard of her; I have heard of the French Laundry restaurant in California though. It has three Michelin stars and is widely regarded as one of the best restaurants in the world. She was the head pastry chef there and has an MBE for cakemaking. She is a big cheese. She is brilliant.

She gives us a two-and-a-half-hour master class and makes a summer trifle. The word doesn't do it justice. It is a work of art on a plate and it tastes amazing. Then we have to copy her. There are more than 50 steps from the almond sponge to the bavarois (no, I had no idea what that was either), and to the wild flowers that have to be placed on top of the perfectly piped dollops of Chantilly cream. I take all the steps with great care and, amazingly, my dessert is all-but-perfect.

Nick gives me 10 out of 10 – a line that is shamefully edited out of the programme as broadcast. Dylan isn't there to see my triumph. He is 'away on business'.

Next up is more dessert but this time it is my own creation. I have conjured up some class of mousse on a base of hazelnut biscuit with a layer of popping candy and I will serve it with a beautiful raspberry coulis, vanilla cream, brandy snap sails and some wild flowers.

Except I won't. After my trifle success I am cocky – too cocky. With just 10 minutes to go, I take the mousse out of the mould but it won't come. It falls apart. Then I fall apart. I cobble together a dessert with the help of Nick. He advises me to put more chocolate on top to hide my sins. The other judges taste it and decide there is too much chocolate on top. Dylan glowers and I think it is game over. But Tracy, who made blue cheese ice-cream, goes instead. She was robbed.

A week on and it is my turn for the bullet. When it comes, the only thing that surprises me is the reason. We are hosting a lunch for our celebrity friends and running a replica restaurant. I have been given another dessert to make – almost as if

the producers are deliberately trying to stress me out – and I know my time is up but I am fine with that. I don't want to suffer another mousse attack so am still kind of stressed, and all through the day I am more Mr Bean than Mrs Beeton.

I make an unholy mess of my work station but am not overly concerned. The day passes and I quite enjoy the experience. Dylan doesn't. He calls me a pig and seems cross because I have gone with square pieces of shortbread rather than the rectangles he wanted (yes, he cares that much). My chef's jacket, which looks like it has been discarded by a serial killer, infuriates him.

I serve the dessert to my celebrity 'friend' – the model Roz Purcell. A woman I have met for the first time today is, for the purpose of the telly, my celebrity friend – I don't have any celebrity friends in real life, you see.

Sidney Gavignet's yacht, **Omanair Musandam,** *with Irish sailor Damian Foxall on board, passes the Fastnet Rock during the biennial Rolex Fastnet Race. Photograph: David Branigan/Oceansport.*

Once the orders are up, I breathe. I think I have done okay, not enough to avoid being sacked, but okay.

We line up. Dylan tells me, in a grave voice, that I have put too much lavender in my Prosecco gloop (not a cheffy term) and my pears now have a soapy taste. I take his criticism on the chin even though it is completely wrong.

There is hardly any lavender in my pears because I completely messed up the recipe. I poached the fruit for an hour and, with seconds to go before they were due to come out, I realised I'd forgotten the poxy lavender. So I dumped a mountain of it in. Then Dylan came along, saw the strong-smelling purple flowers floating in my pears and assumed the worst. It is true what they say about people starting to eat with their eyes.

Lavendergate aside, it was the right decision to take back my apron. The four remaining chefs – Yvonne, Maia, David and Aengus – are all much better than me and I was glad my time had come. Weeks on, I still wake in the middle of the night screaming about collapsing mousse and burnt shortbread.

My *MasterChef* hell is over. For the people left behind, it is only just starting.

TUESDAY, 6 AUGUST 2013

Three Cracked Pillars of a Failed State

Fintan O'Toole

In 1980, in his first Fianna Fáil ardfheis as taoiseach, Charles Haughey described Northern Ireland as a 'failed political entity'. He was right, of course. But: black pots, black kettles; glasshouses, stones. There was, and is, more than one failed political entity on this island.

Back then, when Haughey used this infamous phrase, there was a rather sterile argument about partition. Was it a historical inevitability or a grotesque tragedy? We can now see that the answer, as it usually is in Irish history, is 'both'. Given the lack of any serious engagement with Ulster unionism by Irish nationalists, partition was probably unavoidable. But that does not make its consequences less drastic. It produced two deeply flawed and ultimately unsustainable political entities.

They failed in radically different ways: one through violent explosion, the other through slow implosion. The fate of the southern State is much more complex and ambiguous than that of the northern statelet, and it has the immense advantage of retaining the broad allegiance of most of its citizens. Yet those ambiguities should not mask its ultimate failure. And that failure should be seen as a challenge and an opportunity – it invites us to radically rethink the State.

The failure of the State can be calibrated in many ways: the unwillingness to protect vulnerable citizens from slavery and abuse, the inability to sustain a modest prosperity, the apparently endemic resort to mass emigration, the descent into systemic corruption, the throwing away of hard-won sovereignty, the persistence of structural inequality. But we can also see it even if we look at the State in its simplest expression as a set of institutions.

The State as established under the 1922 and 1937 Constitutions is a classic, three-pillared democracy. It is built on the structure designed in the 18th century by Locke and Montesquieu: the separation of powers between the executive, the legislature and the legal system. But each of these pillars is so badly cracked that any honest inspector would have to condemn the building they support.

This is hardly, at this point, a controversial statement. Every serious observer in recent decades has pointed out, again and again, that the legislature does not originate legislation, scrutinises legislation in a wholly inadequate way (more than half of all Bills under the current government have been rushed through under the guillotine), and seldom holds to account the executive that,

The Middle East peace negotiations back on track . . . as seen by Martyn Turner.

through the whip system, exerts almost complete control over it.

The legal system, meanwhile, has proved itself to be almost entirely powerless in bringing to justice those who commit those crimes that are most corrosive of social order: corruption, fraud, tax evasion, bribery, perjury, market abuse, corporate recklessness. It has therefore failed to uphold its own most basic principle – equality before the law. There is a rough but real distinction: poor criminals go to jail; rich and/or well-connected criminals enjoy a very large measure of impunity.

The weakness of these two pillars of the State is long established. What is new is the virtual collapse of the third. The executive is now crumbling too. The Constitution is clear about what the executive branch of government is: the cabinet acting as a whole. But cabinet government is now itself in crisis. The most consequential

economic decision in the history of the State, the blanket bank guarantee of September 2008, was made when most of the cabinet was not present and when, according to themselves, the absent members had little understanding of what they were agreeing on the phone.

Since then, we have seen that the budget has been passed on for examination by the finance committee of the Bundestag in Berlin before going to the Cabinet in Dublin. And we know, not least from a senior minister such as Joan Burton, that economic and budgetary decisions are being made not by the Cabinet but by the (all-male) Economic Management Council of Enda Kenny, Eamon Gilmore, Michael Noonan and Brendan Howlin, along with unelected and unaccountable advisors. In the most important areas, cabinet government has been replaced by arrangements outside the constitutional structures of the State.

One might argue that there is, in fact, a fourth pillar of the State: direct popular sovereignty through referendums. If so, this pillar is cracked, too. The referendum on the Seanad will present us with a 'choice' scarcely anyone wants: between abolishing bicameral parliaments and keeping a rotten and absurd institution.

Even without considering failures of policy or achievement, it ought to be obvious that the southern State is a 'failed political entity'. Does this mean it is a 'failed State' in the same sense as, say, Somalia is? Of course not: we have a functioning army, police force and bureaucracy and public services that, however strained and inadequate, meet the requirements of a modern society. But it is a failed State in the simple and obvious sense that none of its institutional arms is in working order.

The first step to recovery is honest acknowledgement of the scale of the problem. Piecemeal, symbolic 'reforms' will do nothing except deepen the sense of disillusionment. Facing up to failure can give us the courage to start again.

THURSDAY, 15 AUGUST 2013

Rob Heffernan Has the Walk of His Life

Ian O'Riordan

That good old time again. The where did it all begin. The who is behind it. The when exactly did Rob Heffernan believe he could be world champion. The how on earth did he pull it all off so utterly brilliantly, smiling, both hands waving free, in the most grimacing of athletics events.

Not so easily done, actually. No race ever begins on the starting line, no matter how long or short, and no one knows this better than Heffernan himself. Indeed, his journey to the gold medal in the 50km walk defeats both summary and

economy – which is a good thing, because no moderate or concise praise would be worthy of what went into his moment of triumph in Moscow.

How entirely fitting too that Heffernan must also wait that bit longer to get his hands on that gold medal, and must set out on another little walk, back into the Luzhniki Stadium this evening, for the victory ceremony: because it's been such a long time coming, and if the 35-year-old from Cork hasn't run out of smiles and tears by then it might just be the most emotionally charged medal presentation of these entire World Championships.

One person who won't be there, nor can't be there, will, he believes, be looking down. Because the one person Heffernan will be thinking about more than anyone else is his mother, Maureen, who died tragically in a domestic accident just days before he was set to compete at the last World Championships, two years ago in Daegu.

'My mam would have been so proud of me,' he said, openly addressing the matter on several occasions in the aftermath of his victory. 'People go on about the disappointment of sport. But when she passed away it was the saddest, saddest time of my life, and I wouldn't wish it on my worst enemy. When I was coming through today, feeling good, I realised you have to appreciate the good times, enjoy them while you can. You use that stuff for strength, of course. But this is a big turnaround from a couple of years ago.'

That it all happened exactly 30 years to the day – 14 August – since Eamonn Coghlan won Ireland's first gold medal, at the inaugural World Championships in Helsinki, over 5,000 metres, has elements of both destiny and familiarity. Like Coghlan, who went to Helsinki on the back of a fourth place finish at the Olympics – indeed twice – Heffernan came to Moscow seeking some redemption, not least for his fourth place finish at the 50km walk at the London Olympics almost exactly one year ago.

Robert Heffernan wins the men's 50km walk final at the 2013 IAAF World Championships at the
Luzhniki Stadium in Moscow. Photograph: Loic Venance/AFP.

Challenging for medals

'People go on about medals,' he said, 'but for the last 11 years I've been challenging for medals. For some reason or another I hadn't yet won one. I still thought I had a great performance in London, even though it wasn't a medal. I did everything I could. I still performed. This year I just had a better support team, starting with my wife, Marian. I've trained really well this year, but kept it simple. Marian took a step back from her own athletics career to support me and has been with me all year. All I had to worry about was racing. Everything else is taken care of.'

He noted, however, that he'll be taking care of Marian for the next while, given she's now four months pregnant: 'Yeah I'll have to put the hard yards back in when I get home. The tables will turn.'

What is certain is that none of it happened by accident, and if his support team starts with his wife and now coach, Marian, it continues with his physio, Emma Gallivan, of Athletics Ireland, his strength coach at the Fitness Worx gym in Cork, Robbie Williams, his son Cathal and daughter Meghan, his father Bobby, and the long, long list of previous coaches and mentors, from the time John Hayes took him under his wing at Togher athletic club, the likes of Ray Flynn and Michael Lane at Athletics Ireland, former walkers Yvonne Cassin and Pierce O'Callaghan, and his former physio and chief motivator Liam O'Reilly.

It must also include Irish team manager Patsy McGonagle, who risked possible imprisonment in Moscow yesterday by breaching the stadium security so that Marian could get through the finish line to greet her husband, or indeed when

Clare senior hurling manager Davy Fitzgerald celebrates his side's first goal in their All-Ireland hurling semi-final win over Limerick. Photograph: James Crombie/Inpho.

McGonagle himself kissed Heffernan on the lips, live on Russian television. It was McGonagle who also had to knock on Heffernan's hotel door two years ago, in Daegu, to tell him about his mother's death.

'Sure we've been 15 years on the road together,' said McGonagle, 'and to win that gold medal, in the way he did, was just unbelievable, really. In fairness, all the indications were that Rob was in the shape of his life. But he still had to go out there and deliver. Everything about his body language was perfect, these last few days, and there was a real sense of calm, that he was just ready for the battle.'

A battle was what Heffernan had always expected – so much so that he'd built it up as his Rocky Balboa moment, going to Moscow to take on the Russians in the one event they believed they would be unbeatable. It looked that way, for a brief while, after the Russian pair of Mikhail Ryzhov and Ivan Noskov set off early in search of gold: Heffernan waited patiently, rolling with the little punches, before winning with a knockout – his time of three hours, 37 minutes and 56 seconds – just two seconds off his own Irish record – giving him over a minute to spare on Ryzhov.

'Everything just seemed to align for me today,' he said. 'But I said it earlier in the year, I wanted the Rocky story, to come from a very humble background and make it to the top of the world. It shows as well that anyone can do it, if they have the talent, and if they train right.'

Walking career

If there was an absolute beginning to his walking career it was in second year at Coláiste Chríost Rí, when his PE teacher was looking to fill the last few places for a team they were sending to the Munster schools track and field championships. The last vacancy was in the junior boys walk, so they looked around at the few boys still left waiting for a spot and picked on the little man Heffernan. He was asked to walk one length of the sports hall, then asked to sign the sheet.

By then he'd already tried his hand in several sports, or at least those that would have him. He did taekwondo for four years, and also played some underage Gaelic football with Nemo Rangers, before realising he just wasn't big enough, no matter how hard he tried. He also tried hurling once, too, but broke his thumb, and that put him off that.

When the chance came to walk in the Munster schools for Coláiste Chríost Rí he took it up as a challenge, something different, given he'd already done well enough in cross country running, and did so throughout secondary school. In fifth year, at a time when Sonia O'Sullivan, Marcus O'Sullivan and Mark Carroll were his big heroes, he was actually lined up with a running scholarship in America, but by then he had fallen in love with walking, the intricate technicalities of it, which suited both his body and mind.

He was selected for the 1997 European Junior Championships in Slovenia, where despite travelling with considerable hopes of actually medalling, with a bit of the Roy Keane mentality, he ended up last, about eight minutes behind the winner.

'Later that year I went through a bit of a growth spurt,' he explained, and that meant to the height he now is – five feet, seven and a half inches. He also weighed in at around 55kg, same as he does now, too – except that he does allow himself fill out to around 65kg, in the off season, to give him something to work off in the long, hard months of training. By the time he left school, he was effectively a full-time walker, although he still had plenty more learning to do: he went to the European under-23 championships in Gothenburg in 1999, and while he also finished at the back of the field, it made him realise he wasn't training half hard enough. He upped the tempo again and qualified for the Sydney Olympics, setting off as a 22-year-old which assured him, even though he finished 28th, that race walking was exactly what he wanted to do with his life.

Inquisitive, cranky geese in Ballyduff, Co. Waterford. Photograph: Michael MacSweeney/Provision.

Questioned commitment

Not that Heffernan hasn't sometimes questioned his commitment: his son Cathal and daughter Meghan were among the horde of Irish supporters that lined the route of The Mall last summer for the 50km walk, and after finishing fourth, he looked at them with that sense of double wonder. 'Seeing the kids here reminds me,' he said, 'because you're missing some of them growing up, going to their matches and going to their races, you miss out on a lot of stuff like that. Or not being able to go out and kick around with them because you risk making your leg sore for training. Or having to sleep during the day.'

A year after Sydney, he sent an email to Polish race walker Robert Korzeniowski, widely regarded as the best ever, asking for some advice, and instead ended up joining his group. So began a personally close and yet somewhat professionally distant relationship that lasted a few years, before Heffernan essentially realised he was just a pawn in that game.

'I remember him saying I'd never walk a 50k,' Heffernan recalled yesterday, passing Korzeniowski on each 2km lap of the Moscow course. 'He was my biggest inspiration ever, and my biggest motivation today, as well, to prove him wrong. I knew he'd want me to win it as well, in a good way.'

After that, when Heffernan needed somebody he could trust the most, he trusted himself. 'It's surreal, a great feeling,' he said, not long after crossing the finish line in Moscow yesterday, 'because when I came into the stadium, it felt like an out-of-body experience. I was looking up at the screen, thinking 'this fella looks good, like' . . . So I just rolled with it and enjoyed the last lap.'

216

TUESDAY, 20 AUGUST 2013

Boyfriend Kyle Takes a Gamble on Molly as Roses Stay on Message

Patrick Freyne

So there's Dáithí Ó Sé in a mardi-gras outfit, looking like a member of George Clinton's funk band, grooving alongside mask-wearing New Orleans lady Molly Molloy Gambel.

Then out comes Molly Molloy's boyfriend Kyle Catlett and asks her to marry him in front of around half a million people. 'No, no, no!' she said, before saying 'yes' ('I was saying no because I couldn't believe it was happening,' she said afterwards).

But that's just the most newsworthy part of the evening. Now Dáithí's watching Leitrim woman Edwina Guckian whip part of her dress off (not quite Bucks Fizz-style) in order to dance energetic sean-nós with a barrel and a brush. And now he's being given a certificate of Newfoundland citizenship by Erica Halfyard after kissing a fish and quaffing a shot of rum.

Dáithí probably calls this 'a typical Monday', but the rest of us call it the *Rose of Tralee*, an annual explosion of bizarro-loveliness in which 32 young ladies from across the diaspora ('a sort of positive disease' as Alan Partridge recently explained the word) vie to be named after a tragic tubercular 19th-century maid.

It's kind of amazing – 2,000 family members, escorts, judges, ex-Roses and ex-escorts wave banners and cheer as 18 Roses chat amiably, recite poetry, sing emigrant ballads and Disney songs and play light classical piano.

Performances have titles like Destination Donegal and I am Kerry (guess which Roses did which). None have titles like Laois is a Hole or Get me out of Drogheda!

Last year Daisy the cow got stage fright (Dáithí was going to milk her live). This year Clare Rose Marie Donnellan, who confidently emerged to the theme of *Father Ted* (the festival is impervious to mockery), shows us a safer 'picture' of a cow given as a present by her wellie-wearing escort.

'But what he doesn't realise is that we'll be down with a trailer to collect the calf.'

Monaghan's Eleanor McQuaid emerges with a hurl and a shinty stick to teach Dáithí the difference ('Is it wise to give him a weapon?' a crew member whispers at rehearsal). Later a bed is brought to the stage, Darwin Rose Bridget Haines dons spectacles, and Dáithí is regaled with a bedtime story, 'The Cranky Bear'. She promises to take him back to childhood.

'Don't open that can of worms!' a nation shouts at the telly.

Everyone I meet in Tralee fondly recall past festivals. Dáithí himself has teenage memories of 'sleeping eight or nine of us in someone's sitting room' or 'getting a bus back to Dingle at three in the morning with everyone drunk'.

The mother of a Rosebud tells me about 'a huge tent filled with jockeys who used to stay out the back of my uncle's house'.

My taxi driver, Seán, also remembers gardens

Kyle Catlett proposes to his girlfriend, New Orleans Rose Molly Molloy Gambel, live on stage during the Rose of Tralee festival.
Photograph: Domnick Walsh/Eye Focus.

filled with tents. 'But then at some point the pubs started charging in,' he says. 'And that killed it for a while, the greed.'

There is some sense that since Anthony O'Gara came in and successfully reorganised the financially struggling festival 10 years ago there are two separate events.

There's the family-focused street entertainment in the town and there's a glitzy showbizzy affair on the edge of it. Over breakfast the woman at the B&B said, 'You'll notice that the crowd at the Dome is a little more . . .' she pauses meaningfully, '. . . select than in the town.'

Going to the Dome after being at the parade is like going to the Green Zone in Iraq. It means becoming an embedded journalist. Everyone there is a true believer in a pressed frock/suit or a tight-lipped professional carrying a piece of studio equipment.

At the rehearsals, Dáithí encouraged individual Roses ('that story will get a good reaction') as a stage manager gently manoeuvres them into position.

Sometimes the Roses seem a little tired, their strange wrist-only waves degenerate into flapping, they accidentally utter unRose-like curse words and a coterie of escorts and chaperones step into the breach ('I don't know what to do. I'm a Rose, I need to be led!' jokes one frazzled Rose).

But in general they're self-possessed, relentlessly positive and terrifyingly on message. Even more so en masse. As a crop of Roses march officiously by, heels clacking, fascinators (a type of head sculpture) jauntily perched on their heads, the effect is almost militaristic.

'We say "one team, one dream",' says Donegal Rose Catherine McCarron. 'We support each other. You spend so much time together you do become close, because they're the only people who know how you're feeling. You're sharing this incredible experience with them.'

'It's a sisterhood,' Philadelphia Rose Brittany Killion agrees.

And yes, I joke about the waving and smiling, but sometimes a smile means a lot.

Cork Rose Edel Buckley is raising awareness for Myasthenia Gravis, a neuromuscular auto-immune condition which once affected her so much she couldn't physically smile.

After painful treatments she's now a smiling, waving, tug-of-war playing contender in the *Rose of Tralee*.

'I loved *Rose of Tralee* as a little girl,' she says. 'I loved the girls, the community, the glamour, but then the condition hit me and I couldn't smile. I avoided photos and thought that was never going to happen.'

She smiles. It's happening now.

Up on stage Dáithí Ó Sé is doing a funny dance.

SATURDAY, 24 AUGUST 2013

Andy Moran's Steady Hand on the Mayo Tiller

Keith Duggan

Minutes after Mayo had beaten Dublin in the All-Ireland semi-final of 2006, an elated Mickey Moran recalled a conversation that he had with Andy Moran just before he sent him into the match with 46 minutes gone.

'Andy Moran is a substitute. Usually a half forward. And we were putting him in for James Nallen. He turns to me and says: "I will get you a goal". That's what he said. "I will get you a goal."'

If the Derry man was speaking aloud to somehow make sense of his thoughts and the extraordinary emotional surge through which Mayo somehow recovered from a seven-point deficit to beat Dublin through Ciarán McDonald's late score – half left foot point, half epiphany – then it was understandable.

Andy Moran by James Crombie/Inpho.

Everything about Mayo was predicated on ungovernable emotion in those years and that day of days surpassed all others.

It wasn't just that the Mayo players had provoked the strange stand-off in front of Hill 16 by deciding to warm up at the Dublin end of the ground or that the team was a patchwork of promising young players, veterans from the championship years of 1996/97 and, most evocatively, the returning brilliance of Kevin O'Neill, who had been largely ignored by Mayo selectors since 1993.

It was that everything about the day deepened the conviction that with Mayo, anything could happen. So if Moran was attributing a little bit of prophesy to his player's promise, it didn't seem out of place.

Andy Moran had gone on as a wing back and he had duly concocted a goal that gave Mayo's stunning surge an unstoppable momentum. On that evening, anything seemed possible for Mayo football.

But instead of leading to the long coveted All-Ireland title, it brought only another September defeat, the second in three years at the hands of Kerry. Now, that victory over Dublin is remembered as a moment of isolated splendour rather than the defining moment that set the Westerners on their way.

But seven seasons on, Andy Moran has moved from the versatile cameo player to the embodiment of the new mood and attitude within Mayo football.

By the end of 2006, Moran was at once a young player and a veteran of Mayo's unhappy relationship with All-Ireland finals. In 2004, he was a substitute in the senior final defeat against Kerry and a week later played in the All-Ireland U-21 defeat against Armagh.

'I reckon we need to break our duck,' John Maughan, who managed both sides, said after that U-21 match. 'A victory like that would have lifted our spirits. We need lifting down here, to be honest.'

But nothing, not even the return of John O'Mahony, could nudge the county senior team any closer to All-Ireland victory until the appointment of James Horan – a dark horse choice to succeed O'Mahony – introduced a new directness to the Mayo game. Andy Moran has been central to that.

Last September, he watched as non-playing captain of the team as Mayo lost the third All-Ireland final of his senior career.

In the months afterwards, though, he expressed none of the haunted equivocation which had characterised sentiments in the wake of previous All-Ireland defeats.

'I believe we're going to win more than one, to be honest,' he said a week after Mayo had lost to Donegal. 'If we win, we'll keep going. This is a great group of lads and I wouldn't be surprised in two weeks' time if these lads are back training.'

James Horan since confirmed that he had to dissuade his players from returning to McHale Park such was their anxiety to atone for the loss. And Moran's role in the weeks revolving around that defeat was central. An All-Star in 2011, he had retained that form throughout last summer until his season summarily ended with a cruciate ligament injury in the quarter-final victory over Down.

Horan set the tone by refusing to linger on Moran's injury, stating that the captain would be the first to acknowledge that the injury was an opening for some other player to stake a claim. 'It is disappointing. Andy is the heartbeat of the team – he'd be the first to say that it's an opportunity for someone else.' The refusal to entertain sentiment or to allow the loss to become a reason why Mayo couldn't go on to win set a tone. Moran's luck had been wretched but Mayo went on to decimate Dublin, the All-Ireland champions, in the semi-

final. Suddenly, they were back in a final against Donegal, who had come from nowhere under Jim McGuinness. It was the most novel All-Ireland final in decades and Moran, the captain in crutches, became a cause for the team.

It didn't happen, of course, and so Moran found himself in a Mayo dressing room after an All-Ireland defeat for the third time in his career. And yet just a week after that defeat, he gave a calm and logical appraisal of what he had witnessed from the stands.

'Did we lose to a better team over 70 minutes? We probably did. For the last 60 minutes, how good were we? I'd say we were as good a team as they were.'

The ethos and attitude was plain to see. In those few sentences, Moran did much to dispel the vague notion that there is some hidden force field preventing Mayo from winning an All-Ireland final. It wasn't about the past or curses or collective anxiety or some fatalism within the county; they simply lost because they didn't win.

They just needed to identify their strong points and work on their weaknesses. The lingering concern about Mayo teams has always revolved around the 'baggage' of previous defeats. Yet here was the team captain and a veteran of three huge September losses evincing nothing but can-do positivity and a calm certainty that it wasn't a question of if his Mayo team would win an All-Ireland title, it was a question of how many.

And in the weeks and months after that All-Ireland defeat, it became clear just how immense a figure Andy Moran has become for Mayo. In the space of those seven seasons, he has moved from being Mickey Moran's lucky charm substitute to the Mayo's on- and off-field general. Andy. That's what they call him.

Despite being absent throughout the league as he went through his slow recuperation from injury, Moran's return was to be the signal that all was well within the county. The timing could not have been more perfect, entering late in the day of Mayo's frightening demolition of Galway and scoring a goal. The giddy dance of delight afterwards told everything of how long he had been waiting for that moment. Since then, Moran has, according to himself, tried to reacquaint himself with the pace of championship football. The point he scored in the relentless combination of high-octane quality scores with which Mayo pounded the All-Ireland champions into submission was another private triumph on the long road back.

Now, he is back to where he would have been 12 months ago had injury not ruined his season. At Mayo's press evening last week, Moran sat down to reflect on the season and once again sang of the team ethos, returning to last year's final and the traumatic early minutes when Donegal were 2-1 up and pushing hard for a third goal.

David Clarke's save when Colm McFadden was poised to strike again was of inestimable importance, he argued. Even sitting in the stands, his crutches by his side, he could see that.

'He nearly broke his own leg, he would have broke Colm's leg. But he was going to save that ball. It drove us on.'

And Mayo didn't fall apart. They kept hunting and chasing and were still in the game when the 70 minutes were up.

Despite the disappointment, it gave them more than enough sustenance for the long-term project.

It taught them what they needed to do to win an All-Ireland. So they worked on their tackling, their foot passing, their shooting accuracy and their conditioning. They disguised it well in the league but from the first day out against Galway, their intentions have been clear.

For Moran, much of this year has been about playing catch-up and even as he considered tomorrow's semi-final, he still feels as if he is striving just to return to a place he took for granted for much of his career.

'I don't think I missed a game for six years but the last 24 months have been a bit of a nightmare

in terms of injuries. But I don't worry about the knee. If it is going to go, it is going to go.' And now Mayo and Andy Moran are in a strange position.

Mayo are outright favourites to win this year's All-Ireland. The smart lads expect Andy Moran to become the first Mayo man to lift the Sam Maguire since another Ballaghaderreen man, Sean Flanagan, did so, in the touchstone September of 1951.

Tomorrow they play Tyrone, the most audacious football county of the modern era, managed by the greatest innovator in Mickey Harte. Tyrone didn't so much win three All-Irelands as claim them through Comanche raids. Nobody could live with them.

And yet Mayo are clear favourites to win tomorrow. These are delightful and perilous days for the Westerners. How many boats have gone down with the shore line in sight? In Andy Moran, they have the steadiest captain possible.

SATURDAY, 31 AUGUST 2013

Comfort is Best Found in Seamus Heaney's Poems

Fintan O'Toole

Like all great poets, Seamus Heaney was an alchemist. He turned our disgrace into grace, our petty hatreds into epic generosity, our dull clichés into questioning eloquence, the leaden metal of brutal inevitability into the gold of pure possibility.

He lacked the arrogance to tell us who we are – much more importantly, he told us *what* we are. He reminded us that Ireland is a culture before it is an economy. And in the extraordinary way he bore himself, the dignity and decency and the mellow delight that shone from him, he gave us self-respect.

In *The Tempest,* Miranda exclaims, 'O brave new world, / That has such people in it.'

Seamus Heaney by Neil Drabble/Camera Press.

Seamus Heaney made us gasp in wonder that, for all its follies and terrors, Irish culture had such a person in it.

He was out and about again this spring and summer, reading, opening, presiding, blessing. After he suffered a stroke in 2006, he had cut down on his public engagements, resisting the incessant clamour for his presence. But this year he seemed happy to be a public man again.

He had something to convey – especially, it seemed, to his fellow citizens. It was what his whole life as a poet had articulated with such astounding eloquence. In a speech at the National Museum in March he put it directly: 'We are not simply a credit rating or an economy but a history and a culture, a human population rather than a statistical phenomenon.'

No one did so much to make us feel like

creatures of a long-working imagination rather than figments of a short-term market.

Great poets speak for themselves but they also create the voices through which something beyond themselves finds articulation. What Heaney articulated, above all, was the way in which – in the words of his friend Brian Friel – confusion need not be an ignoble condition. He grew up in a literally divided landscape – 'the lines of sectarian antagonism and affiliation', he wrote, 'followed the boundaries of the land' — and lived through the hopes and horrors of the Troubles.

He was drawn to both Irish and English poetic traditions. He also lived through the death of the ancient rural world into which he was born and the emergence of a globalised modern Ireland. He struggled with contradictions, paradoxes, conflicting impulses.

His genius lay in his ability to hover between them, to give each side of a political or emotional equation its full weight and proper due without becoming the prisoner of either. W.B. Yeats, the poet whose influence he both absorbed and transcended, wrote in a time of Irish violence that 'we are closed in and the key is turned / On our uncertainty'.

Heaney told us that, though we are indeed fated to uncertainty, it need not necessarily be a locked room in which we play out the same scenarios of doom over and over. Uncertainty may simply be the human condition. Heaney humanised uncertainty, made ambiguity rich with possibilities. As he put it in the beautifully homely metaphor of *Terminus*:

'Two buckets were easier carried than one. I grew up in between.'

He was not, in that sense, a national poet. He knew too much about the dangers of tribalism and the foolishness of slogans to ever want to be a spokesman for the collective. He would have agreed with Yeats's dictum that 'We make out of the quarrel with others, rhetoric, but of the quarrel with ourselves, poetry.'

In Heaney's *The Flight Path,* an IRA sympathiser has his demands for political commitment refused:

'When, for fuck's sake, are you going to write Something for us? If I do write something, Whatever it is, I'll be writing for myself.'

But that self was never selfish. It was always open, sensitive, attuned to the signals emanating, not just from nature and memory, but from politics and history too. With the outbreak of the Troubles, as he put it, 'the problems of poetry moved from being simply a matter of achieving the satisfactory verbal icon to being a search for images and symbols adequate to our predicament'. This was his lifelong quest – for images and symbols adequate to the predicament of being alive in his own time.

What forced him to be great, what kept him on his mettle, was that this quest was for him a very hard struggle. His world, the world of his childhood to which he returned so often and with such breathtaking clarity of recall, was archaic: farmers ploughing with horses, thatchers making roofs from rushes, diviners finding hidden sources of water, blacksmiths working in their forges. He could have lived imaginatively only in that world, as a nostalgic romantic, purveyor of hand-woven verbal tweeds. He fought instead to make his art contemporary, to put it under the pressure of its times.

He was often racked, indeed, by a sense that this art was in fact inadequate. The image of his cousin Colum McCartney, murdered in a sectarian attack, haunted him: 'blood and roadside muck in your hair and eyes'.

But he knew too that there was an immense human value in the act of writing with infinite care and utter honesty, in the way poetry acts as an antidote to the murderous clichés of slogans and rhetoric. Heaney recalled of himself and his fellow Belfast-based poets in the early 1960s that they were buoyed by a belief 'that the tolerances and subtleties of their art were precisely what they had to set against the repetitive intolerance of public life'.

That belief may have seemed naive in the bleakest years of the Troubles, but in the longer perspective of history it was vindicated. It was not accidental that, when politicians reached for a language adequate to the unfolding of new possibilities for peace, they took Heaney's 'hope and history rhyme' off the shelf again and again. The poet in Heaney was surely wearied by hearing his new-minted phrase worn away into cliché, but the citizen in him would have regarded the sacrifice as well worth making.

The great maker of such phrases will not be lost, for he is among the immortals now. But the great citizen, the exemplary public man who gave a gentle gravity to our small affairs, who blessed our ordinary days with intimations of the extraordinary, is a devastating loss to Irish life. We can take comfort where we will best find it: in his own luminous poems. There we will find a recurrent image of marks that have been erased in physical reality but go on existing.

He wrote of 'the dotted line my father's ashplant made on Sandymount Strand,' a line long

since washed away but visible to his mind's eye. He wrote of boys continuing to play football after the light has faded and the lines of the pitch have become invisible:

> Youngsters shouting their heads off in a field
> As the light died and they kept on playing
> Because by then they were playing in their heads . . .

Seamus Heaney's grace will play in our heads long after his earthly light has faded.

SATURDAY, 7 SEPTEMBER 2013

Michael Lynn's Second Life

Ruadhán Mac Cormaic

'The World Awaits.' For Michael Lynn the slogan draped across the facade of the Britanic language school must have sounded more like a taunt than a promise. Lynn, the man who amassed millions selling the dream of fortunes in foreign lands, found himself in northeastern Brazil because his own world was contracting, his options narrowing. 'I would say he was already in a sort of open prison,' says Mark Astle, the director of the school.

The archetypal prince of the Irish boom, a small-time solicitor who refashioned himself as a global property tycoon, found himself 8,000km from home, in a country where he didn't speak the language, applying for a €640-a-month job as a part-time tutor.

What Recife did offer, however, thanks to the lack of an extradition treaty between Ireland and Brazil, was sanctuary from the pursuit of the Irish authorities. But even that may now turn out to have been illusory. Last week, six years after Lynn fled Ireland with debts of €80 million and a trail of furious investors in his wake, police in Recife were ordered to act on a 'code red' Interpol alert and

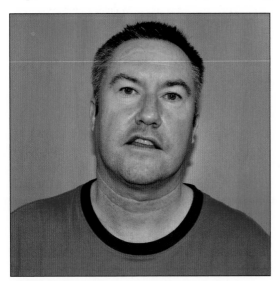

Michael Lynn at the time of his arrest in Recife.
Photograph: Federal Police of Brazil.

Michael Lynn (centre) with pupils from the Britanic
School in Recife, Brazil.
Photograph: Britanic school website.

arrest the 44-year-old Irishman. Within a few hours they had tracked him down.

As Recife awoke from the Brazilian winter this week, blue skies bringing joggers and families to its glorious white-sand beaches, the city looked every bit the rising South American metropolis. Expensive hotels and restaurants stretch along the seafront, a fine new stadium has been built for next year's World Cup, and car dealerships have begun to diversify into the yacht business.

The economy in Recife, the capital of Pernambuco state and Brazil's fifth-largest city, has been outpacing the national juggernaut for years, and unemployment is now running at just 6 per cent. Foreign firms such as Fiat and Microsoft have huge facilities here, and the city has been making a hefty return from regionally produced commodities such as ethanol. The bonanza has been affected only slightly by the global economic downturn.

'For Pernambuco, this is the best moment for 50 years,' says Paulo César Maia Porto, one of Lynn's lawyers.

Yet the spectacular coastline and roaring economy can't mask some of the city's problems, in particular its high rates of poverty and serious crime. Although Rio de Janeiro's drug wars make international headlines, the murder rate in Recife is

58 per 100,000 – more than twice that of Rio. In 2009 there was an average of 12 murders a day, and a screen was mounted in the city centre to keep track of the death toll.

In so many areas of daily life the city's infrastructure has struggled to keep up. Roads can become impassable after a downpour, and traffic is so bad that it can take three hours to travel 40km across the city's outer belt in rush hour. Even the azure sea is notoriously menacing: swimming is prohibited because of frequent shark attacks.

The life that Lynn and his wife, Bríd Murphy, built reflects some of the city's paradoxes. The couple, who have a two-year-old son, rent a house in Candeias, a suburb where middle-class families are buying luxury apartments built alongside favelas and open sewers.

Living in a house is an unusual – and, for most, prohibitively expensive – choice in Recife, where the most sought-after home is an upper-floor apartment facing the sea.

But acquaintances say Lynn was determined to find a house. The family have three dogs, two cats and some birds. They wanted more space. What they found was a large house with a swimming pool and a garden in a walled compound surrounded by barbed wire. The road outside is unpaved and has no street lamps. 'If you want to live in a house there are very few opportunities,' Astle says. 'And if you have one you have to surround yourself with barbed wire, security systems and dogs . . . I wouldn't want it myself.'

Presumably, Lynn accepted these trade-offs because he had a reason to be in Recife. To some of those who know him that reason is obvious: Recife is in the midst of a residential property boom and, as one colleague puts it, 'That's what he knows.'

All along the seafront, family homes have made way for soaring apartment blocks that offer uninterrupted ocean views. Every street in certain parts of Candeias seems to have a glass-fronted Portakabin selling apartments off the plans. In one of these, for a half-built development called Helena Borges, a salesman named Eduardo hands out brochures with pictures of immaculate white living rooms and private gyms. A two-bedroom apartment on the 11th floor costs the equivalent of €103,000. 'It's quiet, it's calm, it's near the beach,' he says. One of his apartments has already been snapped up by an Irishman named Peter, he adds.

Few saw Lynn's arrest coming. He certainly didn't. According to a federal police spokesman, Giovani Santoro, Lynn was calm when he was brought to the station but taken aback by what was happening. 'He said he knew this could happen to him some day, but he didn't think it would happen in Brazil,' Santoro says. 'He was surprised.'

This tallies with other accounts of Lynn's time in Recife, where he lived openly and made little attempt to hide his problems back home. He was also planning for the future: *The Irish Times* has learned that he was building a house for the family on the outskirts of the city.

His confidence was understandable. For six years Lynn had evaded the Irish authorities, a host of financial institutions and the many investors who lost large sums when his property empire collapsed. In Brazil, he believed, the fact that there was no extradition treaty put him beyond Dublin's reach. And if that didn't offer enough protection then the permanent residence status secured through the birth of his son in Brazil surely would.

Sarah King and Amanda Gallagher from Loreto College, St Stephen's Green, react as Joey, the life-sized equine puppet from the English National Theatre's production of War Horse, *operated by puppeteers Jack Parker, Stuart Angel and Mikey Brett, rears up on the stage of the Bord Gáis Energy Theatre in Dublin where the production is to be staged in 2014. Photograph: Alan Betson.*

His arrest is a dramatic turn in an already remarkable story. The man from Crossmolina, Co. Mayo, became a solicitor in the mid-1990s and built a practice specialising in litigation and property conveyancing, giving him a close-up view as Irish property developers' overseas interests began to take off. Lynn wanted a piece of the action.

Working from his law practice in the Capel Building, near the Four Courts, he founded Kendar Holdings, which built apartments in Leitrim and offices in Cavan but soon expanded overseas, starting with a 272-apartment development in the Portuguese Algarve in late 2003.

Specialising in overseas investment property, Kendar grew quickly, earning a reputation for savvy marketing by recruiting celebrities such as the Portuguese footballer Rui Costa. At one point he gave away an apartment in a Bulgarian ski resort on *The Late Late Show*; it was one of the programme's biggest prizes.

By the time Kendar collapsed in 2007, Lynn had 148 properties, 154 bank accounts and assets worth more than €50 million. All the time he had continued to run his legal practice.

Concerns about Lynn's activities came to light in October 2007, when the Law Society, the body that regulates solicitors in Ireland, shut down Lynn's legal practice amid concerns about his property dealings and borrowings. An investigation by the Law Society found he had used his practice's client account for personal dealings and there had been a flow of money between his practice and property business.

In December 2007, the Law Society was due to cross-examine Lynn in the High Court. It intended to press him on his property dealings, particularly his drawing down of multiple mortgages using solicitors' undertakings, a trust mechanism lawyers use in residential-property transactions. It has been alleged that Lynn used these undertakings to draw down multiple loans and build up enormous debts. But Lynn never showed up. A bench warrant was issued for his arrest, but by then he had already fled. He left with bank claims of €80 million against him and owing many millions to investors who paid deposits for his properties in Portugal, Bulgaria, Hungary and Slovakia.

Lynn was struck off the roll of solicitors and looked into by the Garda Bureau of Fraud Investigation. That long-running inquiry culminated in February last year with the Director of Public Prosecutions recommending that he be charged, paving the way for the issuing of an international arrest warrant. According to Brazilian sources, the extradition request from the Irish authorities states that they intend to bring 33 charges against Lynn.

In a rare interview in 2009, Lynn said that although his extensive borrowings were misguided, he does not believe he acted fraudulently. 'The one thing I want to make clear is that I am not going to be a scapegoat for others,' he said. 'I am not going to be used as an example of what was recognised as an acceptable form and practice of business by bankers, lawyers, accountants and auctioneers. I am not going to be the poster boy who ends up in prison to my cost alone.'

Little is known about the solicitor's movements after he left Ireland. He spent some time in Portugal and sightings were reported in Bulgaria, New York and London. In August 2009, he was interviewed by police in Budapest, but he could not be extradited to Ireland because there were no criminal charges against him at the time.

The Brazilian connection had been established well before Lynn's property empire collapsed. Company records for Kendar Holdings showed that, in early 2007, Lynn was planning to buy four plots of land in Brazil worth €686,000. He also planned to set up a 'property speculation arm' in Brazil, according to a draft business plan for the company written in late 2006. The same plan said one of the company's strengths was that it had a 'visionary owner' in Lynn, who was 'prepared to take bold decisions'.

Inquiries by the Brazilian police show Lynn entered the country for the first time in 2007, and then three more times up to 2011. Since settling in the country Lynn has established ties to three cities. He and Murphy were listed as the owners of Golina, a property firm whose papers were first lodged in November 2007 in Fortaleza, a coastal city in the north. Separate files show that in 2011 and 2012 the couple declared their home address in Jardins, a wealthy suburb of São Paulo, the country's commercial capital.

By the summer of 2012, Lynn was working at Britanic language school in Recife, and in October that year he and his wife registered a property company, Quantum Assessoria E Empreendimentos (Quantum Consulting and Ventures) Ltd, which remains active. Lynn is believed to be involved in a venture in Cabo de Santo Agostina, 35km south of Recife, where demand for housing has surged as a result of the expansion of nearby Suape, one of the biggest ports in Brazil. Lynn, it appears, was back in business.

By the time of his arrest in Recife, Lynn had settled into a routine that centred on his home, the school and occasional trips to a golf and country club where he would bring his son to see the horses. 'He had a very regular pattern,' says Santoro, the police spokesman. 'He would go to the school where he taught, go out with his wife, go to the shops.'

In order to get to Lynn, Dublin knew it had to strike a deal with the Brazilians. According to Minister for Justice Alan Shatter, the two states recently decided to begin talks on an extradition treaty; they also agreed that, pending the conclusion of the treaty, they would treat extradition requests from each other on the basis of reciprocity. Once that was agreed, Dublin duly issued a request through Interpol for Lynn to be sent home.

Since his arrest nine days ago, the Irishman has been held in a unit reserved for university graduates and ex-policemen at Cotel prison, on the outskirts of Recife. He can be held for up to 90 days unless his lawyers succeed in having him released on bail. Astle says Lynn appeared calm when he saw him briefly at the police station on the day of his arrest, but Astle recalls Murphy telling him her husband was 'very scared'.

Lynn has made it clear he will resist the attempt to extradite him. The Irish authorities are determined to have him returned. And in the middle are the 11 judges of Brazil's Supreme Federal Court.

The closing act is theirs to write.

SATURDAY, 7 SEPTEMBER 2013

Road to Rio Runs out as Trapattoni Faces Trap Door

Malachy Clerkin

The final curtain fell with a clang and a groan and a crowd that could barely raise a boo. Ireland's efforts to qualify for next year's World Cup in Brazil creaked its last with just about as grim a performance as Giovanni Trapattoni's reign has seen. A Sweden side that wasn't a whole pile better went home with a 2–1 victory that owed most to Zlatan Ibrahimovic, who towered over the night like a lighthouse.

There can't have been many less enjoyable nights down at Lansdowne Road. Neither side came to play with any invention and long before half-time the game was the worst kind of tiresome long-ball ping-pong. The two goalkeepers, David Forde and Andreas Isaksson, spent the night launching kicks through the night sky onto the edge of the opposition box. It was soccer as lottery. Spin the tombola and see what comes out.

The one moment of craft in the evening came when Ibrahimovic sent Anders Svensson through on

THE IRISH TIMES BOOK OF THE YEAR

The Republic of Ireland's Glenn Whelan (left) and John O'Shea dejected after Sweden's second goal at the Aviva Stadium in Dublin all but ended their hopes of qualifying for the World Cup in Brazil in 2014. Photograph: James Crombie/Inpho.

the Irish goal on 56 minutes. It was light and perfectly weighted, and when Glenn Whelan's eagerness to chase down Svensson's run only succeeded in playing him onside, the Swedish veteran struck to beat Forde at his near post. Ireland went the rest of the night without creating a chance.

It means that Trapattoni's time in charge will limp to its conclusion very soon – if not in Vienna on Tuesday night then certainly next month. He was still pretty bullish afterwards, insisting that Ireland's players did their jobs. Damned by his own words, in that case.

'We think about what the others can do for us. We obviously need to win against Austria. We might make one or two changes but the players did not play bad. When we have to recover a

disadvantage, we don't have good morale. We have to think about our attitude, our mentality, our personality.

'We have done a great job. Not a good job, a great job. We have changed many players in the squad. We have to be professional. In football anything can happen. Against Austria, we should have won the game. That would have been an extra two points. Against Sweden in Stockholm, we missed three good opportunities – Shane Long, in front of goal. This is football.'

It needed to be one of those nights. One of those where team was extension of nation, where the Swedes weren't so much playing as wading against a tide. Unique among the managers who have qualified Ireland for major tournaments,

Trapattoni lacked the sort of notch on the bedpost that a man could brag about. There was no equivalent to Mick McCarthy's Netherlands or Jack Charlton's Spain.

Last night's version of Sweden hardly belong in that sort of company. Indeed, the main question raised by their visit to Dublin was how in God's name they managed a 4–4 draw with Germany. The affluent ease of Zlatan Ibrahimovic apart, the Swedes are every bit as lumpen as Ireland. But at least it would have been a win – when badly needed – against a serious group rival.

Ireland were hungry from the start, albeit without being altogether picky about what they feasted on or where their table manners were.

They pressed high and they pressed hard, Jon Walters and Shane Long all scuttle and scud around the Swedish defence. Even James McCarthy's best work in the opening period was toe-in rather than foot-on-ball.

By and large, it was an approach that had its way in those early exchanges. In this sort of hunting, hassling mood, Trap's Ireland are like the show-off kid in the school play – enjoyable enough for what it is but when it's over you're happy enough you don't have it in your life all the time. They had Sweden highly unsettled at the back, leading to a handful of potshots from distance by Walters and Glenn Whelan. It wasn't much but it was more than the visitors were able to claim.

Giovanni Trapattoni's expression says it all as Ireland tumble to a 1–0 defeat against Austria at the Ernst Happel Stadium in Vienna, finally ending hope of participation in the World Cup in Brazil. Photograph: Donall Farmer/Inpho.

And it bought them a lead, albeit one that Ireland held for a grand total of 11 minutes after Robbie Keane scored his 60th international goal. But for those 11 minutes, nobody in the ground was quite able to shift the certainty that a second would be needed.

The Swedish defence was there for the chasing and had Ireland scraped a second, the night could have held some treasure. But when it didn't come, Ireland paid. Johan Elmander equalised on the half hour when he finished off a fine cross from right-back Mikael Lustig.

Richard Dunne was at least embarrassed to take the Man of the Match award afterwards, but he still presented his best face when asked if the campaign was done and dusted now.

'We have to stay positive,' said Dunne. 'We go to Austria on Tuesday and hopefully we can win that and open up the group again. After scoring early on, it's very disappointing to lose. I thought actually a draw would have been harsh on us but to lose is disappointing. We still have a chance; there're still games to play.

'For the first half an hour we were great and then we took our foot off the gas and they got back into it. We gave away two sloppy goals; they put in two good balls and had two good finishes. But we've seen them play every week in the Premier League and we should be able to do better against them.

'It's going to be hard but we still have to believe, otherwise there's no point in carrying on. We just pick our heads up and just go again. We've got a tough game on Tuesday night and then if results go our way, hopefully we can get back into it. They [Sweden] have to go to Kazakhstan and we found out it was a tough place to go. So we just have to hope that they can do us a favour and that we can do ourselves a favour by winning in Austria.'

Fat chance of that.

On 10 September, Austria beat Ireland 1–0, ending all hope of making the World Cup.

An Irishman's Diary/Viking Biking

Frank McNally

On Friday evening last, I cycled into *The Irish Times* office on an errand (well, actually, I cycled on a bicycle; the errand only happened when I dismounted). And because I didn't expect to be there long, I forewent the secure underground car park, instead locking my bike to a pole on Townsend Street.

This, you'll have guessed already, was a mistake. But I had locked the bike to many pieces of street furniture during the three or four years we were together and hadn't lost it. The lock was a reasonably good one, having cost – as cycling lobby groups recommend – at least 10 per cent of the bicycle's value. Besides, it was still daylight.

The street had a regular stream of passersby. And maybe unconsciously, I took added comfort from the fact that my bike was locked under the bronze noses of Countess Markievicz and her dog: a cocker spaniel that in life, apparently, used to annoy republicans so much they wanted to kick it when she wasn't looking.

Anyway, I got delayed at the office. Among the things that delayed me was a rumpus in the street below that sent many of us rushing to the newsroom window to see what was happening. It turned out to be Swedish football fans, departing the city centre en masse for Lansdowne Road: an extraordinary spectacle.

There were thousands of them, almost all in yellow shirts, and many with colourful headgear, ranging from floppy leprechaun hats to horned helmets. Their migration had been carefully co-ordinated. They even had a Garda escort, which was indeed necessary, because it took nearly 10 minutes for them to pass the busy junction with Tara Street where traffic had to wait.

Watching this river of Nordic humanity passing down Townsend Street, it struck me how ominously at home the visitors looked in Dublin. As well they might, since it's their city. Not only did they found it, the part they were now walking through was the historic entry point to Viking Dublin.

Townsend Street marks what was once the Liffey's southern bank, where the longboats came in. Thus, among the landmarks the football fans were passing was a modern replica of the Long Stone: a marker that stood for centuries to warn of sandbanks and that now bears the likeness of a former Viking ruler of the city, Ivar the Boneless.

This is not so much Town's end, you could say, as Town's beginning. So we should have known that home advantage against the Swedes would not count for much in Dublin, and that their modern-day leader, Zlatan-the-ponytailed, would be imposing taxes on the Irish back four before the night was out.

But in the meantime, the game had yet to start. And it was while about to cycle off and watch it somewhere that I returned to the aforesaid pole to find only my broken lock.

No, readers, I'm not suggesting for a moment that Vikings pillaged my bicycle. That would be a stereotype too far. But I wondered afterwards if the spectacle of their mass transit was an unwitting accomplice in the crime, distracting eyes that might otherwise have noticed someone with bolt-cutters or whatever thieves use to cantilever locks against poles until they snap.

Not that much distraction is needed, I know. Bicycle theft happens all the time in Dublin, yet somehow you never see it. And bigger things than my bike have gone missing in the city centre with no apparent witnesses. The original Long Stone was stolen in 1794, I believe. Gardaí at Pearse Street are still waiting for a breakthrough in the case.

This was no consolation as I walked home on Friday, remembering – as always on these occasions – the good times the bike and I had enjoyed together. I'm still too raw now even to think about starting a

new relationship with a bicycle soon. On the contrary, the circumstances of the latest theft have dropped a heavy hint that maybe it's time, belatedly, for me to join the Dublin bike rental scheme.

There happens to be a station right outside *The Irish Times*. And under current expansion plans, there will soon be one where I live too. All right, the bikes are clunky and slow. But on the plus side, you never have to worry about lights or locks again. An enlightened public–private partnership supplies the hardware and risks are shared by the community at large. Not the least impressive thing about the Dublin scheme, in fact, is how free of theft or vandalism it has been. All considered, it may be the closest we have to what I think is called the 'Nordic social model', although, of course, that seems like a bitter irony just now.

FRIDAY, 13 SEPTEMBER 2013

Exasperation in OECD at Snail's Pace of Reform

Dan O'Brien

If it didn't exist, would it be created? That is the most basic test of any public institution (try it on the Seanad). The same test should be applied regularly and rigorously to the myriad schemes, programmes and policies on which governments spend taxpayers' money.

Yesterday's biennial report from the OECD on Ireland masterfully highlighted the failings of the administration to apply that test in two of the most important things it tries to do – boosting employment and increasing entrepreneurship.

Given the State is crying out for more of both, and that it needs to use every cent it spends to maximise the stimulus effect, one might think the government would be working tirelessly to ensure every tax euro is making the greatest possible contribution to hastening recovery.

Alas, it is not. Instead, government is still wasting taxpayers' money on failed schemes when,

Artist Robert Ballagh in the Crawford Art Gallery in Cork before the opening of his exhibition 'Seven'.
Photograph: Michael Mac Sweeney/Provision.

as the OECD says, it should be shutting them down and diverting the money to those which deliver more bang for their buck.

This is all the more disappointing because, during the election campaign, Enda Kenny, who does not habitually go about dropping the names of the giants of the Italian renaissance, quoted Galileo. 'Measure what is measurable, and make measurable what is not,' he said. The remark was as insightful as it was unexpected.

One of the great failings of Irish governance has long been the failure to measure the effectiveness of policies. Managers need data on inputs and outputs and they need information systems. Without this, decision-makers cannot quantify and thus fly blind. Fly blind for any length of time and the outcome will be bad.

Yesterday's report highlights the continued failure to measure. It calls for evaluation of the Momentum programme on vocational education;

JobPlus, which seeks to encourage firms to hire those in long-term unemployment; Springboard, which gives part-time third level courses to the jobless; and 'all' innovation and entrepreneurship programmes.

Richard Bruton at the Department of Enterprise, Jobs and Innovation gets plenty of flak for his inaction in subjecting his sprawling empire to greater rigour.

During the create-a-quango Ahern years, new programmes and agencies were set up to beat the band. The result, the OECD points out, is 'over 170 separate budget lines' in the innovation space 'sometimes for very small amounts of money, and 11 major funding agencies'.

It goes on: 'Fragmentation raises overheads, risks duplication and hampers resource realloc-ation. Gains would be achieved by consolidating funding into a *drastically* smaller number of agencies' (my emphasis).

Enda Kenny strains to hear a reporter's question at the announcement of the government's political reform package in Dublin. Photograph: Brenda Fitzsimons.

Halfway through the coalition's time in office, Bruton is still dithering. As with their technocratic counterparts in the troika, there is evidence of exasperation in the OECD people's report.

Astonishingly, the apprenticeship system is still geared towards the building industry, despite the OECD making clear recommendations for this insanity to stop in its last report. Yesterday they repeated those recommendations with the preface 'as already recommended two years ago in the previous report'.

On the snail's-pace deployment of social welfare case officers to help the jobless find work, the report says that, despite consideration being given to involving the private sector at the beginning of last year, 'no final decision has yet been taken, and it will take at least an additional year to set up the actual service provision'.

Separately, it notes dryly that the establishment of Solas, the agency designed to replace the training agency FÁS, 'was announced in mid-2011 but had not begun operating two years later'.

After two and a half years in office, Enda Kenny can claim a fair number of achievements. But despite a massive mandate and the political cover of the troika, he is not overseeing the rebirth of Ireland's governance structures.

SATURDAY, 14 SEPTEMBER 2013

Another Life: Jellyfish Join the Ecological Anarchists of the Western Lakes

Michael Viney

The great oceanic trout lakes of the west of Ireland, with their rich limestone feeding and plump specimen fish, have no counterpart in continental Europe:

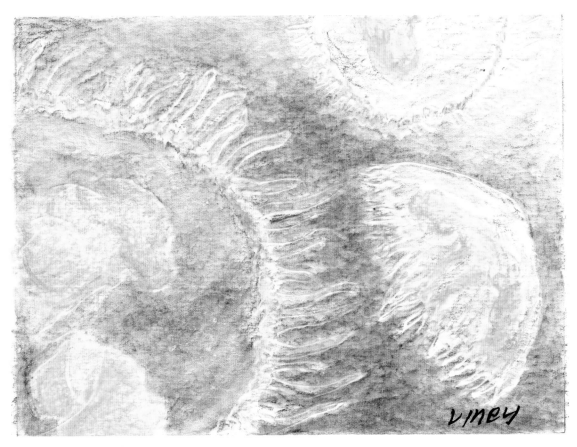

Jellyfish, by Michael Viney.

the summers there simply aren't windy or cool enough. Waves that rock the anglers' boats on Corrib, Mask, Derg or Erne keep the water mixed and full of oxygen from top to bottom. Water temperature rarely reaches 20 degrees, the point at which trout and salmon begin to feel uncomfortable.

In the generally hotter summers of Europe, lakes stratify more readily and severely: they split into layers, warm water above and cold below. The lower layer can lose oxygen as summer progresses and no longer offer fish a cool retreat. In such warm, weedy lakes, salmonids give way to cyprinids, notably carp. Bred to obese sizes by European fish farmers, carp are often sluggishly easy to catch with rod and line.

It is in this context that the recent discovery of minuscule freshwater jellyfish swimming happily in Lough Derg and Lough Erne could become a troubling omen. Their existence as free-swimming little bells, or medusae, was made possible by the preceding weeks of hot sunshine, in which local water temperatures rose, for long periods, above 25 degrees. In various waterways across the world, including those of Europe and most US states, this alien vagrant from China has bloomed only sporadically, when the weather was right.

Craspedacusta sowerbyi is not, strictly speaking, a jellyfish – an extra flap of tissue sorts it from those of the sea – but it looks, acts and reproduces like a jellyfish, and a shoal of their medusae, each the size of a €1 coin, makes an eye-catching glint under the water. The species has travelled widely in its resting forms, as hard-covered microscopic cysts or tiny polyps that grow from them, stuck to transported fish, aquatic plants or even the feet of migrant waterbirds. The polyps then stick to underwater rocks as a cylindrical trunk with a mouth at the top, surrounded by food-catching tentacles.

The polyps can tolerate cold and may live in a static state for years. But if the temperature rises above 25 degrees it may enter a process typical of jellyfish life cycles and bud off a plume of the little free-swimming bells. These medusae have their own tentacles around the fringe, some very long to help in swimming, some toxic-tipped to capture zooplankton food.

The explosion of jellies is often single-sexed (those of Derg and Erne are all female), and their bloom disappears within a few weeks or months, not to be repeated, perhaps, for years. The polyps are insignificantly small and live on unnoticed (they may have been here for decades), which is why Irish scientists are hungry for more sightings of the medusae (tell fisheriesireland.ie, the records centre at nbdc.ie or jellyfish.ie).

As aliens go – or come, rather – this one, in itself, though reckoned invasive, may be relatively harmless, so long as it sticks to the rare explosions of the past. It brings the number of aliens now in Lough Derg to almost 20, however, and so intensifies the ecological anarchy described as invasional meltdown by Dr Dan Minchin of the Lough Derg Science Group, now a leading expert on such threats.

Smothering, plankton-hungry zebra mussels have already wiped out the lake's big native species. They were followed by the equally invasive Asian clam. The alien bloody-red shrimp is preying on native species that feed the lake's last few pollan, an Arctic fish unique to Ireland in western Europe. All these have been introduced by human activity, stuck to the hulls of pleasure craft or pumped out in their bilge or ballast water, imported in anglers' bait boxes or emptied from aquariums stocked with imported fish or decorative aquatic plants. Discarded alien waterweeds are proliferating in many Irish lakes, Derg among them.

The new mussels and clams are clearing the water of plankton and manuring the floor of the lake so that even native plants are growing in the better-lit depths and crowding into long-established fish spawning areas. If the warmth of this summer were to become the norm, explosions of freshwater jellies could add to competition for zooplankton food.

Lough Derg got its name, so one folk tale asserts, from the bloody slaughter of a fairy badger chased into its depths. Some of the proliferating aliens are beginning to seem almost as unlikely, bringing chaos to aquatic ecosystems long shaped and balanced by Ireland's native species. Even without the invaders, rising water temperatures and summer droughts could be bad news for the salmon and trout of the western lakes and rivers, affecting them adversely at every stage of their lives. (The salmon, so a recent report says, have an extra three degrees of thermal tolerance.)

Be careful what you wish for.

MONDAY, 16 SEPTEMBER 2013

How Clueless Irish Pundits Misrepresented Germany

Derek Scally

The German journalist and satirist Kurt Tucholsky, who flourished between the World Wars, once remarked that you have to love the French to understand them – and you have to understand the Germans to love them.

There has not been a lot of love lately in Ireland – particularly in the Irish media – towards

Some of the marchers in paramilitary garb who attended the commemoration of murdered Dublin criminal and so-called Real IRA boss Alan Ryan's first anniversary at Balgriffin. Photograph: Dara Mac Donaill.

the Germans and not a lot of understanding either.

Indeed, one of Ireland's few growth areas in the recession has been in ill-informed German experts. On the airwaves and in print they moan about Chancellor Angela Merkel and shout about her finance minister, Wolfgang Schäuble. Though the voices vary, the rhetoric never changes: the Germans dominate Europe and the Germans demand austerity.

To lend their limp punditry an air of crisp authority, they toss about German words like croutons into a tired salad: *Bild*, Bundestag and even the mouthful that is the Bundesverfassungsgericht, the constitutional court.

For anyone who has any clue, it's like watching a piano teacher who is one lesson ahead of the student. The pundits owe their success to a vicious

circle of lack of interest and lack of information in Ireland about its largest European partner.

While many Irish people understand how the US president is elected by an electoral college of federal states, many are perpetually surprised to hear Germany, too, is a country of federal states.

This gap has allowed three fallacies to dominate mainstream Irish understanding of Germany in the euro crisis.

The first and most insidious is the notion of Germany as the crisis villain. My first experience of this came a few years ago when a researcher called to say a well-known Irish pundit was coming to Germany to film a segment for a crisis documentary. The pundit was anxious to talk to an elderly couple about how German savers fuelled the Irish boom. The aircraft tickets had been bought, now the pundit just needed some pensioners to put a face to their precooked thesis.

That Germans saved and Irish spent in the past decade is one of those sweeping statements rarely challenged from which pundits have extrapolated their Hibernocentric crisis narrative. The Germans were effectively buying the drinks for the Irish, they say, and should thus share the blame, the cost and the consequences for the car now wrapped around the tree.

The trouble is that the financial data to support this argument is at best complex and patchy, and at worst far less compelling than you might think.

Last March the Central Bank supplied *The Irish Times* with previously unpublished data showing that when the music stopped in 2008 it was Britain, not Germany, that was by far the biggest source of funding for Irish banks.

Even the infamous bondholders were, according to consolidated data sets, a quarter Irish and two-thirds non-euro area. The entire euro area, including Germany, held just 13 per cent of total Irish bank bonds. While the data available is far from complete or perfect, it presents a different reality from that peddled by the pundits.

Remember the outrage over the list of 80 Anglo bondholders published by blogger Paul Staines? On his list, a third of the institutions named were German. When I contacted Staines out of curiosity last March he admitted his list presented only a selection of the total Anglo lenders.

Browsing the spreadsheets together, he acknowledged his Anglo bondholder document was 'not a great conspiracy list' because it contained the name of every major institutional investor one would expect to find.

Finally, he acknowledged there was 'more British money than German [in Anglo], which didn't exactly serve my argument that Ireland was bailing out the euro zone'.

His admissions caused far less ruckus than the original Anglo list. Why should they? The narrative was already fixed: of reckless German lending and

Dr Merkel as the Manchurian candidate, activated by big German banks to claw back their reckless, disproportionate investment in Ireland.

The second crisis fallacy is the assumption that everyone thinks, or should think, that it is up to the State to start spending in a downturn to cushion the private-sector slump. The German economic mainstream, however, believes the opposite: that some measure of State financial pruning is necessary in a downturn to reduce borrowing and eventually return to sustainable growth.

Whether you spend or save your way out of a recession is the crux of the euro crisis, and the German view – that you cannot solve a debt crisis with more debt – is deeply frustrating to those who believe otherwise. But trying to win over Germans to your economic thinking, particularly when your economy is on the skids, is like trying to convince Martin Luther about the virgin birth during the Reformation.

Your options: portray yourself as an abused spouse in an abusive marriage; file for divorce and leave the mutual euro zone home; or – the pragmatic option – admit that sharing a currency is a more challenging interfaith marriage of economics than anyone anticipated, and get on with finding a compromise.

The path to compromise, however, requires discarding a third fallacy: expectations of German leadership in Europe. In Ireland and elsewhere, one camp argues Germany is showing too much leadership in the crisis, exploiting the economic weakness of others to ram through its fiscal rule book. The other camp says Germany needs to lead more but in a direction of which it – and not Germany – approves: towards mutualised sovereign debt-buying to mutualised bank rescue funds.

Speaking to German officials – as the Irish pundits don't – they blanch at the idea of German leadership in Europe, where the ideas of *führen* and *Führer* still have terrible connotations. Instead they see a necessity for euro countries to learn to borrow less before, as Berlin admits, a new era of mutualised euro finances become reality.

As their federal election looms, understanding this core concern is a far better way of getting to grips with the Germans than heeding Ireland's cottage industry of crisis pundits.

MONDAY, 23 SEPTEMBER 2013

Dublin Have to Sweat for Victory as Mayo Wilt in the Heat

Sean Moran at Croke Park

Dublin 2-12 Mayo 1-14

Continuing to show the greatest economy in modern All-Ireland history – four final wins by an aggregate five points – Dublin crowned an exceptional season with the county's 24th title.

On a sweltering afternoon the championship showpiece was claustrophobic, intense and exciting, but it disappointed those who had hoped for a firework display between the best teams of the year.

But it wasn't just the temperature – more associated with a good July – that made Jim Gavin's team sweat for the honour, which rounded off the county's first league and championship double since 1976.

As in the semi-final against Kerry, Dublin started poorly and their prospects could have been a speck on the horizon by half time, but again kept afloat by an early goal against the run of play, they got to the break trailing by just a point.

Having taken an apparently firm grip on the match in the third quarter, the Leinster champions

Dublin players run towards Croke Park's Hill 16, clutching their hard-won Sam Maguire, to celebrate with the fans. Photograph: Donall Farmer/Inpho.

Symbolising how Dublin boxed in Mayo's second half attempts to hold onto their early lead, Dublin's Jonny Cooper and Darren Daly overwhelm Mayo's Alan Dillon in the All-Ireland football final at Croke Park. Photograph: Eric Luke.

found themselves pegged back by a Mayo goal against the run of play and although they kept the margin at a goal until injury time, injuries had effectively reduced them to 13 players for the closing 10 minutes – Eoghan O'Gara damaged a hamstring, having menaced Mayo from his first-half introduction, and Rory O'Carroll was visibly dazed after a collision with Enda Varley with all replacements used – and they just about held on to win a second Sam Maguire in three years, a feat not achieved since the 1970s.

Like any team chiselling achievement out of adversity, they needed big performances and just

about found them after the calamitous opening quarter. Stephen Cluxton's kick-outs in the second half were pin-point in their accuracy and helped resource the comeback as well as protect the ball in the fraught closing stages. His two dead-ball kicks were vital in a one-point victory.

Cian O'Sullivan came into the match strongly at centrefield and, when required, dropped back to corner back for fire brigade duty after Jonny Cooper's departure with a concussion at the end of the third quarter. James McCarthy had his best match of the summer once he too had settled, his fast breaks helping to create attacks and his tireless running giving Cluxton a target at the end when legs were tiring and the match was still in the balance.

Michael Darragh Macauley likewise recovered from a static start to get his motor running and launch the pile-driver runs that have characterised his season. Rory O'Carroll gave little change throughout to Alan Freeman and had to stay on the field when injured in the fraught closing minutes.

Above all, Bernard Brogan, a championship of fits and starts behind him, built on the improvement of the semi-final with a match-winning contribution of 2-2 from play.

The first goal in the 16th minute gave Dublin vital breathing space in the opening onslaught: a sprightly leap under Paul Flynn's great, pumped kick and Ger Cafferkey – whose effort and overall effectiveness probably deserved better than an

eight-point invoice – was caught between his man and his goalkeeper as Brogan deftly flicked home.

It was just respite at that stage. Mayo opened up with all the dynamism that had characterised what was until yesterday a season of great promise. Just as they had hustled All-Ireland champions Donegal into oblivion in the quarter-final, they hit Dublin with a high-tempo pressing game but couldn't make it count on the scoreboard.

Keith Higgins – who put in a blameless afternoon between attack and defence – was denied by a fraction, confirmed by Hawk-Eye, within 30 seconds of the start and from then on Dublin didn't appear to know quite what to do about it. They weren't getting forward to put pressure on Mayo and, apparently jittery in the maelstrom, their deliverance from further damage wasn't really any of their doing. Mayo squandered chances: seven

Members of the Mayo minor team celebrate their victory over Tyrone – a win that did not, however, compensate fully for the senior team's defeat against Dublin. Photograph: Lorraine Sullivan/inpho.

wides in the first half plus some poor distribution left the door open for their stricken opponents.

Finals throw up unexpected heroes and Mayo captain Andy Moran, a hard summer of much-debated, underwhelming form behind him, chose the biggest stage to give his best display. A total of 1-2 was begun in the fourth minute with the opening point and he also drew two converted frees.

For Dublin, Ger Brennan, at sea with many of his colleagues in the opening quarter and maybe edging close to substitution, dug in after the break and kicked a miracle point in the 65th minute to keep Mayo at arm's length.

Mayo's decision to start Cillian O'Connor with his shoulder problems was partly vindicated in that although not at his best in open play, his place kicking was customarily high-yield – eight from 10 – but the two missed were the first opportunities and he will have been disappointed with them.

The big hitters on either side in the Footballer of the Year stakes didn't advance their cases as expected. For instance, Aidan O'Shea wasn't the force of nature hoped for at centrefield but his brother Séamus put in another good shift.

It was the half backs as usual who performed best. Lee Keegan had a terrific first half, kicking two points, and held Diarmuid Connolly well over the 70 minutes, whereas Colm Boyle held the centre of the defence as reliably as he had all year and didn't allow Dublin a foothold on the 40. In the second half he persevered when the team was low on inspiration.

It was a sobering afternoon for the high-profile rookies on the Dublin team. Ciarán Kilkenny, Paul Mannion and Jack McCaffrey were all replaced – only Mannion was injured – and although Kilkenny had a number of chances he didn't get on the score board and was replaced by Dean Rock who mightn't have added to his impressive scoring totals for the summer but was involved and busy.

But Dublin's fabled bench had a less obvious impact than on the scoreboard. As they arrived and

raised the tempo they increasingly tied up Mayo's half backs – the team's main source of creativity – and this was seen in the fact that Moran's goal was the only score from play for the Connacht champions.

The end game was tense and fractious. Proponents of the 'beautiful game' for much of the year, Dublin showed themselves as willing as anyone else to commit calculated fouls to forestall attacks and slow the game.

They were, however, deserving winners and Mayo found themselves reliving the familiar nightmare of continuing to run the clock on what will in 2014 be a 63-year gap since their last All-Ireland, now extending to a quarter of a century of seven fruitless finals.

MONDAY, 30 SEPTEMBER 2013

Clare Bask in the Glory of a Perfect Finale to a Glorious Summer of Hurling

Keith Duggan at Croke Park

Monday morning and Clare are the All-Ireland hurling champions and the world is still spinning on its axis. Just about.

The GAA was adventurous enough to scupper protocol and tradition and was rewarded with one of the most beautiful finales not just in the long history of the association, but of sport in general. It was perfection.

Everything about the closing act of a fabulous hurling summer felt strange: a Saturday All-Ireland final replay on a warm autumn evening, the city centre buzzing and a game that began in daylight and finished under lights. It was dreamlike and the watching world was dazzled long before the bulbs lit up the stadium.

Clare's Shane O'Donnell just manages to evade the attention of Cork's Shane O'Neill during the 2013 All-Ireland Senior Hurling Final replay at Croke Park. Photograph: James Crombie/Inpho.

Almost from the throw-in, the hurlers from Clare and Cork mixed it with clean, attacking intent and phenomenal speed, bravery and imagination.

It became clear that the replay would surpass the first day out. Seventy minutes later, it was hard to imagine that there had ever been a better All-Ireland hurling final.

Clare and Cork had played the old game in a way that had not been seen before.

Even the scoreline had a burnished look: 5-16 to 3-16. Central to Clare's five goals was Shane O'Donnell, the 19-year-old Eire Óg flier who was told by Davy Fitzgerald that he was starting just two hours before the throw in. 'He was nearly getting sick on the way in on the bus,' quipped Tony Kelly afterwards.

But on the field, O'Donnell was an incandescent figure as dusk fell across the city. The smoothness with which he finished his three first-half goals was one thing, but the point he scored in the 54th minute when Cork – heroic in the second half – surged with five scores in a row was arguably his most important strike of the game.

It steadied the young Clare team as they cleared their heads for the final win-or-bust shoot-out of the summer.

Twice in the last 15 minutes of action Cork would breach the Clare net and twice the Banner would reply. When Stephen Moylan whipped in Cork's third goal after 71 minutes, just a goal stood between them and the prospect of a third match, of yet another draw, flitted through the mind.

By that stage, those privileged enough to be in the stadium would have been surprised by nothing. But it was Clare's day. With 66 minutes gone, Fitzgerald had withdrawn O'Donnell for the man he had replaced, Darach Honan.

*Teammate Domhnall O'Donovan congratulates Shane O'Donnell on his goal hat-trick after their team's victory
over Cork in the 2013 All-Ireland Senior Hurling Final replay at Croke Park. Photograph: James Crombie/Inpho.*

When O'Donnell took off his helmet, most of
Ireland got a look at him for the first time. Five
minutes later, Honan took a ball on the wing.

Out of all of this bunch, it was Honan's name
that was first whispered as holding the future of
Clare hurling. He took off and half soloed, half
worried the ball past the Cork defence and into the
goal. It trickled into the net. Fitzgerald sank to his
knees. The roar in Croke Park was of that primal,
deafening kind that can only come from a county
that seldom sees All-Ireland splendour. 1914. 1995.
1997. And now 2013 – winners of the finest
hurling summer in living memory.

Jimmy Barry Murphy watched it all calmly.
For a man associated with so many of Cork's
winning Septembers in hurling and football, he is a
class apart in knowing how to lose graciously.

He saw his team shaken by another
unstoppable opening argument from the Claremen
and they were eight points adrift after 26 minutes.

But Cork found a way: from Anthony Nash's
howitzer free into a sardine-tin goalmouth
crowded with Clare men, to Patrick Cronin's
industry to Stephen McDonnell's terrific corner-
back display.

They stayed Cork – positive, innovative and
alive to the half chance – and made the impossible
look likely.

'Both days really we had been playing catch-
up from the word go,' JBM said. 'Difficult thing to
do, I think. You have to get everything right to get
back into a game.

'We did a lot of things right but if you don't
take everything that comes your way . . . it has to

be perfect then at that stage. And eventually our luck ran out. And we were beaten by just a much better team on the day. I think on both days. I've got to acknowledge it – that they deserved it.'

It is odd to think that JBM took instruction from Christy Ring when Croke Park was a hooded place with match-box dressing rooms. Here he was yesterday, still a Cork folk hero, presiding over a game that would surely have thrilled the Cloyne genius.

Tomorrow has never looked better for hurling.

Clare, suddenly, seem to have it all, from born leaders like John Conlon and Brendan Bugler – a source of white fury in the second half – to young wizards like Conor McGrath and Kelly and the unflappable Colin Ryan.

'I love to see them go out and expressing themselves,' Fitzgerald said on Saturday night, his pale eyes watery with the emotion of the evening. 'They'd be out on the field doing things and I'd be watching them thinkin' . . . Jesus.'

He shrugged then when asked if Clare could win more. 'This crowd can do whatever they want.'

It certainly seems that way. Nightfall drew the curtains on a perfect hurling year. The best team won, the most gallant finished runners-up and a jolt of pride travelled across Ireland. What can you say? The kids are alright.

Two of Shane O'Donnell's fans greet him and the rest of the Clare team at their homecoming in Tim Smythe Park in Ennis after their 2013 All-Ireland Senior Hurling Final replay win against Cork.
Photograph: James Crombie/Inpho.

Index

Page numbers set in *italic* indicate a photo/picture.